the ULTIMATE
ground beef
COOKBOOK

the ULTIMATE
ground beef
COOKBOOK

©2008 Reiman Media Group, Inc.
5400 S. 60th Street
Greendale WI 53129

International Standard
Book Number (10):
0-89821-689-3

International Standard
Book Number (13):
978-0-89821-689-9

Library of Congress
Control Number: 2007939533

Front cover photos by Rob Hagen.
Food styled by Jennifer Janz and Diane
Armstrong. Sets styled by Jennifer
Bradley Vent and Stephanie Marchese.

Taco Casserole (p. 275)
Broccoli Meat Roll (p. 136)
Shepherd's Pie (p. 248)
Open-Faced Meatball Sandwiches (p. 89)
Bread Bowl Chili (p. 46)

Back cover photos by Rob Hagen and
Dan Roberts. Food styled by Jennifer
Janz and Julie Herzfeldt. Sets styled
by Grace Natoli Sheldon and Melissa
Haberman.

Hamburger Macaroni Skillet (p. 212)
Cool-Kitchen Meat Loaf (p. 139)
Taco Meatball Ring (p. 19)
Slow-Cooked Spaghetti Sauce (p. 146)
Aloha Burgers (p. 88)

editor Michelle Bretl
vice president, executive editor/books Heidi Reuter Lloyd
art director Gretchen Trautman
creative director Ardyth Cope
senior editor/books Mark Hagen
layout designer Nancy Novak
associate editor Jean Steiner
proofreader Linne Bruskewitz
content production supervisor Julie Wagner
editorial assistant Barb Czysz

food director Diane Werner, RD
test kitchen manager Karen Scales
recipe editors Sue A. Jurack (senior), Mary King, Christine Rukavena
recipe asset system manager Coleen Martin
home economists Tina Johnson, Marie Parker, Annie Rose
test kitchen assistants Rita Krajcir, Kris Lehman

studio photographers
Rob Hagen (senior), Dan Roberts, Jim Wieland, Lori Foy
food stylists
Sarah Thompson (senior), Kaitlyn Besasie, Tamara Kaufman,
Jennifer Janz, Diane Armstrong, Julie Herzfeldt
food stylist assistants
Alynna Malson, Shannon Roum, Leah Rekau
set stylists
Jennifer Bradley Vent (senior), Stephanie Marchese (senior),
Dee Dee Jacq, Grace Natoli Sheldon, Melissa Haberman
photo studio coordinator Kathleen Swaney

president and chief executive officer Mary G. Berner
president, food & entertaining Suzanne M. Grimes
senior vice president, editor in chief Catherine Cassidy

For other *Taste of Home* books and products, visit
www.ShopTasteofHome.com

contents

the ULTIMATE in great ground beef

THE BIGGEST, juiciest burger your hands can hold...piping-hot bowls of perfectly spiced chili...a piled-high plate of Italian spaghetti and meatballs...thick slices of home-style meat loaf...all of those classics rely on one hearty, ever-popular ingredient—ground beef.

With *The Ultimate Ground Beef Cookbook* from *Taste of Home*, you'll get every kind of beefy specialty you and your family crave—plus delicious new twists on old favorites. It all adds up to 450 mouth-watering recipes!

Because this colorful, photo-packed cookbook is from *Taste of Home*, you can trust every recipe you prepare to be a winner every time. Most are shared by cooks just like you from across the country...and all are tested and approved by the expert home economists in the *Taste of Home* Test Kitchen.

To whet your appetite, just look at the generous helping of chapters (12, to be exact) that you can dig into:

Hearty Appetizers
Whether for a Super Bowl party or just an afternoon snack, these meaty bites are sure to satisfy. Munch on Honey-Garlic Glazed Meatballs, Pizza Spread, Beef 'n' Bean Egg Rolls and Bacon Nachos.

Sides, Salads & Breads
These savory, change-of-pace ideas for ground beef just might surprise you. Try Rice Balls with Meat Sauce, Beef Barbecue Biscuits, Chuck Wagon Beans and Patriotic Taco Salad.

Soups, Stews & Chili
Spoon up chunky helpings of Cajun Chili, Beef Minestrone, Meaty Zucchini Stew, Potato Onion Soup or another favorite. You get 52 different bowlfuls!

Home-Style Sandwiches
Of course, you'll find standout burgers such as Sourdough Cheeseburgers and Grilled Burgers with Horseradish Sauce. But you can also enjoy Ground Beef Gyros, Souper Joes and much more.

Meat Loaves & Meatballs
Let ground beef take shape into over 50 crowd-pleasing variations, including Potato-Topped Chili Loaf, Reuben Meatballs, Pinwheel Pizza Loaf and Surprise Meatball Skewers.

Slow Cooker Specialties
A convenient slow cooker lets you "fix and forget it" in the morning, then come home to relaxing, sit-down suppers such

as Beef 'n' Bean Torta, Slow-Cooked Cabbage Rolls, Party-Pleasing Beef Dish and Egg Noodle Lasagna.

Casseroles & Oven Entrees
Mushroom Beef Patties...Chili-Stuffed Peppers...Pizza Rice Casserole...Baked Salisbury Steak...just pop any of these comforting baked dishes into the oven, then pull out a hot and hearty dinner.

Skillet & Stovetop Dishes
Straight from a saucepan or skillet come family-pleasing entrees such as Beef Chow Mein Skillet, Chuck Wagon Tortilla Stack, Hamburger Macaroni Skillet and Beefy Spanish Rice.

Pasta Pleasers
Whether you choose to fix Swiss Cheese Lasagna, Meatball Stroganoff with Noodles, Hearty Mac 'n' Cheese, Beef Mushroom Spaghetti or another dish, you'll serve up a memorable meal-in-one.

Meat Pies & Pizzas
Cut a nice slice—or two—of these all-around winning dinners, including Two-Tater Shepherd's Pie, Grilled Cheeseburger Pizza, Beef and Cheddar Quiche and Pizza English Muffins.

Southwestern Favorites
Olé! Put a south-of-the-border entree such as Beef Quesadillas, Texas Taco Platter, Enchilada Stack or Mexican Chip Casserole on your menu for an instant family fiesta.

Fun Fare for Kids
Children will dig right into these playful and tasty ground beef meals, including Sloppy Joe Wagon Wheels, Hot Dog Pie, Pizzawiches and Chili-Ghetti.

In each chapter of this can't-miss cookbook, you'll also see plenty of delicious, lighter ground beef dishes that include Nutrition Facts at the end of the recipe. Just look for the hamburger-shaped icon next to each dish that's lower in calories, fat and sodium.

Page through, and you'll also spot dozens of handy cooking tips from our Test Kitchen...as well as two convenient indexes at the back of the book. The General Recipe Index and Alphabetical Recipe Index will help you locate exactly the kind of dishes you need.

With all of that—plus 450 unbeatable, family-favorite recipes—you know that *The Ultimate Ground Beef Cookbook* from *Taste of Home* truly is the ultimate!

HEARTY
appetizers

excellent ENTREE

Served with colorful toothpicks, Polynesian Meatballs make terrific party appetizers. But you'll want to consider this recipe for dinnertime, too. Just serve the meatballs over hot cooked rice, and you'll have a satisfying main course.

polynesian meatballs

prep 30 minutes | **cook** 15 minutes

carol wakley

north east, pennsylvania

With pretty bits of pineapple, these meatballs are sure to attract attention…and the sweet-tart sauce brings people back for seconds.

1	can (5 ounces) evaporated milk
1/3	cup chopped onion
2/3	cup crushed saltines
1	teaspoon seasoned salt
1-1/2	pounds lean ground beef

sauce

1	can (20 ounces) pineapple tidbits
2	tablespoons cornstarch
1/2	cup cider vinegar
2	tablespoons soy sauce
2	tablespoons lemon juice
1/2	cup packed brown sugar

In a bowl, combine the milk, onion, saltines and seasoned salt. Crumble beef over mixture and mix well. With wet hands, shape into 1-in. balls. In a large skillet over medium heat, brown meatballs in small batches, turning often. Remove with a slotted spoon and keep warm. Drain skillet.

Drain pineapple, reserving juice; set pineapple aside. Add enough water to juice to measure 1 cup. In a bowl, combine the cornstarch, pineapple juice mixture, vinegar, soy sauce, lemon juice and brown sugar until smooth. Add to skillet.

Bring to a boil; cook and stir for 2 minutes or until thickened. Add meatballs. Reduce heat; cover and simmer for 15 minutes. Add the pineapple; heat through. **yield:** about 6 dozen.

bacon nachos

prep/total time 20 minutes

1/2	pound ground beef
4	cups tortilla chips
1/4	cup real bacon bits
2	cups (8 ounces) shredded cheddar cheese
1/2	cup guacamole dip
1/2	cup sour cream

Chopped tomatoes and green onions, optional

In a small skillet, cook beef over medium heat until no longer pink; drain. Place the chips on a microwave-safe serving plate. Layer with the beef, bacon and cheese.

Microwave, uncovered, on high for 1-2 minutes or until cheese is melted. Top with guacamole and sour cream. Sprinkle with tomatoes and onions if desired. **yield:** 4-6 servings.

editor's note: This recipe was tested in a 1,100-watt microwave.

ruth ann bott

lake wales, florida

These crispy nachos have always been a big hit in our house. They're topped with kid-friendly ingredients like bacon bits and cheese.

pizza roll-ups

prep 20 minutes | **bake** 15 minutes

1/2 pound ground beef
1 can (8 ounces) tomato sauce
1/2 cup shredded part-skim mozzarella cheese
1/2 teaspoon dried oregano
2 tubes (8 ounces *each*) refrigerated crescent rolls

In a skillet, cook beef over medium heat until no longer pink; drain. Remove from the heat. Add tomato sauce, mozzarella cheese and oregano; mix well.

Separate crescent dough into eight rectangles, pinching seams together. Place about 3 tablespoons of meat mixture along one long side of each rectangle. Roll up jelly-roll style, starting with a long side. Cut each roll into three pieces. Place seam side down 2 in. apart on greased baking sheets. Bake at 375° for 15 minutes or until golden brown. **yield:** 2 dozen.

donna klettke
wheatland, missouri

Ever since I received this recipe through 4-H, it's been a regular after-school snack. The bite-size treats are especially good served with warmed pizza sauce or spaghetti sauce for dipping.

mexican pizza

prep 20 minutes + chilling | **bake** 10 minutes + cooling

sandra mckenzie
braham, minnesota

My husband and I came up with the recipe for these loaded snack squares. Our whole family likes the Southwestern flavor.

2 tubes (8 ounces *each*) refrigerated crescent rolls
1 package (8 ounces) cream cheese, softened
1 cup (8 ounces) sour cream
1 pound ground beef
1 envelope taco seasoning
1 can (2-1/4 ounces) sliced ripe olives, drained
1 medium tomato, chopped
3/4 cup shredded cheddar cheese
3/4 cup shredded part-skim mozzarella cheese
1 cup shredded lettuce

Unroll crescent roll dough and place in an ungreased 15-in. x 10-in. x 1-in. baking pan. Flatten dough to fit the pan, sealing seams and perforations. Bake at 375° for 8-10 minutes or until light golden brown; cool.

In a small bowl, blend cream cheese and sour cream with a wire whisk; spread over crust. Chill 30 minutes.

Meanwhile, in a large skillet, cook beef over medium heat until no longer pink; drain. Stir in taco seasoning. Add water according to package directions and simmer for 5 minutes, stirring occasionally. Spread over cream cheese layer. Top with olives, tomato, cheeses and lettuce. Cut into serving-size pieces. Serve immediately or refrigerate. **yield:** 12-16 servings.

sweet 'n' soy snack meatballs

prep 25 minutes | bake 20 minutes

1 egg
1/4 cup finely chopped onion
1 tablespoon ketchup
1-1/2 teaspoons salt
1/2 teaspoon pepper
1/2 teaspoon seasoned salt
1/2 teaspoon Worcestershire sauce
2 pounds ground beef
3/4 cup dry bread crumbs

sauce

2 tablespoons plus 1-1/2 teaspoons cornstarch
1 cup orange marmalade
3 to 4 tablespoons soy sauce
2 tablespoons lemon juice
2 garlic cloves, minced

In a large bowl, combine the first seven ingredients. Crumble meat over mixture. Sprinkle with crumbs; mix gently. Shape into 1-in. balls.

Place meatballs on a greased rack in a shallow baking pan. Bake, uncovered, at 350° for 20-25 minutes or until meat is no longer pink; drain.

Meanwhile, in a small saucepan, combine the sauce ingredients. Bring to a boil; cook and stir for 2 minutes or until thickened. Remove meatballs to a serving dish; serve with sauce. **yield:** 5 dozen.

jodi klassen
coaldale, alberta

When I got married years ago, my mom gave me this recipe. The mouth-watering meatballs are easy to make and always disappear quickly.

jalapeno bean dip

prep 15 minutes | cook 30 minutes

lorene goodwin
belle fourche, south dakota

This is the snack my family usually requests on cold winter nights. We also like to make this zippy dip on camping trips.

2 pounds ground beef
1 medium onion, chopped
1 garlic clove, minced
2 cans (8 ounces *each*) tomato sauce
1 can (15-1/2 ounces) chili beans, undrained
1 can (16 ounces) kidney beans, rinsed and drained
2 medium jalapeno peppers, seeded and chopped
1/2 teaspoon salt
1/8 teaspoon cayenne pepper
1 package (10-1/2 ounces) corn chips
1 cup (4 ounces) shredded cheddar cheese
1 cup (8 ounces) sour cream

In a large skillet, cook the beef, onion and garlic over medium heat until meat is no longer pink; drain. Stir in the tomato sauce, beans and jalapeno peppers. Bring to a boil. Add salt and cayenne. Reduce heat; cover and simmer for 20 minutes.

To serve, spoon beef mixture over chips; sprinkle with cheese. Top with sour cream. **yield:** 12 servings.

editor's note: When cutting or seeding hot peppers, use rubber or plastic gloves to protect your hands. Avoid touching your face.

best **BACON**

Always check the date that's stamped on packages of vacuum-sealed bacon to make sure the bacon is fresh. The date reflects the last date of sale. Once the package has been opened, the bacon should be used within a week. For longer storage, freeze it for up to 1 month.

bacon cheeseburger balls

prep 25 minutes | **cook** 10 minutes

cathy lendvoy
boharm, saskatchewan

When I serve these, my husband and sons are often fooled into thinking we're having plain meatballs— until they cut into the golden filling inside.

1 egg
1 envelope onion soup mix
1 pound ground beef
2 tablespoons all-purpose flour
2 tablespoons milk
1 cup (4 ounces) shredded cheddar cheese
4 bacon strips, cooked and crumbled

coating

2 eggs
1 cup crushed saltines (about 30 crackers)
5 tablespoons vegetable oil

In a large bowl, combine egg and soup mix. Crumble beef over mixture and mix well. Divide into 36 portions; set aside. In another large bowl, combine the flour and milk until smooth. Add cheese and bacon; mix well.

Shape cheese mixture into 36 balls. Shape one beef portion around each cheese ball. In a shallow bowl, beat the eggs. Place cracker crumbs in another bowl. Dip meatballs into egg, then coat with crumbs.

In a large skillet, cook meatballs over medium heat in oil for 10-12 minutes or until the meat is no longer pink and coating is golden brown. **yield:** 3 dozen.

cheesy sausage dip

prep/total time 20 minutes

1 pound ground beef
1 pound bulk pork sausage
2 tablespoons all-purpose flour
1 can (10-3/4 ounces) condensed cream of mushroom soup, undiluted
1 can (10 ounces) diced tomatoes and green chilies, undrained
1 medium onion, chopped
1 tablespoon garlic powder
2 pounds process cheese (Velveeta), cubed
Tortilla chips

In a large saucepan, cook beef and sausage over medium heat until no longer pink; drain. Sprinkle with flour. Stir in the soup, tomatoes, onion and garlic powder.

Bring to a boil; cook and stir for 2 minutes or until thickened. Reduce the heat. Stir in cheese until melted. Serve warm with chips. Refrigerate leftovers. **yield:** 8 cups.

curtis cole
dallas, texas

The garlic flavor really comes through in this crowd-pleasing cheese dip, which is one of our family's all-time favorites. I serve it in a slow cooker with a big basket of tortilla chips.

chili cups

prep 45 minutes | bake 15 minutes

1 pound ground beef
1 medium green pepper, diced
1 medium onion, diced
3 garlic cloves, minced
1 can (8 ounces) tomato sauce
2 tablespoons water
1/2 teaspoon salt
1/2 to 1 teaspoon ground cumin
1/2 teaspoon dried oregano
1/4 teaspoon celery seed
1/4 teaspoon dill weed
1/8 to 1/4 teaspoon cayenne pepper
2 loaves (1 pound *each*) sliced Italian bread
Grated Parmesan cheese

In a large skillet, cook beef, green pepper, onion and garlic over medium heat until meat is no longer pink; drain. Stir in the tomato sauce, water and seasonings. Bring to a boil over medium heat. Reduce heat; cover and simmer for 30 minutes, stirring occasionally.

Meanwhile, cut circles from bread slices using a 2-1/2-in. biscuit cutter. Press the circles into greased miniature muffin cups.

Bake at 400° for 5-6 minutes or until lightly toasted. Remove from tins and cool on wire racks. Fill each bread cup with about 1 tablespoon chili mixture; sprinkle with Parmesan cheese. Broil for 2-3 minutes or until cheese is golden brown. **yield:** about 5 dozen.

nutrition facts: 3 chili cups equals 114 calories, 4 g fat (1 g saturated fat), 15 mg cholesterol, 255 mg sodium, 13 g carbohydrate, 1 g fiber, 7 g protein.

editor's note: Some slices of bread will yield two 2-1/2-in. circles and some slices only one. There may be bread slices left over.

This beef recipe is lighter in calories, fat and sodium.

diane hixon
niceville, florida

Nothing tickles appetites quicker than these spicy bits. They're like eating chili in a muffin. I like to prepare and freeze them ahead of time for the Christmas season.

picadillo dip

prep 10 minutes | cook 65 minutes

This beef recipe is lighter in calories, fat and sodium.

lisa revell
vernon, new jersey

For a hot dip that's both sweet and savory, try this easy stovetop recipe. The unusual combination of ingredients is delicious.

1 pound ground beef
1 cup water
1 garlic clove, minced
1/2 teaspoon salt
1/4 teaspoon pepper
1 can (14-1/4 ounces) diced tomatoes, undrained
1 can (6 ounces) tomato paste
1/2 cup raisins
1/2 cup slivered almonds
1/4 cup sliced pimiento-stuffed olives
1/2 teaspoon sugar
Tortilla chips

In a large saucepan, cook beef over medium heat until no longer pink. Add the water, garlic, salt and pepper. Cover and simmer for 20 minutes; drain. Stir in the next six ingredients. Cover and simmer for 45 minutes, stirring occasionally. Serve hot with chips. **yield:** 4 cups.

nutrition facts: 1/4 cup equals 97 calories, 5 g fat (1 g saturated fat), 14 mg cholesterol, 178 mg sodium, 8 g carbohydrate, 2 g fiber, 6 g protein.

saucy cherry meatballs

prep 10 minutes | **cook** 25 minutes

marina castle-henry
burbank, california

Water chestnuts lend crunch to these moist ground beef and pork sausage meatballs. The baked bites are glazed with a sweet sauce made with cherry pie filling.

- 1/2 cup milk
- 1 tablespoon soy sauce
- 7 slices bread, crusts removed and cut into 1/2-inch cubes
- 1 teaspoon garlic salt
- 1/4 teaspoon onion powder
- 1/2 pound lean ground beef
- 1/2 pound bulk pork sausage
- 1 can (8 ounces) water chestnuts, drained and chopped

cherry sauce

- 1 can (21 ounces) cherry pie filling
- 1/3 cup apple juice
- 1/4 cup cider vinegar
- 1/4 cup steak sauce
- 2 tablespoons brown sugar
- 2 tablespoons soy sauce

In a bowl, combine the milk, soy sauce, bread cubes, garlic salt and onion powder. Crumble beef and sausage over mixture and mix well. Stir in water chestnuts. Shape into 1-in. balls.

Line a 15-in. x 10-in. x 1-in. baking pan with foil; place meatballs in pan. Broil 4-6 in. from the heat for 10 minutes or until meat is no longer pink; drain.

In a large skillet, combine the sauce ingredients. Bring to a boil. Reduce heat; simmer, uncovered, until thickened. Add meatballs; cook and stir until heated through. **yield:** about 4 dozen.

pizza spread

prep/total time 15 minutes

- 1 pound ground beef
- 1 jar (26 ounces) marinara *or* spaghetti sauce
- 1 teaspoon dried oregano
- 4 cups (16 ounces) shredded part-skim mozzarella cheese
- 1 loaf Italian *or* French bread, cubed *or* sliced

In a large saucepan, cook beef over medium heat until no longer pink; drain. Stir in marinara sauce and oregano. Gradually stir in cheese until melted. Pour into a fondue pot or small slow cooker to keep warm. Serve with bread. **yield:** 8-10 servings.

beverly mong
middletown, new york

For a satisfying snack, spread slices of Italian or French bread with this thick, cheesy mixture. My guests always say it's irresistible.

starry night taco cups

prep 15 minutes | **bake** 20 minutes

- 1 pound ground beef
- 1/2 cup chopped onion
- 1/4 cup salsa
- 1/4 cup ketchup
- 1 tablespoon chili powder
- 1 teaspoon salt
- 16 flour tortillas (7 inches)

Shredded lettuce, chopped tomatoes, shredded cheddar cheese *and/or* sour cream

In a large skillet, cook beef and onion over medium heat until meat is no longer pink; drain. Add the salsa, ketchup, chili powder and salt; heat through.

Cut each tortilla into a 4-in. square; set scraps aside. Microwave eight squares at a time for 20 seconds. Press onto the bottom and up the sides of greased muffin cups; set aside.

Cut tortilla scraps into stars with a 1-in. cookie cutter; place on greased baking sheet. Bake at 350° for 6 minutes or until golden brown; set aside.

Fill each tortilla cup with 2 tablespoons meat mixture. Bake for 12-15 minutes or until tortillas are golden brown. Serve with toppings of your choice; garnish with toasted stars. **yield:** 16 servings.

taste of home test kitchen

greendale, wisconsin

These Southwestern bites will add sparkle to just about any event. We lined muffin cups with tortillas, then filled them with a not-too-spicy beef mixture and garnished them with taco toppings.

cheesy beef taco dip

prep/total time 20 minutes

carol smith

sanford, north carolina

For a warm, hearty snack with a bit of a kick, try this recipe. It's great for parties because it makes a big potful. The only "utensil" you'll need to serve it with is a bowl of chips.

2 pounds ground beef
1 large onion, finely chopped
1 medium green pepper, finely chopped
1 pound process cheese (Velveeta), cubed
1 pound pepper Jack cheese, cubed
1 jar (16 ounces) taco sauce
1 can (10 ounces) diced tomatoes and green chilies, drained
1 can (4 ounces) mushroom stems and pieces, drained and chopped
1 can (2-1/4 ounces) sliced ripe olives, drained
Tortilla chips

In a large skillet, cook the beef, onion and green pepper over medium heat until meat is no longer pink; drain. Stir in the cheeses, taco sauce, tomatoes, mushrooms and olives. Cook and stir over low heat until cheese is melted. Serve warm with tortilla chips. **yield:** 10 cups.

beef 'n' bean egg rolls

prep 40 minutes | **bake** 20 minutes

- 1/2 pound ground beef
- 1/4 cup chopped onion
- 2 tablespoons chopped green pepper
- 1 cup refried beans
- 1/4 cup shredded cheddar cheese
- 1 tablespoon ketchup
- 1-1/2 teaspoons chili powder
- 1/4 teaspoon ground cumin
- 32 wonton wrappers
- Oil for deep-fat frying
- Salsa

In a large skillet, cook the beef, onion and green pepper over medium heat until meat is no longer pink; drain. Remove from the heat; stir in beans, cheese, ketchup, chili powder and cumin.

Position a wrapper with one point toward you. Place 1 tablespoon meat mixture in the center. Fold bottom corner over filling; fold sides toward center over filling. Roll toward the remaining point. Moisten top corner with water; press to seal. Repeat with remaining wrappers and filling.

In an electric skillet or deep-fat fryer, heat oil to 375°. Fry egg rolls, a few at a time, for 2 minutes or until golden brown. Drain on paper towels. Serve egg rolls with salsa. **yield:** 32 egg rolls.

editor's note: Fill wonton wrappers a few at a time, keeping the others covered with a damp paper towel until ready to use.

laura mahaffey
annapolis, maryland

Unlike traditional egg rolls filled with cabbage, this version uses spiced-up beef and beans. These are a regular part of our annual New Year's Eve "snack fest."

honey-garlic glazed meatballs

prep 25 minutes | **bake** 15 minutes

marion foster
kirkton, ontario

My husband and I raise cattle on our farm here in Southwestern Ontario. These saucy meatballs are one of our favorite snacks.

- 2 eggs
- 3/4 cup milk
- 1 cup dry bread crumbs
- 1/2 cup finely chopped onion
- 2 teaspoons salt
- 2 pounds ground beef
- 4 garlic cloves, minced
- 1 tablespoon butter
- 3/4 cup ketchup
- 1/2 cup honey
- 3 tablespoons soy sauce

In a large bowl, combine the eggs and milk. Add the bread crumbs, onion and salt. Crumble the beef over the mixture and mix well. Shape into 1-in. balls. Place on greased racks in shallow baking pans. Bake, uncovered, at 400° for 12-15 minutes or until the meat is no longer pink.

Meanwhile, in a large saucepan, saute garlic in butter until tender. Stir in the ketchup, honey and soy sauce. Bring to a boil. Reduce heat; cover and simmer for 5 minutes. Drain meatballs; add to sauce. Carefully stir to evenly coat. Cook for 5-10 minutes. **yield:** 5-1/2 dozen.

ginger meatballs

prep 30 minutes | **cook** 30 minutes

 This beef recipe is lighter in calories, fat and sodium.

sybil leson
houston, texas

After tasting these sweet and tangy meatballs, many of my guests have asked, "What's that great flavor?" I often increase the recipe and keep the meatballs warm in a slow cooker.

1 egg
1/2 cup finely crushed gingersnaps (about 11 cookies)
1 teaspoon salt
1-1/2 pounds ground beef
1 cup ketchup
1/4 cup packed brown sugar
2 tablespoons Dijon mustard
1/2 teaspoon ground ginger

In a large bowl, combine the egg, cookie crumbs and salt. Crumble beef over mixture and mix well. Shape into 1-in. balls.

Place on greased racks in shallow baking pans. Bake, uncovered, at 350° for 15-20 minutes or until no longer pink; drain.

In a large skillet, combine the ketchup, brown sugar, mustard and ginger. Add meatballs. Simmer, uncovered, for 15-20 minutes or until heated through, gently stirring several times. **yield:** about 3-1/2 dozen.

nutrition facts: 2 meatballs prepared with lean ground beef equals 97 calories, 4 g fat (1 g saturated fat), 22 mg cholesterol, 322 mg sodium, 8 g carbohydrate, trace fiber, 7 g protein.

snack pizzas

prep/total time 30 minutes

1 pound ground beef
1 medium onion, chopped
1/2 cup chopped green pepper
1 garlic clove, minced
1 can (6 ounces) tomato paste
3/4 cup water
4-1/2 teaspoons minced fresh oregano *or* 1-1/2 teaspoons dried oregano
1-1/2 teaspoons minced fresh thyme *or* 1/2 teaspoon dried thyme
1/2 teaspoon fennel seed
1/2 to 1 teaspoon garlic salt
36 slices snack rye bread
Grated Parmesan cheese

 This beef recipe is lighter in calories, fat and sodium.

margaret wagner allen
abingdon, virginia

These filling bites on snack rye bread resemble sloppy joe sandwiches. They're hard for meat-lovers—and just about everyone else—to resist.

In a large skillet, cook the beef, onion, green pepper and garlic over medium heat until meat is no longer pink; drain. Add tomato paste, water and seasonings; cook over low heat until thickened, about 10 minutes. Spread 1 tablespoonful on each slice of bread. Place on ungreased baking sheets; sprinkle with cheese. Bake at 350° for 8-10 minutes or until heated through. **yield:** 3 dozen.

nutrition facts: 3 pizzas equals 134 calories, 4 g fat (2 g saturated fat), 19 mg cholesterol, 250 mg sodium, 15 g carbohydrate, 2 g fiber, 9 g protein.

taco meatball ring

prep 20 minutes | **cook** 30 minutes

- 2 cups (8 ounces) shredded cheddar cheese, *divided*
- 2 tablespoons water
- 2 to 4 tablespoons taco seasoning
- 1/2 pound ground beef
- 2 tubes (8 ounces *each*) refrigerated crescent rolls
- 1/2 medium head iceberg lettuce, shredded
- 1 medium tomato, chopped
- 4 green onions, sliced
- 1/2 cup sliced ripe olives

Sour cream

- 2 small jalapeno peppers, seeded and sliced

Salsa, optional

In a large bowl, combine 1 cup cheese, water and taco seasoning. Crumble beef over mixture and mix well. Shape into 16 balls.

Place meatballs on a greased rack in a shallow baking pan. Bake, uncovered, at 400° for 12 minutes or until meat is no longer pink. Drain meatballs on paper towels. Reduce heat to 375°.

Arrange crescent rolls on a greased 15-in. pizza pan, forming a ring with pointed ends facing the outer edge of the pan and wide ends overlapping.

Place a meatball on each roll; fold point over meatball and tuck under wide end of roll (meatballs will be visible). Bake for 15-20 minutes or until rolls are golden brown.

Fill the center of ring with lettuce, tomato, onions, olives, remaining cheese, sour cream, jalapenos and salsa if desired. **yield:** 8 servings.

editor's note: When cutting or seeding hot peppers, use rubber or plastic gloves to protect your hands. Avoid touching your face.

brenda johnson
davison, michigan

This attractive, meat-filled ring may look complicated, but it's really very easy to assemble. Serve it as a party appetizer or even as a main course.

meatball and sausage bites

prep 20 minutes | **bake** 40 minutes

deb henderson
maroa, illinois

A friend of mine prepared this meaty snack for my wedding. It's convenient to assemble pans of these a day ahead of time, cover them and store them in the refrigerator. Just remove the bites from the fridge 30 minutes before baking them as directed, and serve them from a slow cooker or electric roaster.

2 eggs
1 small onion, finely chopped
1 cup dry bread crumbs
1/2 teaspoon garlic salt
1/2 teaspoon pepper
2 pounds ground beef
2 packages (1 pound *each*) miniature smoked sausages
2 cans (20 ounces *each*) pineapple chunks, drained
1 jar (10 ounces) pimiento-stuffed olives, drained
1 cup packed brown sugar
2 bottles (20 ounces *each*) barbecue sauce

In a large bowl, combine the first five ingredients. Crumble the beef over the mixture and mix well. Shape into 1-in. balls. Place meatballs on a greased rack in a shallow baking pan.

Bake, uncovered, at 350° for 15 minutes or until no longer pink; drain. With a slotted spoon, transfer meatballs to two shallow 3-qt. baking dishes. Add sausages, pineapple and olives to each; toss gently to mix.

Combine brown sugar and barbecue sauce; pour half over each casserole. Bake, uncovered, at 350° for 25 minutes or until heated through. **yield:** about 40 servings.

horseradish meatballs

prep 30 minutes | **bake** 35 minutes

2 eggs
1 tablespoon prepared horseradish
1/2 cup dry bread crumbs
1/4 cup chopped green onions
1/2 teaspoon salt
1/4 teaspoon pepper
1-1/2 pounds ground beef
1/2 pound ground pork *or* turkey

sauce

1/2 cup water
1/2 cup ketchup
1/2 cup chili sauce
1 small onion, finely chopped
1/4 cup packed brown sugar
1/4 cup cider vinegar
1 tablespoon prepared horseradish
1 tablespoon Worcestershire sauce
1 garlic clove, minced
1 teaspoon ground mustard
1/4 teaspoon hot pepper sauce

In a large bowl, combine the first six ingredients. Crumble meat over mixture and mix well. Shape into 1-1/2-in. balls.

Place meatballs on a greased rack in a shallow baking pan. Bake, uncovered, at 350° for 35-40 minutes or until no longer pink; drain.

Meanwhile, in a large saucepan, combine the sauce ingredients. Bring to a boil, stirring often. Reduce heat; simmer, uncovered, for 10 minutes. Add meatballs; stir gently to coat. **yield:** 3 dozen.

joyce benninger
owen sound, ontario

With their thick and savory sauce, these spicy meatballs are a popular party food. I also like to serve them with rice for a hearty meal.

cheeseburger mini muffins

prep 20 minutes | **bake** 15 minutes

teresa kraus
cortez, colorado

I invented these cute little muffins so I could enjoy the flavor of cheeseburgers without resorting to fast food. I often freeze a batch and reheat however many I need.

1/2 pound ground beef
1 small onion, finely chopped
2-1/2 cups all-purpose flour
1 tablespoon sugar
2 teaspoons baking powder
1 teaspoon salt
3/4 cup ketchup
3/4 cup milk
1/2 cup butter, melted
2 eggs
1 teaspoon prepared mustard
2 cups (8 ounces) shredded cheddar cheese

In a large skillet, cook the beef and onion over medium heat until the meat is no longer pink; drain.

In a small bowl, combine the flour, sugar, baking powder and salt. In another bowl, combine the ketchup, milk, butter, eggs and mustard; stir into the dry ingredients just until moistened. Fold in the beef mixture and cheese.

Fill greased miniature muffin cups three-fourths full. Bake at 425° for 15-18 minutes or until a toothpick comes out clean. Cool for 5 minutes before removing from pans to wire racks. Refrigerate leftovers. **yield:** 5 dozen.

editor's note: Muffins may be baked in regular-size muffin cups for 20-25 minutes; recipe makes 2 dozen.

SIDES, SALADS & breads

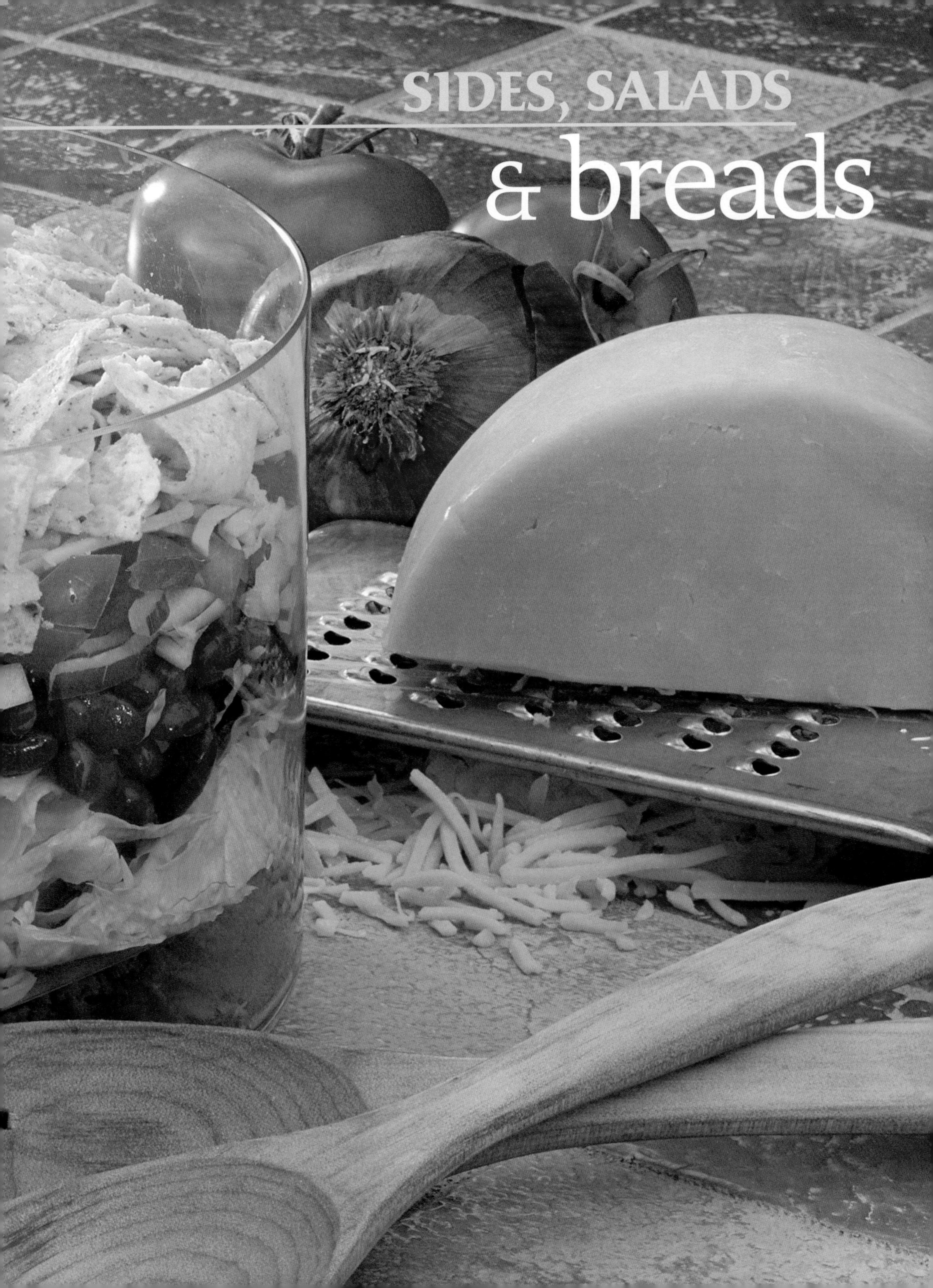

hearty bean bake

prep 15 minutes | **bake** 45 minutes + standing

barb wilkin
coshocton, ohio

Because it makes such a big batch, this popular four-bean bake is a super addition to potlucks. I'll even serve it as a main course to my family because we like the leftovers.

1 pound ground beef
1 medium onion, chopped
1/2 pound sliced bacon, cooked and crumbled
1 can (28 ounces) baked beans
1 can (16 ounces) kidney beans, rinsed and drained
1 can (14-1/2 ounces) wax beans, drained
1 can (14-1/2 ounces) cut green beans, drained
1/2 cup packed brown sugar
1/2 cup ketchup
3 tablespoons honey
2 tablespoons cider vinegar

In a large skillet, cook beef and onion over medium heat until meat is no longer pink; drain. Stir in bacon and beans. Transfer to a greased 2-1/2-qt. baking dish.

In a small bowl, combine the brown sugar, ketchup, honey and vinegar. Pour over the bean mixture. Bake, uncovered, at 325° for 45-50 minutes or until heated through and bubbly. Let stand for 10 minutes; stir before serving. **yield:** 12 servings.

tangy beef turnovers

prep/total time 30 minutes

1 pound ground beef
1 medium onion, chopped
1 jar (16 ounces) sauerkraut, rinsed, drained and chopped
1 cup (4 ounces) shredded Swiss cheese
3 tubes (8 ounces *each*) refrigerated crescent rolls

In a large skillet, cook beef and onion over medium heat until meat is no longer pink; drain. Add sauerkraut and cheese.

Unroll crescent roll dough and separate into rectangles. Place on greased baking sheets; pinch seams to seal. Place 1/2 cup beef mixture in the center of each rectangle. Bring corners to the center and pinch to seal. Bake at 375° for 15-18 minutes or until golden brown. **yield:** 1 dozen.

claudia bodeker
ash flat, arkansas

My mom's recipe for these flavorful pockets called for dough made from scratch, but I streamlined it by using refrigerated crescent rolls. My children love the turnovers plain or dipped in ketchup.

braided pizza loaf

prep 50 minutes + rising | **bake** 30 minutes

1 loaf (1 pound) frozen bread dough, thawed
1 pound ground beef
1 medium onion, finely chopped
1 teaspoon salt
1 teaspoon pepper
1 can (8 ounces) tomato sauce
1 teaspoon dried oregano
1 teaspoon paprika
1/2 teaspoon garlic salt
1 cup (4 ounces) shredded cheddar cheese
1 cup (4 ounces) shredded part-skim mozzarella cheese

Melted butter

Place dough in a greased bowl, turning once to grease top. Cover and let rise in a warm place until doubled, about 1 hour.

Meanwhile, in a large skillet, cook the beef, onion, salt and pepper over medium heat until meat is no longer pink; drain. Stir in tomato sauce, oregano, paprika and garlic salt. Bring to a boil. Reduce heat; cover and simmer for 30 minutes, stirring occasionally. Cool completely.

Punch the dough down. Turn onto a lightly floured surface; roll into a 15-in. x 12-in. rectangle. Place on a greased baking sheet. Spread the beef filling lengthwise down the center third of the rectangle. Sprinkle with the cheeses.

On each long side, cut 1-1/2-in.-wide strips about 2-1/2 in. into center. Starting at one end, fold alternating strips at an angle across filling. Brush with butter. Bake at 350° for 30-35 minutes or until golden brown. Serve warm. Refrigerate leftovers. **yield:** 1 loaf.

debbie meduna
plaza, north dakota

This special bread has terrific pizza taste that appeals to all ages. Remember to let the simmered beef filling cool completely before spreading it on the rolled dough.

taco-topped potato

prep/total time 15 minutes

linda brausen
janesville, wisconsin

Quick and easy, this recipe fits in well with a busy schedule. I like to serve the baked potato with a small broiled steak…or even with a green salad for a light meal.

1 large baking potato
1/4 pound ground beef
1 tablespoon chopped onion
1/4 cup salsa
1/4 teaspoon Worcestershire sauce
2 tablespoons shredded cheddar cheese

Sour cream

Scrub and pierce potato; place on a microwave-safe plate. Microwave, uncovered, on high for 3-4 minutes on each side or until tender; set aside.

Crumble the ground beef into a shallow microwave-safe bowl; add the onion. Cover and microwave on high for 1-1/2 to 2 minutes or until the meat is no longer pink, stirring once; drain. Stir in the salsa and Worcestershire sauce.

Cut potato in half lengthwise; fluff pulp with fork. Top each half with meat mixture, cheese and sour cream. **yield:** 2 servings.

editor's note: This recipe was tested in a 1,100-watt microwave. To prepare in a conventional oven, bake potato at 400° for 40 minutes or until tender. Cook beef and onion in a skillet until meat is no longer pink; drain. Stir in salsa and Worcestershire sauce. Assemble as directed.

taco braid

prep 40 minutes + rising | **bake** 20 minutes

 This beef recipe is lighter in calories, fat and sodium.

lucile proctor

panguitch, utah

This pretty braided sandwich loaf is a proven winner. My daughter entered the recipe in a state 4-H beef contest and won a trip to the national competition.

1 teaspoon active dry yeast
2 tablespoons sugar, *divided*
3/4 cup warm water (110° to 115°), *divided*
2 tablespoons butter, softened
2 tablespoons nonfat dry milk powder
1 egg, lightly beaten
1/2 teaspoon salt
2 cups all-purpose flour

filling

1 pound lean ground beef
1/4 cup sliced fresh mushrooms
1 can (8 ounces) tomato sauce
2 tablespoons taco seasoning
1 egg, lightly beaten
1/2 cup shredded cheddar cheese
1/4 cup sliced ripe olives

In a large mixing bowl, dissolve yeast and 1 teaspoon sugar in 1/2 cup water; let stand for 5 minutes. Add the butter, milk powder, egg, salt and remaining sugar and water. Stir in enough flour to form a soft dough.

Turn onto a floured surface; knead until smooth and elastic, about 6-8 minutes.

Place in a greased bowl, turning once to greased top. Cover and let rise in a warm place until doubled, about 1 hour.

In a large skillet, cook beef and mushrooms over medium heat until meat is no longer pink; drain. Stir in tomato sauce and taco seasoning. Set aside 1 tablespoon beaten egg. Stir remaining egg into beef mixture. Cool completely.

Punch dough down. Turn onto a lightly floured surface; roll into a 15-in. x 12-in. rectangle. Place on a greased baking sheet. Spread filling lengthwise down center third of rectangle. Sprinkle with cheddar cheese and olives.

On each long side, cut 1-in.-wide strips about 2-1/2 in. into center. Starting at one end, fold alternating strips at an angle across filling. Pinch ends to seal and tuck under. Cover and let rise for 30 minutes.

Brush with reserved egg. Bake at 350° for 20-25 minutes or until golden brown. Remove from pan to a wire rack to cool. **yield:** 12-16 servings.

nutrition facts: 1 piece equals 154 calories, 5 g fat (3 g saturated fat), 48 mg cholesterol, 328 mg sodium, 16 g carbohydrate, 1 g fiber, 9 g protein.

meat buns

prep 25 minutes + rising | **bake** 20 minutes

dough

1-1/2	teaspoons active dry yeast
1/2	cup plus 1 tablespoon warm water (110° to 115°)
3	tablespoons sugar
1	egg
1/2	teaspoon salt
2 to 2-1/4	cups bread flour

filling

1	pound ground beef
1-1/2	cups chopped cabbage
1/2	cup chopped onion
	and pepper to taste
	shredded cheddar cheese
2	spoons butter, melted

In a large mixing b___ ___ssolve yeast in water. Add sugar, egg, sal___ ___ cup flour; beat on low for 3 minutes. Add ___ ___h remaining flour to form a soft dough.

Turn onto a floured surface; knea___ ___il smooth and elastic, about 6-8 minute___. Place in a greased bowl; turn once to grease top. Cover and let rise in a warm place until doubled, about 1 hour.

Meanwhile, in a large skillet, cook beef over medium heat until no longer pink; drain. Add cabbage, onion, salt and pepper. Cover and cook over medium heat for 15 minutes or until vegetables are tender. Stir in cheese. Remove from the heat; set aside to cool.

Punch dough down and divide into 12 pieces. Gently roll out each piece into a 5-in. circle. Top each with about 1/4 cup filling. Fold dough over filling to meet in the center; pinch edges to seal.

Place seam side down on a greased baking sheet. Cover and let rise in a warm place until doubled, about 30 minutes. Brush with butter. Bake at 350° for 20 minutes or until golden brown. Serve warm. **yield:** 1 dozen.

nutrition facts: 1 meat bun equals 199 calories, 8 g fat (4 g saturated fat), 53 mg cholesterol, 172 mg sodium, 19 g carbohydrate, 1 g fiber, 12 g protein.

editor's note: The dough may be prepared in a bread machine. Place dough ingredients (using water that is 70°-80° and only 2 cups of bread flour) in bread pan in order suggested by manufacturer. Select dough setting (check dough after 5 minutes of mixing; add 1 to 2 tablespoons of water or flour if needed). When cycle is completed, turn dough onto a floured surface and punch down. Prepare buns as directed.

 This beef recipe is lighter in calories, fat and sodium.

sharon leno
keansburg, new jersey

On the outside, these golden buns resemble ordinary dinner rolls. But one bite reveals the tasty, cheesy beef filling inside.

safe STIRRING

When cooking ground beef, you should stir it often to break up large pieces. But as a general rule, you should not use the spoon (or other utensil) that was used to prepare the uncooked beef for later stirring or to serve the cooked food.

To prevent cross-contamination, wash the utensil in hot soapy water before reusing it, or just use a different spoon.

patriotic taco salad

prep 10 minutes | **cook** 20 minutes

glenda jarboek

oroville, california

When my daughter asked to have a patriotic theme for her July birthday party, I made this refreshing dish. If you want to prepare your salad in advance, omit the layer of chips and serve them on the side.

1 pound ground beef
1 medium onion, chopped
1-1/2 cups water
1 can (6 ounces) tomato paste
1 envelope taco seasoning
6 cups tortilla or corn chips
4 to 5 cups shredded lettuce
9 to 10 pitted large olives, sliced lengthwise
2 cups (8 ounces) shredded cheddar cheese
2 cups cherry tomatoes, halved

In a large skillet, cook beef and onion over medium heat until meat is no longer pink; drain. Stir in the water, tomato paste and taco seasoning. Bring to a boil. Reduce heat; simmer, uncovered, for 20 minutes.

Place chips in an ungreased 13-in. x 9-in. x 2-in. dish. Spread beef mixture evenly over the top. Cover with lettuce. For each star, arrange five olive slices together in the upper left corner. To form stripes, add cheese and tomatoes in alternating rows. Serve immediately. **yield:** 8 servings.

ground beef bundles

prep 20 minutes | **bake** 20 minutes

1/2 pound ground beef
2 cups shredded cabbage
1/2 cup chopped onion
2 tablespoons butter
1 teaspoon Worcestershire sauce
1/4 teaspoon salt
1/8 teaspoon pepper
1 loaf (1 pound) frozen bread dough, thawed
1/2 cup shredded Swiss cheese
Melted butter

In a large skillet, cook beef over medium heat until no longer pink; drain. Add the cabbage, onion, butter, Worcestershire sauce, salt and pepper. Cook and stir until cabbage is crisp-tender.

Meanwhile, cut bread dough into eight equal pieces; roll each into a 5-in. square. Place 1/4 cup meat mixture in the center of each square; sprinkle with about 1 tablespoon cheese. Bring corners together in the center; pinch edges to seal.

Place bundles on an ungreased baking sheet; brush tops with melted butter. Bake at 350° for 16-18 minutes. Serve warm. **yield:** 8 servings.

denise goedeken

platte center, nebraska

These little bundles are simple to create using frozen bread dough. And with the beef and cabbage stuffing, they're sure to satisfy your family.

broccoli beef braids

prep/total time 30 minutes

- 1 pound ground beef
- 1/2 cup chopped onion
- 3 cups frozen chopped broccoli
- 1 cup (4 ounces) shredded part-skim mozzarella cheese
- 1/2 cup sour cream
- 1/4 teaspoon salt
- 1/4 teaspoon pepper
- 2 tubes (8 ounces *each*) refrigerated crescent rolls

In a large skillet, cook beef and onion over medium heat until meat is no longer pink; drain. Add broccoli, cheese, sour cream, salt and pepper; heat through.

Unroll one tube of dough on a greased baking sheet; seal the seams and perforations, forming a 12-in. x 8-in. rectangle. Spread half of beef mixture lengthwise down the center. On each side, cut 1-in.-wide strips 3 in. into center.

Starting at one end, fold alternating strips at an angle across filling; seal ends. Repeat with second tube of dough. Bake at 350° for 15-20 minutes or until golden brown. **yield:** 2 loaves (8 servings each).

nutrition facts: 1 piece equals 141 calories, 8 g fat (4 g saturated fat), 24 mg cholesterol, 201 mg sodium, 7 g carbohydrate, 1 g fiber, 8 g protein.

 This beef recipe is lighter in calories, fat and sodium.

penny lapp
north royalton, ohio

Each slice of this fast-to-fix, golden bread is like a hot sandwich packed with beef, broccoli and mozzarella. Served with a green salad, the braid-shaped loaf makes a great lunch or dinner.

black-eyed pea casserole

prep 20 minutes | **bake** 20 minutes

This beef recipe is lighter in calories, fat and sodium.

kathy rogers
natchez, mississippi

This side dish recipe is perfect for a group because it makes two big casseroles. People always come back for "just a little more."

2 packages (6 ounces *each*) long grain and wild rice mix
2 pounds ground beef
2 medium onions, chopped
2 small green peppers, chopped
4 cans (15-1/2 ounces *each*) black-eyed peas with jalapenos, rinsed and drained
2 cans (10-3/4 ounces *each*) condensed cream of mushroom soup, undiluted
1-1/3 cups shredded cheddar cheese

In a large saucepan, cook the rice mixes according to package directions. Meanwhile, in a large skillet, cook the beef, onions and green peppers over medium heat until the meat is no longer pink; drain.

In a large bowl, combine the peas, soup, rice and beef mixture. Transfer to two greased 2-1/2-qt. baking dishes.

Cover and bake at 350° for 20-25 minutes or until heated through. Uncover; sprinkle with cheese. Bake 5 minutes longer or until cheese is melted. **yield:** 2 casseroles (10-12 servings each).

nutrition facts: 1 cup equals 122 calories, 6 g fat (3 g saturated fat), 26 mg cholesterol, 247 mg sodium, 8 g carbohydrate, 1 g fiber, 9 g protein.

grilled pizza bread

prep 20 minutes | **bake** 15 minutes

edna hoffman

hebron, indiana

Both kids and adults love this fun French bread covered with pizza toppings. It's great grilled fare for a picnic and can also be baked in the oven.

1 pound ground beef
1/2 cup chopped onion
1 can (8 ounces) tomato sauce
1/2 teaspoon salt
1/2 teaspoon dried oregano
1 loaf (1 pound) French bread
1 cup (4 ounces) shredded part-skim mozzarella cheese
1 can (2-1/4 ounces) sliced ripe olives, drained
Sliced pepperoni, optional

In a large skillet, cook beef and onion over medium heat until meat is no longer pink; drain. Stir in the tomato sauce, salt and oregano; simmer for 5-10 minutes.

Cut bread in half lengthwise and then widthwise. Spread meat mixture on cut side of bread; sprinkle with cheese, olives and pepperoni if desired.

Loosely wrap bread individually in pieces of heavy-duty foil (about 24 in. x 18 in.); seal. Grill, covered, over medium heat for 15-20 minutes or until heated through. **yield:** 4-6 servings.

texican rice salad

prep/total time 30 minutes

1 pound ground beef
1/2 cup chopped onion
1/2 cup chili sauce
2 garlic cloves, minced
1/2 teaspoon salt
1 teaspoon chili powder
3 cups cooked long grain rice
1 can (15 ounces) garbanzo beans, rinsed and drained
1 can (4 ounces) chopped green chilies
1 to 2 medium tomatoes, seeded and chopped
Shredded lettuce
Shredded cheddar cheese

In a large skillet, cook ground beef and onion over medium heat until the meat is no longer pink; drain. In a small bowl, combine the chili sauce, garlic, salt and chili powder; add to meat mixture. Stir in the rice, beans and chilies. Cover and cook over medium until heated through. Add tomato; cook 5 minutes longer.

For each serving, spoon 1 cup meat mixture over lettuce and sprinkle with cheese. **yield:** 8-10 servings.

rebecca mininger

jeromesville, ohio

This salad supper is a favorite of my husband's and makes use of the plentiful rice grown in our area. I fix this all the time, and we never tire of it.

spaghetti squash boats

prep 60 minutes | **bake** 20 minutes

 This beef recipe is lighter in calories, fat and sodium.

vickey lorenger
detroit, michigan

With a bounty of fresh ingredients, this recipe makes a fun summer dish. Spaghetti squash has an interesting texture that's delightfully different.

1   medium spaghetti squash (2 to 2-1/2 pounds)
1/4 pound lean ground beef
1/2 cup chopped onion
1/2 cup chopped green pepper
1/2 cup sliced fresh mushrooms
1   garlic clove, minced
1/2 teaspoon dried basil
1/2 teaspoon dried oregano
1/4 teaspoon salt
1/8 teaspoon pepper
1   can (14-1/2 ounces) diced tomatoes, drained
1/3 cup shredded part-skim mozzarella cheese

Cut squash in half lengthwise; scoop out seeds. Place squash cut side down in a baking dish. Fill pan with hot water to a depth of 1/2 in. Bake, uncovered, at 375° for 30-40 minutes or until tender.

When cool enough to handle, scoop out squash, separating strands with a fork; set shells and squash aside.

In a skillet, cook beef, onion and green pepper over medium heat until the meat is no longer pink and the vegetables are tender; drain.

Add mushrooms, garlic, basil, oregano, salt and pepper; cook and stir for 2 minutes. Add tomatoes; cook and stir for 2 minutes. Add squash; mix well.

Cook, uncovered, until liquid has evaporated, about 10 minutes. Fill shells; place in shallow baking dish.

Bake, uncovered, at 350° for 15 minutes. Sprinkle with cheese; bake 5 minutes longer or until cheese is melted. **yield:** 4-6 side-dish servings or 2 main-dish servings.

nutrition facts: 1 cup equals 102 calories, 3 g fat (1 g saturated fat), 13 mg cholesterol, 246 mg sodium, 13 g carbohydrate, 3 g fiber, 7 g protein.

oriental meatball salad

prep/total time 30 minutes

1 egg
6 teaspoons soy sauce, *divided*
1 can (8 ounces) water chestnuts, drained and chopped
1/3 cup thinly sliced green onions
1/4 cup dry bread crumbs
1 pound ground beef
1 tablespoon cornstarch
1 teaspoon sugar
1-1/2 cups chicken broth
1/2 teaspoon white vinegar
1 medium head iceberg lettuce, finely shredded
Additional green onions
1 medium lemon, cut into wedges

In a large bowl, beat egg and 4 teaspoons soy sauce; add water chestnuts, green onions and bread crumbs. Crumble ground beef over mixture and mix well. Shape into 1-in. balls.

Place meatballs on a greased rack in a shallow baking pan. Bake, uncovered, at 400° for 10-12 minutes or until meat is no longer pink.

Meanwhile, for dressing, combine cornstarch and sugar in a saucepan. Whisk in broth, vinegar and remaining soy sauce until smooth. Bring to a boil; cook and stir for 2 minutes or until thickened.

Arrange meatballs over lettuce; garnish with green onions and lemon. Serve with the dressing. **yield:** 4 servings.

le ane wohlgemuth
rimbey, alberta

To jazz up iceberg lettuce, I tossed in some tangy meatballs flavored with soy sauce and water chestnuts. The homemade dressing is the perfect accompaniment.

barbecued corn muffins

prep 20 minutes | bake 15 minutes

shawn roland
madison, mississippi

When I was growing up ~~in~~ ~~mississippi~~ I was encouraged to cook by my grandmother and mother. I rarely use written recipes, but this one is a classic.

1/2 pound ground beef
1/4 cup packed brown sugar
1/4 cup ketchup
1 tablespoon Worcestershire sauce
1 teaspoon prepared mustard
1/2 teaspoon salt
1/4 teaspoon pepper
1/4 teaspoon garlic powder
1 package (8-1/2 ounces) corn bread/muffin mix
2/3 cup shredded cheddar cheese

In a large skillet, cook beef over medium heat until no longer pink; drain and place in a bowl. Add the brown sugar, ketchup, Worcestershire sauce, mustard, salt, pepper and garlic powder.

Prepare corn bread mix according to package directions. Fill greased muffin cups with a scant 2 tablespoons of batter. Top each with 2 tablespoons beef mixture; sprinkle with cheese. Top with remaining corn bread mix.

Bake at 400° for 12-15 minutes or until a toothpick comes out clean. Cool for 5 minutes before removing from pan to a wire rack. Serve warm. Refrigerate leftovers. **yield:** 1 dozen.

cheeseburger buns

prep 30 minutes + rising | **bake** 10 minutes

nancy holland
morgan hill, california

My mother stuffs soft, homemade yeast rolls with ground beef, tomato sauce and cheese to make these sandwich-like buns. Any leftovers taste just as good for lunch the next day.

2 packages (1/4 ounce *each*) active dry yeast
1/2 cup warm water (110° to 115°)
3/4 cup warm milk (110° to 115°)
1/4 cup sugar
1/4 cup shortening
1 egg
1 teaspoon salt
3-1/2 to 4 cups all-purpose flour
1-1/2 pounds ground beef
1/4 cup chopped onion
1 can (8 ounces) tomato sauce
8 slices process American cheese, quartered

measuring **METHOD**

To measure 1/4 cup solid shortening for the Cheeseburger Buns, spoon it into a dry measuring cup. Pack the shortening into the cup with a spatula to be sure the cup is completely filled.

In a large mixing bowl, dissolve yeast in warm water. Add the milk, sugar, shortening, egg, salt and 2 cups flour; beat until smooth. Stir in enough remaining flour to form a soft dough.

Turn onto a floured surface; knead until smooth and elastic, about 4-6 minutes. Place in a greased bowl, turning once to grease top. Cover and let rise in a warm place until doubled, about 30 minutes.

In a large skillet, cook beef and onion over medium heat until meat is no longer pink; drain. Stir in tomato sauce. Remove from the heat; set aside.

Punch the dough down; divide into 16 pieces. On a lightly floured surface, gently roll out and stretch each piece into a 5-in. circle. Top each circle with two pieces of cheese and about 3 tablespoons beef mixture. Bring dough over filling to center; pinch edges to seal.

Place seam side down on a greased baking sheet. Cover and let rise in a warm place until doubled, about 20 minutes. Bake at 400° for 8-12 minutes or until golden brown. Serve warm. Refrigerate leftovers.
yield: 16 sandwiches.

chuck wagon beans

prep 30 minutes | **bake** 40 minutes

2 pounds lean ground beef
1/2 cup chopped celery
1/2 cup chopped green pepper
1/2 cup chopped onion
2 cans (15 ounces *each*) pork and beans
1 can (10-3/4 ounces) reduced-sodium condensed tomato soup, undiluted
1/4 cup water
2 tablespoons cider vinegar
1 tablespoon brown sugar
1 teaspoon ground mustard

In a nonstick skillet, cook the beef, celery, green pepper and onion over medium heat until meat is no longer pink; drain. In a large bowl, combine the pork and beans, tomato soup, water, vinegar, brown sugar, mustard and beef mixture.

Transfer to a shallow 2-1/2-qt. baking dish coated with nonstick cooking spray. Bake, uncovered, at 375° for 40-50 minutes or until heated through and mixture reaches desired thickness. **yield:** 8 servings.

connie staal
greenbrier, arkansas

I don't have to ring the dinner bell twice when these Western-style beans are on the menu. Using lean beef and reduced-sodium soup makes them a little lighter.

salad in a bread bowl

prep 20 minutes + rising | **bake** 25 minutes

barbara hayes
meadville, pennsylvania

In the past, I served salad with fresh bread alongside as an accompaniment. This fun recipe combines those

1 loaf (1 pound) frozen white bread dough, thawed
8 cups torn lettuce
1 cup quartered cherry tomatoes
1 cup fresh cauliflowerets
1 cup quartered thinly sliced cucumber
1/2 cup thinly sliced celery
1/2 cup s̶l̶i̶c̶e̶d̶
1 pound ground beef
1/2 cup chopped onion
Italian salad dressing *or* dressing of your choice

Divide bread dough into four equal portions; pat each into an 8-in. circle. Coat the outside of four 5-in. x 2-in. round ovenproof bowls with nonstick cooking spray. Place upside down on a baking sheet. Shape dough circles around bowls. Cover and let rise in a warm place for 1 hour.

Bake at 350° for 25-30 minutes or until golden brown. Meanwhile, combine lettuce, tomatoes, cauliflower, cucumber, celery and carrots; set aside.

In a skillet, cook beef and onion over medium heat until meat is no longer pink; drain. Place 2-1/2 cups of lettuce mixture into each bread bowl. Top with 1/4 cup beef mixture. Serve with dressing. **yield:** 4 servings.

hearty baked beans

prep 15 minutes | **bake** 1 hour

cathy swancutt

junction city, oregon

This saucy dish is chock-full of ground beef, bacon and four varieties of beans. I always turn to this recipe when I need to satisfy big appetites at a family party or neighborhood potluck.

1 pound ground beef

2 large onions, chopped

3/4 pound sliced bacon, cooked and crumbled

4 cans (15 ounces *each*) pork and beans

1 bottle (18 ounces) honey barbecue sauce

1 can (16 ounces) kidney beans, rinsed and drained

1 can (15-1/4 ounces) lima beans, rinsed and drained

1 can (15 ounces) black beans, rinsed and drained

1/2 cup packed brown sugar

3 tablespoons cider vinegar

1 tablespoon Liquid Smoke, optional

1 teaspoon salt

1/2 teaspoon pepper

In a large skillet, cook beef and onions over medium heat until meat is no longer pink; drain. Transfer to a 5-qt. Dutch oven. Stir in the remaining ingredients. Cover and bake at 350° for 1 hour or until heated through. **yield:** 18 servings.

onion **EASE**

To reduce tears, freeze onions for about 20 minutes before chopping them. Use a very sharp knife and chop quickly.

To save time, chop many onions at once and freeze the extras in an airtight container for up to 3 months. (Before sauteing, thaw the onions and pat them dry. Frozen chopped onions may be added directly to soups or casseroles.)

handy meat pies

prep 20 minutes + chilling | **bake** 15 minutes

3/4 pound ground beef
3/4 pound bulk pork sausage
1 medium onion, chopped
1/3 cup chopped green onions
1 garlic clove, minced
2 tablespoons minced fresh parsley
1 tablespoon water
2 teaspoons all-purpose flour
1/2 teaspoon baking powder
1/2 teaspoon salt
1/4 teaspoon pepper
2 tubes (12 ounces *each*) buttermilk biscuits

In a large skillet, cook beef and sausage over medium heat until no longer pink; drain. Add onions and garlic; cook until tender. Stir in parsley, water, flour, baking powder, salt and pepper. Heat through. Cover and refrigerate for at least 1 hour.

On a floured surface, pat 10 biscuits into 4-in. circles. Top each with about 1/3 cup of the meat mixture. Pat remaining biscuits into 5-in. circles and place over filling; seal edges with water. Press edges together with a fork dipped in flour; pierce the top.

Place on an ungreased baking sheet. Bake at 375° for 12-14 minutes or until biscuits are golden brown and filling is hot. **yield:** 10 servings.

amy stumpf
hampton, virginia

With plenty of beef and sausage inside, these mini pies are sure to tide you over when you want a snack or quick meal. Using refrigerated biscuit dough really speeds up the preparation.

SOUPS, STEWS
& chili

bread bowl chili

prep/total time 30 minutes

tonya michelle burkhard
port charlotte, florida

Served in hollowed-out rolls, this hearty chili gets extra zip from jalapeno pepper. Sometimes I serve the chili in one large, round bread loaf from a specialty store.

1/2 pound ground beef
1/2 pound ground pork
  2 cans (16 ounces *each*) kidney beans, rinsed and drained
  2 cans (14-1/2 ounces *each*) diced tomatoes with garlic and onion, undrained
  1 can (14-1/2 ounces) beef broth
  1 can (8 ounces) tomato sauce
  2 tablespoons chili powder
  1 jalapeno pepper, seeded and chopped
 12 hard rolls (about 4-1/2 inches), optional
Shredded cheddar cheese, sliced green onions and sour cream, optional

In a large saucepan, cook beef and pork over medium heat until no longer pink; drain. Stir in the beans, tomatoes, broth, tomato sauce, chili powder and jalapeno. Bring to a boil. Reduce heat; cover and simmer for 20 minutes.

Serve in soup bowls, or if desired, cut the top fourth off of each roll; carefully hollow out bottom, leaving a 1/2-in. shell. Cube removed bread. Spoon chili into bread bowls. Serve with cubed bread, sliced green onions, shredded cheddar cheese and sour cream if desired. **yield:** 12 servings.

editor's note: When cutting or seeding hot peppers, use rubber or plastic gloves to protect your hands. Avoid touching your face.

potato onion soup

prep 50 minutes | **bake** 10 minutes

- 2 large onions, chopped
- 3 tablespoons vegetable oil
- 1 pound ground beef
- 4 cups water
- 2 medium potatoes, peeled and cubed
- 2 tablespoons red wine vinegar
- 1 tablespoon beef bouillon granules
- 1 teaspoon salt
- 1/2 teaspoon pepper
- 2 tablespoons minced fresh parsley
- 1 cup (4 ounces) shredded Swiss cheese
- 2 tablespoons grated Parmesan cheese
- 7 slices French bread (1 inch thick)

In a Dutch oven or soup kettle, saute onions over medium heat in oil for 10-12 minutes or until golden brown. Remove and set aside. In the same kettle, brown beef; drain.

Add water, potatoes, vinegar, bouillon, salt, pepper and reserved onions; bring to a boil. Reduce heat; cover and simmer for 30 minutes or until potatoes are tender.

Stir in parsley. Ladle into ovenproof bowls. Top each with Swiss cheese, a slice of bread and Parmesan cheese. Bake at 375° for 10 minutes or until cheeses are bubbly. **yield:** 7 servings.

mary brombaugh
mt. pleasant, iowa

In our house, meaty soups are popular suppertime fare. This recipe uses ground beef and potatoes to give traditional onion soup a new twist.

harvest soup

prep 10 minutes | **cook** 25 minutes

This beef recipe is lighter in calories, fat and sodium.

janice mitchell
aurora, colorado

Loaded with squash, tomatoes and two kinds of potatoes, this colorful soup makes a great meal-in-one. Feel free to replace some of the vegetables with those that better suit your taste.

- 1 pound lean ground beef
- 3/4 cup chopped onion
- 2 garlic cloves, minced
- 3-1/2 cups water
- 2-1/4 cups chopped peeled sweet potatoes
- 1 cup chopped red potatoes
- 1 cup chopped peeled acorn squash
- 2 teaspoons beef bouillon granules
- 2 bay leaves
- 1/2 teaspoon chili powder
- 1/2 teaspoon pepper
- 1/8 teaspoon ground allspice
- 1/8 teaspoon ground cloves
- 1 can (14-1/2 ounces) diced tomatoes, undrained

In a large saucepan, cook the beef, onion and garlic over medium heat until meat is no longer pink; drain well. Add the water, potatoes, squash, bouillon, bay leaves, chili powder, pepper, allspice and cloves. Bring to a boil. Reduce heat; cover and simmer for 15-20 minutes or until vegetable are tender.

Add the tomatoes. Cook and stir until heated through. Discard bay leaves. **yield:** 6 servings.

nutrition facts: 1-1/2 cups equals 241 calories, 7 g fat (3 g saturated fat), 28 mg cholesterol, 493 mg sodium, 26 g carbohydrate, 4 g fiber, 18 g protein.

zucchini beef soup

prep 20 minutes | **cook** 20 minutes

betty claycomb
alverton, pennsylvania

As soon as my homegrown zucchini is plentiful, I make this chunky, fresh-tasting soup. I often double the recipe and freeze the leftovers to enjoy later.

- 1/2 pound ground beef
- 2 celery ribs, thinly sliced
- 1/3 cup chopped onion
- 1/2 cup chopped green pepper
- 1 can (28 ounces) diced tomatoes, undrained
- 3 medium zucchini, cubed
- 2 cups water
- 1-1/2 teaspoons Italian seasoning
- 1 teaspoon salt, optional
- 1 teaspoon beef bouillon granules
- 1/2 teaspoon sugar
- Pepper to taste
- Shredded Parmesan cheese, optional

In a large saucepan, cook the beef, celery, onion and green pepper over medium heat until meat is no longer pink and vegetables are tender; drain. Stir in the tomatoes, zucchini, water, Italian seasoning, salt if desired, bouillon, sugar and pepper.

Bring to a boil. Reduce heat; cover and simmer for 20-25 minutes or until zucchini is tender. Garnish with Parmesan cheese if desired. **yield:** 6 servings.

beefy tomato pasta soup

prep 15 minutes | **cook** 45 minutes

- 1 pound lean ground beef
- 2 medium green peppers, cut into 1-inch chunks
- 1 medium onion, cut into chunks
- 2 garlic cloves, minced
- 5 to 6 cups water
- 2 cans (14-1/2 ounces *each*) Italian diced tomatoes, undrained
- 1 can (6 ounces) tomato paste
- 1 tablespoon brown sugar
- 2 to 3 teaspoons Italian seasoning
- 1 teaspoon salt
- 1/4 teaspoon pepper
- 2 cups uncooked spiral pasta
- Croutons, optional

nancy rollag
kewaskum, wisconsin

If you're a fan of Italian food, you'll love this hearty creation. The taste reminds me of lasagna, but the soup is easier to fix.

In a Dutch oven, cook the beef, green peppers, onion and garlic over medium heat until meat is no longer pink; drain. Add the water, tomatoes, tomato paste, brown sugar, Italian seasoning, salt and pepper.

Bring to a boil. Add pasta. Cook for 10-14 minutes or until pasta is tender, stirring occasionally. Serve with croutons if desired. **yield:** 10 servings (about 2-1/2 quarts).

speedy chili

prep/total time 30 minutes

1 pound ground beef
1 large onion, chopped
1 garlic clove, minced
2 cans (8 ounces *each*) tomato sauce
1 tablespoon chili powder
1 tablespoon red wine vinegar
2 teaspoons baking cocoa
1/4 teaspoon ground cinnamon
Dash ground allspice
1 can (16 ounces) kidney beans, rinsed and drained
Hot cooked macaroni, shredded cheddar cheese and sliced green onions, optional

In a microwave oven, cook beef, onion and garlic on high for 2 minutes in a covered 2-qt. microwave-safe dish; stir to crumble meat. Cover and cook for 2-minutes; drain.

Add the next six ingredients; cover and cook on high for 3-1/2 minutes. Stir in the beans. Cover and cook 2-1/2 minutes more. Let stand 3-5 minutes. If desired, serve over macaroni and top with cheese and onions.

yield: 4 servings (about 1 quart).

editor's note: This recipe was tested in a 1,100-watt microwave.

betty ruenholl
syracuse, nebraska

Want chili in just half an hour? Try this microwave recipe. It speeds up the preparation but still uses all of the classic ingredients that people crave.

vegetable meatball stew

prep 30 minutes | **cook** 25 minutes

elaine grose
elmira, new york

Everyone who tries this chock-full stew remarks on the sweet potatoes. But people can never quite guess the recipe's secret ingredient—parsnips!

4 cups water
2 medium peeled potatoes, cut into 1-inch cubes
2 medium carrots, cut into 3/4-inch chunks
1 large onion, cut into eighths
2 tablespoons beef bouillon granules
1 bay leaf
1 teaspoon dried thyme
1 teaspoon dried basil
1/2 teaspoon salt
1/2 teaspoon pepper
1/2 cup seasoned dry bread crumbs
1 egg, lightly beaten
1 teaspoon Worcestershire sauce
1 pound ground beef
2 medium sweet potatoes, peeled and cut into 1-inch cubes
2 medium parsnips, peeled and cut into 3/4-inch slices
1 cup frozen peas
1/3 cup all-purpose flour
1/2 cup cold water
1/4 teaspoon browning sauce, optional

In a large Dutch oven or soup kettle, bring water to boil. Add potatoes, carrots, onion and seasonings; return to a boil. Reduce heat; cover and simmer for 10 minutes.

Meanwhile, in a small bowl, combine the crumbs, egg and Worcestershire sauce. Crumble beef over mixture and mix well.

Shape into 1-in. balls; add to Dutch oven along with sweet potatoes and parsnips. Bring to a boil. Reduce heat; cover and simmer for 15 minutes or until vegetables are tender.

Discard the bay leaf. Stir in the peas. Combine flour, cold water and browning sauce if desired until smooth; gradually stir into the stew. Bring to a boil; cook and stir for 2 minutes or until thickened. **yield:** 6 servings.

ground beef noodle soup

prep 15 minutes | **cook** 20 minutes

1-1/2   pounds ground beef
1/2   cup *each* chopped onion, celery and carrot
7   cups water
1   envelope au jus mix
2   tablespoons beef bouillon granules
2   bay leaves
1/8   teaspoon pepper
1-1/2   cups uncooked egg noodles

In a large saucepan or Dutch oven, cook the beef, onion, celery and carrot over medium heat until meat is no longer pink and vegetables are tender; drain.

Add the water, au jus mix, beef bouillon, bay leaves and pepper; bring to a boil. Stir in the noodles. Return to a boil. Cook, uncovered, for 15 minutes or until the noodles are tender, stirring occasionally. Discard the bay leaves before serving the soup. **yield:** 8 servings (2 quarts).

judy brander
two harbors, minnesota

Want a change of pace from the usual noodle soups? Try this ground beef recipe. It's quick to put together, so it's a great choice for busy weeknights.

cheeseburger soup

prep 45 minutes | **cook** 10 minutes

joanie shawhan
madison, wisconsin

When I requested the recipe for a cheeseburger-flavored soup served at a restaurant, they wouldn't reveal it. So I developed my own version by modifying a recipe for potato soup, and I was really pleased with the results.

1/2   pound ground beef
3/4   cup chopped onion
3/4   cup shredded carrots
3/4   cup diced celery
1   teaspoon dried basil
1   teaspoon dried parsley flakes
4   tablespoons butter, *divided*
3   cups chicken broth
4   cups diced peeled potatoes (1-3/4 pounds)
1/4   cup all-purpose flour
2   cups (8 ounces) process cheese (Velveeta)
1-1/2   cups milk
3/4   teaspoon salt
1/4   to 1/2 teaspoon pepper
1/4   cup sour cream

In a 3-qt. saucepan, brown beef; drain and set aside. In the same saucepan, saute onion, carrots, celery, basil and parsley in 1 tablespoon butter until vegetables are tender, about 10 minutes. Add broth, potatoes and beef; bring to a boil. Reduce heat; cover and simmer for 10-12 minutes or until potatoes are tender.

Meanwhile, in a small skillet, melt remaining butter. Add flour; cook and stir for 3-5 minutes or until bubbly. Add to soup; bring to a boil. Cook and stir for 2 minutes. Reduce heat to low. Add cheese, milk, salt and pepper; cook and stir until cheese melts. Remove from the heat; blend in sour cream. **yield:** 8 servings (2-1/4 quarts).

dumpling vegetable soup

prep 15 minutes | **cook** 1 hour

peggy linton
cobourg, ontario

*Delicious rice dumplings
give a homemade touch
to this irresistible soup,
which takes advantage of
convenience products.
It's a quick, nourishing,
all-in-one-pot meal.*

1/2 pound ground beef
4 cups water
1 can (28 ounces) diced tomatoes, undrained
1 package (10 ounces) frozen mixed vegetables
1 envelope dry onion soup mix
1/2 teaspoon dried oregano
1/4 teaspoon pepper

rice dumplings

1-1/4 cups all-purpose flour
1 teaspoon baking powder
1/2 teaspoon salt
1 tablespoon shortening
1/3 cup cooked rice, room temperature
1 tablespoon minced fresh parsley
1 egg, lightly beaten
1/2 cup milk

In a Dutch oven, cook beef over medium heat until no longer pink; drain. Add the water, tomatoes, mixed vegetables, soup mix, oregano and pepper; bring to a boil. Reduce heat; cover and simmer for 30-40 minutes or until the vegetables are tender.

For dumplings, combine the flour, baking powder and salt in a bowl. Cut in shortening until the mixture resembles coarse crumbs. Add rice and parsley; toss.

In a small bowl, combine egg and milk. Add to rice mixture; stir just until moistened. Drop by teaspoonfuls onto simmering soup. Cover and simmer for 15 minutes or until a toothpick inserted in a dumpling comes out clean (do not lift the cover while simmering). Serve immediately. **yield:** 6-8 servings (2 quarts).

green chili stew

prep 10 minutes | **cook** 50 minutes

1 pound ground beef
1 pound ground pork
8 to 10 Anaheim chilies, roasted, peeled and chopped *or* 3 cans (4 ounces *each*) chopped green chilies, drained
4 medium potatoes, peeled and diced
1 can (28 ounces) diced tomatoes, undrained
2 cups water
1 garlic clove, minced
1 teaspoon salt, optional
1/2 teaspoon dried oregano
1/4 teaspoon pepper
1/4 teaspoon dried coriander

mary spill
tierra amarilla, new mexico

*Roasted Anaheim chilies
add plenty of spark to this
ground beef-and-pork stew.
The savory blend of herbs
provides even more flavor.*

In a large kettle or Dutch oven, brown beef and pork; drain. Add remaining ingredients. Cover and simmer for 45 minutes. **yield:** 10 servings.

editor's note: When cutting or seeding hot peppers, use rubber or plastic gloves to protect your hands. Avoid touching your face.

count on **CUMIN**

Spicing up chili is a cinch with cumin, which dates back to 5,000 B.C. Used in chili powder, Indian curries and Middle Eastern cuisine, this spice has a warm, earthy taste and bold aroma.

Cumin seed is the fruit of a small annual herb in the parsley family. The tiny, nutty seeds resemble caraway seeds and come in white, amber and black.

You can purchase cumin in seed form or ground. The whole seeds will keep for up to 3 years. The ground variety, like other spices, may be stored for up to 1 year in an airtight container.

chili with potato dumplings

prep 25 minutes | **cook** 55 minutes

- 1 pound ground beef
- 1 pound ground turkey
- 1/2 cup chopped onion
- 1 can (16 ounces) kidney beans, rinsed and drained
- 1 can (15-1/2 ounces) mild chili beans, undrained
- 1/2 cup chopped green pepper
- 4 teaspoons chili powder
- 1 teaspoon salt
- 1 teaspoon paprika
- 1 teaspoon cumin seeds
- 1/2 teaspoon garlic salt
- 1/2 teaspoon dried oregano
- 1/4 teaspoon crushed red pepper flakes
- 3 cups V8 juice

dumplings
- 1 cup mashed potato flakes
- 1 cup all-purpose flour
- 1 tablespoon minced fresh parsley
- 2 teaspoons baking powder
- 1/2 teaspoon salt
- 1 cup milk
- 1 egg, beaten

In a Dutch oven or large soup kettle, cook beef, turkey and onion until meat is browned; drain. Add next 11 ingredients; bring to a boil. Reduce heat; cover and simmer for 30 minutes, stirring occasionally.

In a large bowl, combine the first five dumpling ingredients. Add milk and egg; stir just until moistened. Let rest for 3 minutes. Drop by tablespoonfuls into simmering chili. Cover and cook for 15 minutes. **yield:** 8 servings (2 quarts).

shirley marshall
michigantown, indiana

Now that my husband has retired, we eat out a lot. But when we stay home, he usually asks if we're going to have this chili! I've been making it, with a few changes here or there, most of my married life.

spice it up soup

prep 10 minutes | **cook** 40 minutes

guyla cooper
enville, tennessee

Jalapeno peppers and spicy sausage give a nice kick to this chunky soup. The original recipe called for three cooking pots, but I simplified it so I can use just one.

1 pound uncooked hot turkey Italian sausage links, sliced
1/2 pound lean ground beef
1 large onion, chopped
1 medium green pepper, chopped
3 garlic cloves, minced
2 cans (14-1/2 ounces *each*) beef broth
2 cups water
2 cups fresh *or* frozen corn
1 can (14-1/2 ounces) diced tomatoes with green chilies, undrained
1 cup diced carrots
1/3 cup minced fresh cilantro
2 jalapeno peppers, seeded and chopped
1/2 teaspoon salt
1/2 teaspoon ground cumin

In a large saucepan, cook sausage, beef, onion, green pepper and garlic over medium heat until meat is no longer pink; drain. Stir in the remaining ingredients. Bring to a boil. Reduce heat; cover and simmer for 30-40 minutes or until heated through. **yield:** 8 servings.

editor's note: When cutting or seeding hot peppers, use rubber or plastic gloves to protect your hands. Avoid touching your face.

meaty three-bean chili

prep 25 minutes | **cook** 1 hour 40 minutes

3/4 pound Italian sausage links, cut into 1/2-inch chunks

3/4 pound ground beef

1 large onion, chopped

1 medium green pepper, chopped

1 jalapeno pepper, seeded and minced

2 garlic cloves, minced

1 cup beef broth

1/2 cup Worcestershire sauce

1-1/2 teaspoons chili powder

1 teaspoon pepper

1 teaspoon ground mustard

1/2 teaspoon celery seed

1/2 teaspoon salt

6 cups chopped fresh plum tomatoes (about 2 pounds)

6 bacon strips, cooked and crumbled

1 can (16 ounces) kidney beans, rinsed and drained

1 can (15 ounces) pinto beans, rinsed and drained

1 can (15 ounces) garbanzo beans, rinsed and drained

Additional chopped onion, optional

In a 4-qt. kettle or Dutch oven, cook the sausage and beef over medium heat, until the meat is no longer pink; drain, reserving 1 tablespoon drippings. Set meat aside.

Saute onion, peppers and garlic in the reserved drippings for 3 minutes. Add the beef broth, Worcestershire sauce and seasonings; bring to a boil over medium heat. Reduce the heat; cover and simmer for 10 minutes.

Add tomatoes, bacon and browned sausage and beef; return to a boil. Reduce heat; cover and simmer for 30 minutes.

Add the kidney, pinto and garbanzo beans. Simmer for 1 hour, stirring occasionally. Garnish with chopped onion if desired.

yield: 10-12 servings (3 quarts).

editor's note: When cutting or seeding hot peppers, use rubber or plastic gloves to protect your hands. Avoid touching your face.

sandra miller

lees summit, missouri

Doubling this recipe is a habit for me—just about everyone wants more than one bowl! If I do end up with leftovers, I freeze them for a quick and easy meal another day.

hearty chili mac

prep 20 minutes | **cook** 1 hour 15 minutes

2 pounds ground beef
1 medium onion, chopped
1 can (46 ounces) tomato juice
1 can (28 ounces) diced tomatoes, undrained
2 celery ribs without leaves, chopped
3 tablespoons brown sugar
2 tablespoons chili powder
1 teaspoon salt
1 teaspoon prepared mustard
1/4 teaspoon pepper
2 cans (16 ounces *each*) kidney beans, rinsed and drained
1/2 cup uncooked elbow macaroni

fannie wehmas
saxon, wisconsin

Everyone asks for a second bowl of this macaroni chili, so it's a good thing the recipe makes a lot. You'll love the leftovers, too… that is, if you have any!

In a Dutch oven or large kettle, cook beef and onion over medium heat until meat is no longer pink; drain. Stir in the tomato juice, tomatoes, celery, brown sugar, chili powder, salt, mustard and pepper. Bring to a boil. Reduce heat; simmer, uncovered, for 1 hour, stirring occasionally.

Add the beans and macaroni; simmer 15-20 minutes longer or until macaroni is tender. **yield:** 10-12 servings.

vegetable beef chili

prep 10 minutes | **cook** 30 minutes

This beef recipe is lighter in calories, fat and sodium.

amy baxter
bishop, california

People who like their chili hot really get a kick out of this zippy recipe. I serve steaming bowls of it with oven-fresh corn bread.

1 pound lean ground beef
1 large onion, chopped
1 medium zucchini, diced
1 medium yellow summer squash, diced
1 medium sweet red pepper, chopped
1 can (15-1/2 ounces) hominy, drained
1 can (15 ounces) black beans, rinsed and drained
1 can (14-1/2 ounces) diced tomatoes with green peppers and onions, undrained
1 cup light beer *or* beef broth
1 can (4 ounces) chopped green chilies
1 tablespoon minced fresh parsley
2 garlic cloves, minced
2 teaspoons ground cumin
2 teaspoons dried coriander
1 teaspoon minced fresh cilantro
1 teaspoon chili powder
1/4 teaspoon cayenne pepper

In a large saucepan, cook beef and onion over medium heat until meat is no longer pink; drain. Add the zucchini, yellow squash and red pepper; cook and stir until crisp-tender. Stir in the remaining ingredients. Bring to a boil. Reduce heat; cover and simmer for 20 minutes or until the vegetables are tender. **yield:** 8 servings (2 quarts).

nutrition facts: 1 cup equals 223 calories, 6 g fat (2 g saturated fat), 21 mg cholesterol, 439 mg sodium, 23 g carbohydrate, 7 g fiber, 17 g protein.

shaker herb 'n' meatball soup

prep 30 minutes | **cook** 2 hours

8 cups beef broth
2 cans (14-1/2 ounces *each*) diced tomatoes, undrained
3 medium potatoes, peeled and cubed
3 medium carrots, sliced
1 cup shredded cabbage
1 large onion, chopped
1/2 cup chopped fresh parsley
6 whole peppercorns
1/2 teaspoon dried marjoram
1/2 teaspoon celery seed
1/2 teaspoon dried thyme
1/8 teaspoon ground cumin
1 pound lean ground beef
1/2 cup soft bread crumbs
1 egg, beaten
1 teaspoon Worcestershire sauce
1/4 teaspoon salt
1/8 teaspoon pepper

In a Dutch oven or soup kettle, combine the first 12 ingredients; bring to a boil. Reduce heat; cover and simmer for 1 hour.

In a bowl, combine the beef, bread crumbs, egg, Worcestershire sauce, salt and pepper. Shape into 1-in. balls; drop into soup. Cover and simmer for 2 hours. **yield:** 12-14 servings (3-1/2 quarts).

nutrition facts: 1 cup equals 114 calories, 3 g fat (1 g saturated fat), 31 mg cholesterol, 594 mg sodium, 12 g carbohydrate, 2 g fiber, 9 g protein.

 This beef recipe is lighter in calories, fat and sodium.

carolyn milke
north canton, connecticut

This filling soup is one of my favorite ways to warm up during the cold winter season in New England. The meatballs are fuss-free because they cook in the soup—there's no need to brown them beforehand.

onion meatball stew

prep 20 minutes | **cook** 25 minutes

valerie warner
north manchester, indiana

When fall arrives, I start to crave comforting fare such as homemade soups and stews. This meaty recipe is one of the first I reach for.

1 egg, lightly beaten
1/2 cup soft bread crumbs
1 garlic clove, minced
1/2 teaspoon salt
1/2 teaspoon dried savory
1 pound ground beef
1 tablespoon vegetable oil
1 can (10-1/2 ounces) condensed French onion soup, undiluted
2/3 cup water
3 medium carrots, cut into 3/4-inch chunks
2 medium potatoes, peeled and cut into 1-inch chunks
1 medium onion, cut into thin wedges
1 tablespoon minced fresh parsley

In a large bowl, combine the egg, bread crumbs, garlic, salt and savory. Crumble beef over mixture and mix well. Shape into 1-1/4-in. balls.

In a large skillet, brown meatballs in oil over medium heat; drain. Stir in the soup, water, carrots, potatoes and onion. Bring to a boil. Reduce heat; cover and simmer for 25-30 minutes or until vegetables are tender. Sprinkle with parsley. **yield:** 4 servings.

mom's tomato vegetable soup

prep 15 minutes | **cook** 3 hours

 This beef recipe is lighter in calories, fat and sodium.

sandra davis
brownsville, tennessee

I created this vegetable-based soup using a recipe my mom made when I was a child. The robust, down-home taste brings back memories of growing up on the farm.

1 broiler/fryer chicken (3 to 3-1/2 pounds), cut up
8 cups water
1 celery rib, halved
1 medium onion, halved
3 medium potatoes, peeled and cut into 1/2-inch cubes
2 cups reduced-sodium tomato juice
1 can (16 ounces) mixed vegetables, drained
1 can (15-1/2 ounces) black-eyed peas, rinsed and drained
1 can (14-1/2 ounces) reduced-sodium stewed tomatoes
1/2 cup chopped onion
2-1/2 teaspoons salt, optional
1 teaspoon pepper
1/2 pound lean ground beef
1 can (15 ounces) cream-style corn

In an 8-qt. soup kettle, place chicken, water, celery and onion. Cover and bring to a boil; skim fat. Reduce the heat; cover and simmer for 1-1/2 hours or until the chicken falls off the bones.

Strain broth and skim fat; return broth to kettle. Add the next eight ingredients. Debone chicken and cut into chunks; return to kettle. Bring to a boil.

Meanwhile, in a medium skillet, cook beef until no longer pink; drain and add to soup. Reduce heat; cover and simmer for 1 hour. Stir in corn; cook, uncovered, for 30 minutes, stirring occasionally. **yield:** 18 servings (4-1/2 quarts).

nutrition facts: 1 cup (calculated without added salt) equals 178 calories, 6 g fat (2 g saturated fat), 35 mg cholesterol, 241 mg sodium, 17 g carbohydrate, 2 g fiber, 15 g protein.

beefy wild rice soup

prep 15 minutes | **cook** 1 hour 15 minutes

1 pound ground beef
1/2 teaspoon Italian seasoning
6 cups water, *divided*
2 large onions, chopped
3 celery ribs, chopped
1 cup uncooked wild rice
2 teaspoons beef bouillon granules
1/2 teaspoon pepper
1/4 teaspoon hot pepper sauce
3 cans (10-3/4 ounces *each*) condensed cream of mushroom soup, undiluted
1 can (4 ounces) mushroom stems and pieces, drained

 This beef recipe is lighter in calories, fat and sodium.

marilyn chesbrough
wautoma, wisconsin

Here in central Wisconsin, we experience many days of snow and cold temperatures. I like to serve hot soup often, especially this creamy one.

In a Dutch oven or soup kettle, cook beef and Italian seasoning over medium heat until the meat is no longer pink; drain. Add 2 cups water, onions, celery, wild rice, beef bouillon, pepper and hot pepper sauce; bring to a boil.

Reduce heat; cover and simmer for 45 minutes. Stir in the soup, mushrooms and remaining water. Cover and simmer for 30 minutes. **yield:** 10-12 servings (3 quarts).

nutrition facts: 1 cup equals 166 calories, 6 g fat (2 g saturated fat), 26 mg cholesterol, 372 mg sodium, 17 g carbohydrate, 2 g fiber, 11 g protein.

hearty italian chili

prep 15 minutes | **cook** 30 minutes

chloe buckner
edinburg, pennsylvania

When I was a girl, I was my grandmother's constant helper in the kitchen. And, like her, I can't seem to use a recipe without changing it! When I got bored with plain chili, I came up with this Italian version full of beef and sausage.

1 pound ground beef
1/2 pound bulk Italian sausage
1 medium onion, chopped
1/2 cup chopped green pepper
1 can *or* jar (26-1/2 to 30 ounces) spaghetti sauce
1 can (16 ounces) kidney beans, rinsed and drained
1 can (14-1/2 ounces) diced tomatoes, undrained
1 jar (4-1/2 ounces) sliced mushrooms, drained
1 cup water
1/3 cup halved sliced pepperoni
5 teaspoons chili powder
1/2 teaspoon salt
Pinch pepper

In a large saucepan, cook beef, sausage, onion and green pepper over medium heat until the meat is no longer pink; drain.

Add the remaining ingredients; bring to a boil. Reduce the heat; simmer, uncovered, for 30 minutes. **yield:** 6-8 servings (2-1/4 quarts).

meaty zucchini stew

prep 10 minutes | **cook** 30 minutes

1 pound ground beef
1 pound bulk pork sausage
2 cans (14-1/2 ounces *each*) diced tomatoes
2 medium green peppers, cut into 1/2-inch pieces
2 cups thinly sliced celery
1 cup chopped onion
6 medium zucchini, halved and cut into 1/2-inch slices
1 cup tomato juice
1 teaspoon salt
1 teaspoon Italian seasoning
1 teaspoon dried oregano
Grated Parmesan cheese, optional

In a Dutch oven or large saucepan, cook beef and sausage over medium heat until no longer pink; drain and set aside.

Drain tomatoes, reserving the juice; set tomatoes aside. In the same pan, combine the peppers, celery, onion and reserved juice. Cover and cook over medium heat for 10 minutes.

Add the meat, tomatoes, zucchini, tomato juice and seasonings. Cover and cook for 15 minutes or until zucchini is tender, stirring occasionally. Garnish with cheese if desired. **yield:** 12 servings.

phyllis bertin
thunder bay, ontario

Slices of zucchini are mixed with ground beef, pork sausage and an assortment of other vegetables to create this one-dish wonder. It's a favorite choice for potlucks.

mexican bean soup

prep 20 minutes | **cook** 45 minutes

vivian christian
stephenville, texas

For the annual party my family has in fall, I make a big pot of this Southwestern soup and serve it with corn bread. Everyone loves to garnish a brimming bowlful with cheese and sour cream.

2 pounds ground beef
1 medium onion, chopped
1 quart water
3 cans (14-1/2 ounces *each*) diced tomatoes, undrained
2 cans (15-1/2 ounces *each*) hominy, drained
2 cans (15-1/2 ounces *each*) ranch-style *or* chili beans
1 can (16 ounces) kidney beans, rinsed and drained
1 can (4 ounces) chopped green chilies
2 envelopes taco seasoning
1 envelope (1 ounce) original ranch dressing mix
2 tablespoons brown sugar
1/4 teaspoon cayenne pepper
Shredded cheddar cheese and sour cream, optional

In a Dutch oven or soup kettle, brown beef and onion; drain. Add the next 10 ingredients; bring to a boil. Reduce heat; cover and simmer for 30 minutes. Garnish with cheese and sour cream if desired. **yield:** 14-16 servings (4 quarts).

great GARNISHES

Shredded cheddar cheese and a dollop of sour cream make delicious garnishes for Mexican Bean Soup...and they create an attractive presentation, too.

Want more ideas for topping off your favorite soup recipe? Finish off a bowlful with crumbled cooked bacon, slices of green onion or strips of sweet pepper.

Or, try fried tortilla strips, shredded carrot, parsley, Chinese noodles or seasoned or plain croutons.

hearty meatball soup

prep 20 minutes | **cook** 45 minutes

2 eggs
1 cup soft bread crumbs
1 teaspoon salt
1/2 teaspoon pepper
1 pound lean ground beef
1 pound ground pork
1/2 pound ground turkey
4 cups beef broth
1 can (46 ounces) tomato juice
2 cans (14-1/2 ounces *each*) stewed tomatoes
8 cups shredded cabbage
1 cup thinly sliced celery
1 cup thinly sliced carrots
8 green onions, sliced
3/4 cup uncooked long grain rice
2 teaspoons dried basil
3 tablespoons minced fresh parsley
2 tablespoons soy sauce

In a large bowl, combine the egg, bread crumbs, salt and pepper. Crumble beef, pork and turkey over mixture and mix well. Shape into 1-in. balls.

In a soup kettle, bring broth to a boil. Carefully add the meatballs. Add the tomato juice, tomatoes, vegetables, rice and basil. Cover and simmer for 30 minutes.

Add the parsley and soy sauce. Simmer, uncovered, for 10 minutes or until meatballs are no longer pink and vegetables are tender. **yield:** 22-24 servings (5-3/4 quarts).

janice thompson
lansing, michigan

Ground pork, turkey and beef make flavorful meatballs for this thick soup. A little bit goes a long way, so it's a terrific choice for potlucks.

pronto chili

prep 10 minutes | **cook** 30 minutes

taste of home test kitchen
greendale, wisconsin

When your busy schedule won't allow you to have chili simmering all day on the stove, try this recipe. Your family will never guess this homemade version takes just minutes to make.

1 pound ground beef
1 medium onion, chopped
1 medium green pepper, chopped
2 to 3 teaspoons chili powder
1 teaspoon ground cumin
1 teaspoon salt
1 can (14-1/2 ounces) Mexican stewed tomatoes
1 can (15-3/4 ounces) chili beans in gravy
1 cup frozen corn
Shredded cheddar cheese, optional

In a large saucepan, cook the beef, onion and green pepper over medium heat until the meat is no longer pink; drain. Add the next six ingredients; cover and simmer for 20 minutes. Serve with cheese if desired. **yield:** 6 servings.

country-style stew

prep 20 minutes | **cook** 2 hours

ladonna reed
ponca city, oklahoma

When my husband and I got married, I came up with this recipe and was delighted by the delicious results. It's still our favorite stew.

2 pounds ground beef
1 can (32 ounces) tomato juice
4 cups water
4 medium carrots, sliced
1 large onion, diced
2 cups frozen sliced okra
1-1/2 cups shredded cabbage
1-1/2 cups diced celery
1 cup frozen green beans
1 cup frozen peas
2 cans (14-1/2 ounces *each*) diced tomatoes, undrained
1 can (15-1/2 ounces) great northern beans, rinsed and drained
1 can (15-1/2 ounces) black-eyed peas, rinsed and drained
1 can (15-1/4 ounces) lima beans, rinsed and drained
1 can (11 ounces) Mexican-style corn
5 teaspoons beef bouillon granules
1 teaspoon seasoned salt
1/2 teaspoon dried oregano
1/2 teaspoon garlic powder
1/2 teaspoon pepper
1/4 teaspoon celery salt

In a Dutch oven or soup kettle, brown beef; drain. Add remaining ingredients; bring to a boil. Reduce heat; cover and simmer for 2 hours or until vegetables are tender. **yield:** 18-22 servings (5-1/2 quarts).

baked bean chili

prep/total time 30 minutes

2 pounds ground beef
3 cans (28 ounces *each*) baked beans
1 can (46 ounces) tomato juice
1 can (11-1/2 ounces) V8 juice
1 envelope chili seasoning

nancy wall
bakersfield, california

Who says a good chili has to simmer all day long? This zippy chili—with a touch of sweetness from the baked beans—can be made on the spur of the moment. It's great for drop-in guests.

In a Dutch oven, cook beef over medium heat until no longer pink; drain. Stir in the remaining ingredients. Bring to a boil. Reduce heat; simmer, uncovered, for 10 minutes. **yield:** 24 servings.

hearty black-eyed pea soup

prep 10 minutes | **cook** 1 hour

1 pound bulk pork sausage
1 pound ground beef
1 large onion, chopped
4 cups water
3 cans (15-1/2 ounces *each*) black-eyed peas, rinsed and drained
1 can (28 ounces) diced tomatoes, undrained
1 can (10 ounces) diced tomatoes and green chilies, undrained
1 can (4 ounces) chopped green chilies
4 beef bouillon cubes
4 teaspoons molasses
1 teaspoon Worcestershire sauce
3/4 teaspoon garlic salt
1/2 teaspoon salt
1/4 teaspoon pepper
1/4 teaspoon ground cumin

In a Dutch oven or soup kettle, cook sausage, beef and onion over medium heat until meat is no longer pink; drain. Add remaining ingredients; bring to a boil. Reduce heat; cover and simmer for 45 minutes. **yield:** 12-16 servings (4 quarts).

going DUTCH

A Dutch oven is a heavy covered pan that can be used both on the stovetop and in the oven. Available in a variety of sizes from 2-1/2 quarts to 6 quarts, a Dutch oven is often called for in recipes for soups, stews and chili. This pot is also handy for browning meats before roasting—you need just one pan and keep the flavor of the drippings.

alice jarrell
dexter, missouri

I'd eaten this flavorful, meaty soup countless times at a small restaurant in our town. When the owner finally retired, he said I deserved the secret recipe and passed it along. Now, my family enjoys it at least once a month!

chili for a crowd

prep 25 minutes | **cook** 1 hour

lisa humphreys
wasilla, alaska

My aunt gave me the basis of this recipe, which combines ground beef with kielbasa. It's a great chili for a Super Bowl party or other event.

3 pounds ground beef

2 cans (28 ounces *each*) diced tomatoes, undrained

4 cans (16 ounces *each*) kidney beans, rinsed and drained *or* 4 cans (15 ounces) pinto beans *or* black beans, rinsed and drained

1 pound smoked kielbasa, sliced and halved

2 large onions, halved and thinly sliced

2 cans (8 ounces *each*) tomato sauce

2/3 cup hickory-flavored barbecue sauce

1-1/2 cups water

1/2 cup packed brown sugar

5 fresh banana peppers, seeded and sliced

2 tablespoons chili powder

2 teaspoons ground mustard

2 teaspoons instant coffee granules

1 teaspoon *each* dried oregano, thyme and sage

1/2 to 1 teaspoon cayenne pepper

1/2 to 1 teaspoon crushed red pepper flakes

2 garlic cloves, minced

In an 8-qt. kettle or Dutch oven, cook beef over medium heat until beef is no longer pink; drain.

Add the remaining ingredients; bring to a boil. Reduce the heat; cover and simmer for 1 hour, stirring soup occasionally. **yield:** 20-24 servings (6 quarts).

pepper **POINTERS**

Banana peppers add distinctive flavor to Chili for a Crowd. The flavor of banana peppers is sweet and mild.

Look for peppers with evenly colored skins that are free of blemishes. Banana peppers stay fresh in a plastic bag in the refrigerator for about 1 week.

cheesy chili

prep/total time 25 minutes

- 2 pounds ground beef
- 2 medium onions, chopped
- 2 garlic cloves, minced
- 3 cans (10 ounces *each*) diced tomatoes and green chilies, undrained
- 1 can (28 ounces) diced tomatoes, undrained
- 2 cans (4 ounces *each*) chopped green chilies
- 1/2 teaspoon pepper
- 2 pounds process cheese (Velveeta)

In a large saucepan, cook the beef, onions and garlic until meat is no longer pink; drain. Stir in the tomatoes, chilies and pepper; bring to a boil. Reduce heat; simmer, uncovered, for 10-15 minutes. Stir in cheese until melted. Serve immediately or allow to cool before freezing. May be frozen for up to 3 months.

TO USE FROZEN CHILI: Thaw in the refrigerator; heat in a saucepan or microwave. **yield:** 12 servings (about 3 quarts).

codie ray
tallulah, louisiana

My grandchildren like digging into big bowls of this zesty chili. It's so rich and cheesy, you could even serve it as a dip for chips.

quick beef stew

prep 35 minutes | **cook** 20 minutes

 This beef recipe is lighter in calories, fat and sodium.

laura mccormick
lebanon, missouri

This family-friendly recipe proves that comforting, home-style stews don't have to simmer for hours. You'll love the plentiful veggies and blend of seasonings.

- 5 medium red potatoes, cubed
- 2 cups water
- 2 pounds ground beef
- 1 medium onion, chopped
- 1 package (16 ounces) frozen mixed vegetables
- 1 can (14-1/2 ounces) diced tomatoes, undrained
- 1 can (10 ounces) diced tomatoes and green chilies, undrained
- 1 can (8 ounces) tomato sauce
- 1/2 teaspoon chili powder
- 1/2 teaspoon salt
- 1/4 teaspoon garlic powder

Place the potatoes and water in a microwave-safe dish; microwave on high until almost tender, about 7-9 minutes. Set aside (do not drain).

In a 3-qt. microwave-safe dish, cook beef and onion on medium until beef is browned, about 8 minutes; drain. Add potatoes and remaining ingredients. Cover and microwave on medium for 12 minutes or until potatoes are tender and vegetables are heated through. **yield:** 12 servings.

nutrition facts: 1-1/2 cups equals 195 calories, 7 g fat (3 g saturated fat), 37 mg cholesterol, 391 mg sodium, 17 g carbohydrate, 4 g fiber, 16 g protein.

editor's note: This recipe was tested in a 1,100-watt microwave.

cabbage patch soup

prep 10 minutes | **bake** 30 minutes

This beef recipe is lighter in calories, fat and sodium.

fran strother
wasilla, alaska

People are always glad to see this slightly sweet and mildly zippy soup on the menu. The amount of cabbage flavor is just right.

1/2 pound ground beef
1-1/2 cups chopped onion
1/2 cup sliced celery
2 cups water
1 can (16 ounces) kidney beans, rinsed and drained
1 can (14-1/2 ounces) stewed tomatoes
1 cup shredded cabbage
1 teaspoon chili powder
1/2 teaspoon salt
Hot mashed potatoes, optional

In a large saucepan over medium heat, brown beef; drain. Add onion and celery; cook until tender. Stir in the water, beans, tomatoes, cabbage, chili powder and salt; bring to a boil. Reduce heat; cover and simmer for 20-30 minutes or until cabbage is tender. Top each bowl with mashed potatoes if desired. **yield:** 4-6 servings.

nutrition facts: 1 cup equals 180 calories, 5 g fat (2 g saturated fat), 25 mg cholesterol, 476 mg sodium, 22 g carbohydrate, 5 g fiber, 14 g protein.

southwest beef stew

prep/total time 30 minutes

2 pounds lean ground beef
1-1/2 cups chopped onions
1 can (28 ounces) diced tomatoes, undrained
1 package (16 ounces) frozen corn, thawed
1 can (15 ounces) black beans, rinsed and drained
1 cup picante sauce
3/4 cup water
1 teaspoon ground cumin
3/4 teaspoon salt
1/2 teaspoon garlic powder
1/2 teaspoon pepper
1/2 cup shredded cheddar cheese

janet brannan
sidney, montana

Add your family's favorite picante sauce to this tasty stew, then watch how quickly they empty their bowls! I like to make an extra batch and freeze it for another day.

In a Dutch oven, cook beef and onions over medium heat until meat is no longer pink; drain. Stir in the tomatoes, corn, beans, picante sauce, water, cumin, salt, garlic powder and pepper. Bring to a boil. Reduce heat; cover and simmer for 15 minutes or until corn is tender. Sprinkle with cheese. **yield:** 8 servings.

four-bean taco chili

prep 15 minutes | cook 30 minutes

amy martell
canton, pennsylvania

Heat up the dinner table on a cold night with this zesty chili. It's chock-full of ground beef, beans, green chilies and taco seasoning.

2 pounds ground beef
3 cups tomato juice
1 jar (16 ounces) salsa
1 can (16 ounces) kidney beans, rinsed and drained
1 can (15-1/2 ounces) great northern beans, rinsed and drained
1 can (15 ounces) butter beans, rinsed and drained
1 can (15 ounces) black beans, rinsed and drained
1 can (8 ounces) tomato sauce
1 can (6 ounces) tomato paste
1 can (4 ounces) chopped green chilies
1 envelope taco seasoning

In a Dutch oven or soup kettle, cook beef over medium heat until no longer pink; drain. Stir in the remaining ingredients. Bring to a boil. Reduce heat; simmer, uncovered, for 15 minutes, stirring occasionally. **yield:** 12 cups.

italian vegetable bowl

prep 15 minutes | cook 1 hour 20 minutes

1 pound lean ground beef
2 cups water
1 can (16 ounces) kidney beans, rinsed and drained
1 can (15 ounces) tomato sauce
1 can (14-1/2 ounces) Italian stewed tomatoes
1 cup chopped carrots
1 cup chopped celery
1 cup chopped onion
3 beef bouillon granules
2 garlic cloves, minced
3/4 teaspoon dried oregano
3/4 teaspoon dried basil
1/2 teaspoon pepper
2 cups shredded cabbage
1 cup cooked elbow macaroni
1 tablespoon minced fresh parsley

In a Dutch oven or soup kettle over medium heat, cook beef until no longer pink; drain. Add the next 12 ingredients; bring to a boil. Reduce heat; cover and simmer for 1 hour or until the vegetables are tender. Add cabbage, macaroni and parsley. Cook 20 minutes longer or until cabbage is tender. **yield:** 10 servings (2-1/2 quarts).

nutrition facts: 1 cup equals 164 calories, 3 g fat (1 g saturated fat), 22 mg cholesterol, 716 mg sodium, 19 g carbohydrate, 5 g fiber, 14 g protein.

 This beef recipe is lighter in calories, fat and sodium.

lynn sager
north richland hills, texas

I love to fix this hamburger vegetable stew on chilly fall and winter days. Pair it with oven-fresh bread or a green salad for an unbeatable meal.

chunky beef chili

prep 20 minutes | **cook** 5 hours

vicki flowers
knoxville, tennessee

When I first sampled this chili, which came from my brother, I couldn't wait to share it. It's the best I've ever had! The recipe mixes ground beef with chunks of beef stew meat.

1/2 cup all-purpose flour
1-1/2 teaspoons *each* dried thyme and rosemary, crushed
1-1/2 pounds beef stew meat, cut into 1-inch cubes
1/2 pound ground beef
1 can (14-1/2 ounces) beef broth
1 large onion, finely chopped
1/2 cup chopped green pepper
1 garlic clove, minced
1 can (4 ounces) chopped green chilies
1 to 2 jalapeno peppers, seeded and minced
1 can (15 ounces) crushed tomatoes
2 cans (15-1/2 ounces *each*) chili beans, undrained
1 can (15-1/2 ounces) pinto beans, rinsed and drained
1 can (15 ounces) white *or* red kidney beans, rinsed and drained
1 can (6 ounces) tomato paste
2 tablespoons ground cumin
1 teaspoon dried oregano
1/2 teaspoon *each* pepper, white pepper and cayenne pepper
3 to 4 drops hot pepper sauce
Shredded cheddar cheese, optional

In a plastic bag, combine flour, thyme and rosemary; add beef cubes, a few at a time, and shake to coat. In a 4-qt. kettle or Dutch oven, cook ground beef and the beef cubes over medium heat until beef is no longer pink; drain.

Add all of the remaining ingredients except the cheese. Cover and simmer for 5 hours. Garnish with cheese if desired. **yield:** 10-12 servings (3 quarts).

editor's note: When cutting or seeding hot peppers, use rubber or plastic gloves to protect your hands. Avoid touching your face.

zesty **CAYENNE**

Chunky Beef Chili gets a tongue-tingling kick from cayenne pepper. Sometimes called red pepper, this spice has an extremely hot, pungent flavor that lives up to its fiery, red-orange appearance.

Cayenne pepper is made by grinding up dried pods from several varieties of hot chili peppers. Just a little cayenne pepper in a recipe can go a long way.

cajun chili

prep 15 minutes | **cook** 35 minutes

2 pounds ground beef
1 cup chopped onion
1 cup chopped green pepper
1 garlic clove, minced
1 can (15 ounces) pinto beans, undrained
1 can (14-1/2 ounces) diced tomatoes, undrained
1 can (8 ounces) tomato sauce
1 to 2 tablespoons chili powder
1 tablespoon honey
1 teaspoon dried parsley flakes
1 teaspoon dried oregano
1 teaspoon ground cumin
1 teaspoon Cajun seasoning

In a Dutch oven, brown beef, onion, green pepper and garlic. Meanwhile, in a blender or food processor, process beans with liquid until smooth. Drain fat from Dutch oven; add the beans and remaining ingredients. Simmer, uncovered, for 35 to 45 minutes. **yield:** 6 servings.

james harris
columbus, georgia

Cajun cooking is one of my specialties. When I'm hungry for a meaty meal with a bit of zip to it, this is the recipe I reach for.

hearty hamburger soup

prep/total time 30 minutes

diane mrozinski
essexville, michigan

This veggie-packed soup gets a thumbs-up from everyone. The recipe yields two servings, but you can easily double or triple it for more people.

1/4 pound ground beef
1/4 cup chopped onion
1-1/2 cups water
1/4 cup thinly sliced carrot
1-1/2 teaspoons beef bouillon granules
1 can (5-1/2 ounces) V8 juice
1/4 cup frozen corn
1/4 cup frozen peas
1/4 cup sliced fresh mushrooms
1/4 cup sliced zucchini
1/8 teaspoon dried basil
Dash pepper
1/2 cup cooked elbow macaroni

In a small saucepan, cook beef and onion over medium heat until meat is no longer pink; drain. Add water, carrot and bouillon. Bring to a boil. Reduce heat; simmer, uncovered, for 5 minutes.

Add V8 juice, corn, peas, mushrooms, zucchini, basil and pepper. Simmer 6-8 minutes longer or until vegetables are tender. Add macaroni; heat through. **yield:** 2 servings.

cowpoke chili

prep 10 minutes | **bake** 40 minutes

1 pound ground beef
1 small onion, chopped
1 garlic clove, minced
1 can (10-1/2 ounces) condensed beef broth, undiluted
1 can (8 ounces) tomato sauce
1 can (6 ounces) tomato paste
1 can (15-1/2 ounces) hot chili beans
1 can (15 ounces) black beans, rinsed and drained
2 tablespoons sugar
1 tablespoon butter
1 teaspoon chili powder
1/4 teaspoon salt
1/4 teaspoon dried oregano
1/8 teaspoon ground cumin
1/8 teaspoon crushed red pepper flakes
Dash cayenne pepper
2 cups frozen lima beans, thawed
Cherry tomatoes, fresh oregano and small chili peppers, optional

ramona nelson
fairbanks, alaska

Many of my friends and family members have requested this chili recipe, which I've been making for 25 years. It won first place in a local cooking contest.

In a large saucepan, cook beef, onion and garlic over medium heat until meat is no longer pink; drain. Stir in the broth, tomato sauce and paste until blended. Add the next 10 ingredients. Bring to a boil. Reduce heat; cover and simmer for 30 minutes.

Add lima beans; cook 5-10 minutes longer or until beans are tender. Garnish with tomatoes, oregano and peppers if desired. **yield:** 7 servings.

country carrot soup

prep/total time 30 minutes

marlane jones
allentown, pennsylvania

I used ground beef to jazz up a traditional carrot soup recipe. This meaty, creamy meal-in-a-bowl always hits the spot.

1 pound ground beef
1/4 cup chopped onion
2 cans (10-3/4 ounces *each*) condensed cream of celery soup, undiluted
3 cups tomato juice
2 cups shredded carrots
1 cup water
1 bay leaf
1/2 teaspoon sugar

1/2 teaspoon dried marjoram
1/2 teaspoon salt
1/4 teaspoon garlic powder
1/4 teaspoon pepper

In a large saucepan, brown beef and onion over medium heat until beef is no longer pink; drain. Add remaining ingredients; bring to a boil. Reduce heat; cover and simmer for 15 minutes or until carrots are tender. Remove bay leaf. **yield:** 6-8 servings.

beef minestrone

prep 20 minutes | **cook** 1 hour

- 1 pound lean ground beef
- 1 cup chopped onion
- 6 cups water
- 1 cup cubed peeled potatoes
- 1 cup chopped tomatoes
- 1 cup shredded cabbage
- 1 cup chopped carrots
- 1/2 cup chopped celery
- 1/4 cup uncooked long grain rice
- 1/2 teaspoon dried basil
- 1/2 teaspoon dried thyme
- 1 bay leaf
- 1/4 teaspoon pepper
- 5 teaspoons grated Parmesan cheese

In a Dutch oven, cook beef and onion until meat is browned and onion is tender; drain. Add next 11 ingredients; bring to a boil. Reduce heat; cover and simmer for 1 hour.

Discard the bay leaf. Sprinkle each serving with 1/2 teaspoon of Parmesan cheese. **yield:** 10 servings.

nutrition facts: 1 cup equals 141 calories, 7 g fat (0 saturated fat), 31 mg cholesterol, 58 mg sodium, 10 g carbohydrate, 0 fiber, 11 g protein.

 This beef recipe is lighter in calories, fat and sodium.

ann lape

richmondville, new york

This recipe pleasantly proves that eating lighter doesn't have to mean saying farewell to ground beef's full-bodied flavor. A steaming bowl of this soup tastes like a treat.

cincinnati chili

prep 20 minutes | **cook** 1-1/2 hours

edith joyce

parkman, ohio

Cinnamon and cocoa give rich color to this hearty chili, which is served over spaghetti noodles. It never fails to warm me up on a cold day.

- 1 pound ground beef
- 1 pound ground pork
- 4 medium onions, chopped
- 6 garlic cloves, minced
- 2 cans (16 ounces *each*) kidney beans, rinsed and drained
- 1 can (28 ounces) crushed tomatoes
- 1/4 cup white vinegar
- 1/4 cup baking cocoa
- 2 tablespoons chili powder
- 2 tablespoons Worcestershire sauce
- 4 teaspoons ground cinnamon
- 3 teaspoons dried oregano
- 2 teaspoons ground cumin
- 2 teaspoons ground allspice
- 2 teaspoons hot pepper sauce
- 3 bay leaves
- 1 teaspoon sugar

Salt and pepper to taste

Hot cooked spaghetti

Shredded cheddar cheese, sour cream, chopped tomatoes and green onions

In a Dutch oven or soup kettle, cook beef, pork, onions and garlic over medium heat until meat is no longer pink; drain. Add the beans, tomatoes, vinegar, cocoa and seasonings; bring to a boil. Reduce heat; cover and simmer for 1-1/2 hours or until heated through.

Discard bay leaves. Serve over spaghetti. Garnish with cheese, sour cream, tomatoes and onions. **yield:** 8 servings.

root vegetable beef stew

prep 15 minutes | **cook** 40 minutes

This beef recipe is lighter in calories, fat and sodium.

mary rea
orangeville, ontario

I discovered this recipe in our local newspaper a number of years ago. The chunky beef stew is so satisfying on a cold fall or winter day.

1 pound lean ground beef
1 medium onion, chopped
2 cans (14-1/2 ounces *each*) reduced-sodium beef broth
1 medium sweet potato, peeled and cubed
1 cup cubed carrots
1 cup cubed peeled rutabaga
1 cup cubed peeled parsnips
1 cup cubed peeled potatoes
2 tablespoons tomato paste
1 teaspoon Worcestershire sauce
1/2 teaspoon dried thyme
1/4 teaspoon salt
1/4 teaspoon pepper
1 tablespoon cornstarch
2 tablespoons water

In a Dutch oven or large kettle, cook beef and onion over medium heat until meat is no longer pink; drain. Add the broth, vegetables, tomato paste, Worcestershire sauce, thyme, salt and pepper. Bring to a boil. Reduce heat; cover and simmer for 30-40 minutes or until vegetables are tender.

In a small bowl, combine the cornstarch and water until smooth; stir into the stew. Bring to a boil; cook and stir for 2 minutes or until thickened. **yield:** 6 servings.

nutrition facts: 1-1/3 cups equals 246 calories, 6 g fat (3 g saturated fat), 37 mg cholesterol, 659 mg sodium, 29 g carbohydrate, 5 g fiber, 18 g protein.

sausage onion chili

prep/total time 25 minutes

1 pound bulk pork sausage
1 pound ground beef
1 can (10-1/2 ounces) condensed French onion soup, undiluted
2 tablespoons chili powder
1 teaspoon ground cumin
1/2 teaspoon salt
1/2 teaspoon pepper
1 can (16 ounces) kidney beans, rinsed and drained
1 can (8 ounces) tomato sauce
1 can (6 ounces) tomato paste
1/2 cup water

In a large saucepan, brown sausage and beef; drain. Stir in the remaining ingredients. Bring to boil. Reduce heat; cook and stir for 10-15 minutes or until thickened. **yield:** 6 servings (about 1-1/2 quarts).

making the CUT

Ground beef is often labeled using the cut of meat it is ground from, such as ground chuck or ground round. (Ground beef comes from a mix of beef cuts.)

It can also be labeled according to the fat content of the ground mixture or the percentage of lean meat to fat, such as 85% lean. The higher the percentage, the leaner the meat.

denise vonstein
shiloh, ohio

With both sausage and ground beef, this chili is a meat-lover's delight. French onion soup makes it different and adds extra flavor.

pepperoni pizza chili

prep 5 minutes | **cook** 40 minutes

marilouise wyatt
cowen, west virginia

I came up with this recipe one day when I was craving pizza but didn't want to fuss with making a crust. I just put the pizza in a bowl instead!

1 pound ground beef
1 can (16 ounces) kidney beans, rinsed and drained
1 can (15 ounces) pizza sauce
1 can (14-1/2 ounces) Italian stewed tomatoes
1 can (8 ounces) tomato sauce
1-1/2 cups water
1 package (3-1/2 ounces) sliced pepperoni
1/2 cup chopped green pepper
1 teaspoon pizza seasoning *or* Italian seasoning
1 teaspoon salt
Shredded part-skim mozzarella cheese, optional

In a large saucepan, cook beef over medium heat until no longer pink; drain. Stir in the beans, pizza sauce, tomatoes, tomato sauce, water, pepperoni, green pepper, pizza seasoning and salt. Bring to a boil. Reduce heat; simmer, uncovered, for 30 minutes or until chili reaches desired thickness. Sprinkle with cheese if desired. **yield:** 8 servings.

sensational SIDE

The recipe for tasty Pinto Bean Chili also makes simple Chili Cheese Quesadillas as a side dish. Consider pairing these irresistible, four-ingredient quesadillas with other Southwestern recipes in this chapter, such as Mexican Bean Soup (p. 62) or Four-Bean Taco Chili (p. 69).

pinto bean chili

prep 20 minutes + standing | **cook** 1 hour 40 minutes

sandy dilatush

denver, colorado

Plenty of cumin and chili powder season this chili, which includes homemade quesadillas served on the side. It all makes a terrific Southwestern meal.

1 pound dried pinto beans
2 pounds ground beef
1 medium onion, chopped
3 celery ribs, chopped
3 tablespoons all-purpose flour
4 cups water
2 tablespoons chili powder
2 tablespoons ground cumin
1/2 teaspoon sugar
1 can (28 ounces) crushed tomatoes
2 teaspoons cider vinegar
1-1/2 teaspoons salt

chili cheese quesadillas

2 cans (4 ounces *each*) chopped green chilies
12 flour tortillas (6 inches)
3 cups (12 ounces) shredded cheddar cheese
3 teaspoons vegetable oil

Place beans in a Dutch oven or soup kettle; add water to cover by 2 in. Bring to a boil; boil for 2 minutes. Remove from the heat; cover and let stand for 1 hour. Drain and rinse beans, discarding liquid.

In a Dutch oven, cook the beef, onion and celery over medium heat until meat is no longer pink; drain. Stir in flour until blended. Gradually stir in water. Add the beans, chili powder, cumin and sugar. Bring to a boil. Reduce heat; cover and simmer for 1-1/2 hours or until beans are tender. Stir in the tomatoes, vinegar and salt; heat through, stirring occasionally.

Meanwhile, for quesadillas, spread about 1 tablespoon of chilies on half of each tortilla. Sprinkle with 1/4 cup of cheese; fold in half. In a large skillet, cook tortillas in 1 teaspoon of oil over medium heat until lightly browned on each side, adding more oil as needed. Cut each in half. Serve with chili. **yield:** 8 servings.

aloha chili

prep/total time 30 minutes

- 2 pounds ground beef
- 1 large onion, finely chopped
- 1 can (16 ounces) kidney beans, rinsed and drained
- 1 can (15-3/4 ounces) pork and beans
- 1 can (20 ounces) pineapple chunks, undrained
- 1 cup ketchup
- 1/4 cup packed brown sugar
- 1/4 cup white vinegar

In a large saucepan, brown beef and onion; drain. Stir in remaining ingredients. Cover and simmer for 20 minutes. **yield:** 8 servings (2-1/4 quarts).

dyan cornies
 vernon, british columbia

Pineapple and brown sugar give this out-of-the-ordinary chili a tropical taste. Everyone who samples it is pleasantly surprised—and they often request a second bowl.

ravioli soup

prep 20 minutes | **cook** 30 minutes

This beef recipe is lighter in calories, fat and sodium.

shelley way
cheyenne, wyoming

My family's love of pasta inspired me to create this thick, special-looking soup. We really enjoy the rich tomato base and tender, cheese-filled ravioli.

- 1 pound ground beef
- 2 cups water
- 1 can (28 ounces) crushed tomatoes
- 1 can (14-1/2 ounces) crushed tomatoes
- 1 can (6 ounces) tomato paste
- 1-1/2 cups chopped onion
- 1/4 cup minced fresh parsley
- 2 garlic cloves, minced
- 3/4 teaspoon dried basil
- 1/2 teaspoon dried oregano
- 1/2 teaspoon onion salt
- 1/2 teaspoon sugar
- 1/2 teaspoon salt
- 1/4 teaspoon pepper
- 1/4 teaspoon dried thyme
- 1 package (9 ounces) refrigerated cheese ravioli
- 1/4 cup grated Parmesan cheese

In a Dutch oven, cook beef over medium heat until no longer pink; drain. Add the water, tomatoes, tomato paste, onion, parsley, garlic cloves and seasonings; bring to a boil. Reduce the heat; cover and simmer for 30 minutes.

Meanwhile, cook ravioli according to package directions; drain. Add to soup and heat through. Stir in the Parmesan cheese. **yield:** 10 servings (2-1/2 quarts).

nutrition facts: 1 cup equals 235 calories, 8 g fat (4 g saturated fat), 42 mg cholesterol, 542 mg sodium, 25 g carbohydrate, 4 g fiber, 17 g protein.

HOME-STYLE
sandwiches

sausage-stuffed loaf

prep 20 minutes | **bake** 15 minutes

mary koehler
portland, oregon

For this impressive sandwich, I stuff a saucy mixture of beef and sausage inside a loaf of French bread. Sprinkled with pepper and Parmesan, it's a crowd-pleaser every time.

2 Italian sausage links
1/2 pound ground beef
1/2 cup chopped onion
1/4 cup chopped green pepper
1 medium tomato, chopped
1 can (15 ounces) chunky Italian-style tomato sauce
1/2 teaspoon dried basil
1/2 teaspoon dried oregano
1/2 teaspoon sugar
1/4 teaspoon aniseed
1/4 teaspoon salt
1/8 teaspoon garlic powder
1 loaf (1 pound) French bread
1/4 to 1/2 cup shredded Parmesan cheese
Coarsely ground pepper

In a large skillet, cook sausages over medium heat until no longer pink. Remove and set aside. In the same skillet, cook the beef, onion and green pepper until beef is no longer pink; drain. Stir in tomato, tomato sauce and seasonings. Cut sausages in half lengthwise and slice; add to meat sauce.

Cut a wedge out of top of the bread, about 1 in. wide and three-fourths of the way through the loaf. Discard cut portion or save for another use.

Fill loaf with meat sauce. Sprinkle with Parmesan cheese and pepper. Wrap in heavy-duty foil. Bake at 400° for 15-20 minutes or until heated through. **yield:** 6 servings.

baked beef patties

prep 15 minutes | **bake** 25 minutes

4-1/2　teaspoons minced fresh thyme *or* 1-1/2 teaspoons dried thyme, *divided*
　　3　tablespoons water
　1/2　teaspoon garlic salt
　1/2　teaspoon dried oregano
Dash paprika
Dash pepper
1-1/4　pounds lean ground beef
　1/4　cup all-purpose flour
　　1　egg, beaten
　1/4　cup seasoned bread crumbs
　　2　tablespoons butter
　　1　cup spaghetti sauce, *divided*
　3/4　cup shredded cheddar cheese
　　2　tablespoons grated Parmesan cheese
　　4　to 6 hamburger buns, split, optional

In a large bowl, combine 1-1/2 teaspoons of fresh thyme (or 1/2 teaspoon dried), water, garlic salt, oregano, paprika and pepper. Add beef; mix well. Shape into four to six patties. Coat patties with flour; dip into egg and then crumbs.

In a skillet, brown patties in butter. Arrange in a greased shallow baking dish. Pour half of the spaghetti sauce over patties. Sprinkle with cheeses; top with remaining sauce. Bake at 400° for 25 minutes or until meat is no longer pink. Sprinkle with remaining thyme. Serve patties and sauce on buns if desired. **yield:** 4-6 servings.

diane hixon
niceville, florida

Turn ordinary burgers into something special with this simple recipe. Topped with cheese and spaghetti sauce, the tasty beef patties can even be served without buns.

deluxe bacon burgers

prep/total time 20 minutes

bernadine dirmeyer
harpster, ohio

This hearty, contest-winning recipe is like meat loaf in a sandwich. When I prepare this for dinner, I always feel that my family is well fed.

　2　large carrots, grated
　1　large onion, grated
　1　cup mashed potato flakes
　2　eggs, lightly beaten
　1　garlic clove, minced
　1　teaspoon salt
Pepper to taste
　2　pounds ground beef
　8　bacon strips
　8　lettuce leaves, optional
　8　hamburger buns, split, optional

In a large bowl, combine the first seven ingredients. Crumble beef over mixture and mix gently. Shape into eight patties. Wrap a bacon strip around each patty; secure with toothpicks.

In a large skillet, cook burgers until meat is no longer pink and bacon is crisp. Remove toothpicks. Serve on lettuce-lined buns if desired. **yield:** 8 servings.

chalupa joes

prep/total time 20 minutes

nancy means

moline, illinois

Ordinary sloppy joes get a lift from the extra seasonings and picante sauce in this fun recipe. Try serving the sandwiches with refried beans and chips for a complete meal.

1 pound ground beef
1 cup picante sauce
2 tablespoons soy sauce
1 tablespoon olive oil
1 teaspoon Dijon mustard
1/2 teaspoon lemon-pepper seasoning
1/4 teaspoon garlic powder
1/8 teaspoon ground nutmeg
1/8 teaspoon ground cardamom
1 cup (4 ounces) shredded Monterey Jack cheese
6 Italian-style buns, split
1/4 cup sliced green onions

In a large skillet, cook beef over medium heat until no longer pink; drain. Add the picante sauce, soy sauce, oil, mustard, lemon-pepper, garlic powder, nutmeg and cardamom; simmer for 3-4 minutes.

Remove from the heat. Stir in the cheese. Spoon onto buns and sprinkle with onions. **yield:** 6 servings.

decked-out burgers

prep/total time 20 minutes

1 cup (4 ounces) shredded cheddar cheese
1 jar (4-1/2 ounces) sliced mushrooms, drained
1/3 cup mayonnaise
6 bacon strips, cooked and crumbled
1-1/2 pounds lean ground beef
1/4 cup finely chopped onion
1 teaspoon salt
1/2 teaspoon pepper
1/4 teaspoon garlic powder
1/8 teaspoon hot pepper sauce
6 hamburger buns, split
Lettuce leaves and tomato slices, optional

karen bourne

magrath, alberta

Guests always enjoy this burger's topping of bacon, cheese, mushrooms and mayonnaise. The hot pepper sauce mixed with the ground beef adds a bit of a kick.

In a bowl, combine cheese, mushrooms, mayonnaise and bacon; cover and refrigerate. In another bowl, combine the beef, onion, salt, pepper, garlic powder and hot pepper sauce. Shape mixture into six 1/2-in.-thick patties.

Grill, covered, over medium-hot heat for 4-5 minutes on each side. Spoon cheese mixture on top of each burger. Grill 1-2 minutes longer or until the cheese begins to melt. Serve on buns with lettuce and tomato if desired. **yield:** 6 servings.

taco sandwich

prep/total time 20 minutes

1 pound ground beef
1 loaf (1 pound) unsliced Italian bread
4 ounces cream cheese, softened
1/2 cup salsa
2 tablespoons taco seasoning
1 cup shredded lettuce
1 large tomato, sliced
6 slices American cheese

In a large skillet, cook beef over medium heat until no longer pink. Meanwhile, cut bread in half lengthwise; hollow out top and bottom of loaf, leaving a 1/2-in. shell (discard removed bread or save for another use). In a small mixing bowl, beat cream cheese and salsa until blended. Spread inside bread shell; set aside.

Drain beef. Stir in taco seasoning. Layer lettuce and tomato in bottom of bread shell; top with beef mixture and cheese. Replace bread top. **yield:** 6 servings.

melody stoltzfus
parkesburg, pennsylvania

This delicious sandwich tastes just like a taco on French bread. It's great when you're craving Southwestern food but don't have taco shells or tortillas on hand.

zesty sloppy joes

prep 15 minutes | **cook** 1 hour

sharon mckee
denton, texas

My mother-in-law created this recipe in the early 1950s. Our family likes these classic sloppy joes best served with pickles and potato chips.

2 pounds ground beef
1 large green pepper, chopped
2 cans (14-1/2 ounces *each*) diced tomatoes, undrained
2 cans (8 ounces *each*) tomato sauce
1 can (6 ounces) tomato paste
2 tablespoons Worcestershire sauce
1 tablespoon sugar
2 teaspoons celery salt *or* celery seed
2 teaspoons onion salt *or* onion powder
1 teaspoon paprika
1/4 to 1/2 teaspoon cayenne pepper
3 bay leaves
16 hamburger buns, split

In a Dutch oven or large kettle, cook the beef and green pepper over medium heat until the meat is no longer pink; drain. Stir in the tomatoes, tomato sauce, tomato paste and seasonings. Bring to a boil. Reduce the heat; cover and cook over low heat for 30 minutes.

Uncover; cook 30-40 minutes longer or until thickened. Discard bay leaves. Serve 1/2 cup of meat mixture on each bun. **yield:** 16 servings.

sourdough cheeseburgers

prep/total time 20 minutes

michelle dommel
quakertown, pennsylvania

*I came up with this burger
one night when I realized I'd
run out of hamburger buns.
My husband loved the tang
and toasty crunch of the
sourdough bread.*

3 tablespoons mayonnaise
1 tablespoon ketchup
1 tablespoon sweet pickle relish
1/2 pound ground beef
Salt and pepper to taste
1 small onion, sliced and separated into rings
4 tablespoons butter, *divided*
4 slices sourdough bread
4 slices Swiss cheese

In a small bowl, combine the mayonnaise, ketchup and relish; cover and refrigerate.

Shape beef into two oval patties. In a large skillet, cook burgers over medium heat for 4-5 minutes on each side or until a meat thermometer reads 160°. Season with salt and pepper; remove and keep warm. In the same skillet, saute onion in 1 tablespoon butter until tender. Remove and keep warm.

Using 2 tablespoons butter, butter one side of each slice of bread. Melt remaining butter in the skillet. Place bread buttered side up in the skillet; cook for 2-3 minutes or until golden brown. Turn; top two of the bread slices with the cheese. Cook 2 minutes longer or until cheese is melted.

To serve, place toast cheese side up on a plate. Top with a burger, relish mixture, onion and remaining toast. **yield:** 2 servings.

chili burgers

prep/total time 20 minutes

1 pound ground beef
1-1/2 teaspoons chili powder
1 can (15 ounces) chili with beans
4 hamburger buns, split and toasted
1/2 cup shredded cheddar cheese
1 can (2.8 ounces) french-fried onions

sue ross
casa grande, arizona

*These easy-to-assemble
sandwiches require only
five ingredients in addition
to the ground beef. Canned
chili and french-fried onions
make fun alternatives to the
usual burger toppings such as
ketchup and mustard.*

In a large bowl, combine beef and chili powder. Shape into four patties. Pan-fry, grill or broil until meat is no longer pink.

Meanwhile, in a small saucepan, bring chili to a boil. Reduce heat; simmer for 5 minutes or until heated through. Place burgers on bun bottoms; top with chili, cheese and onions. Replace bun tops. **yield:** 4 servings.

pumpkin sloppy joes

prep/total time 30 minutes

 This beef recipe is lighter in calories, fat and sodium.

donna musser

pearl city, illinois

Mixing canned pumpkin into sloppy joe meat may seem strange, but everyone is delightfully surprised by these fall-flavored sandwiches. I add cloves, nutmeg and chili powder for extra zest.

2 pounds ground beef
1 medium onion, finely chopped
1 cup ketchup
1/2 cup tomato juice
1 teaspoon chili powder
3/4 teaspoon salt
1/4 teaspoon *each* ground cloves, nutmeg and pepper
2 cups canned pumpkin
Hamburger buns, split

In a large skillet over medium heat, cook beef and onion until meat is no longer pink; drain. Add ketchup, tomato juice, chili powder, salt, cloves, nutmeg and pepper; mix well. Bring to a boil. Stir in pumpkin. Reduce heat; cover and simmer for 15-20 minutes. Serve on buns. **yield:** 6-8 servings.

nutrition facts: 1 sandwich equals 240 calories, 11 g fat (5 g saturated fat), 56 mg cholesterol, 713 mg sodium, 15 g carbohydrate, 3 g fiber, 22 g protein.

baked barbecued beef

prep 15 minutes | **bake** 2 hours

2-1/2 pounds ground beef
2 small onions, chopped
1 large green pepper, chopped
1 can (10-3/4 ounces) condensed tomato soup, undiluted
1 cup chili sauce
1 tablespoon white vinegar
1 teaspoon prepared mustard
1 teaspoon sugar
1/4 teaspoon salt
1/4 teaspoon pepper
10 to 12 hamburger buns, split

 This beef recipe is lighter in calories, fat and sodium.

mercia miner

canfield, ohio

This was among the first American dishes I tasted after arriving in the United States from New Zealand years ago. The lip-smacking beef recipe is now the one I use most.

In a Dutch oven, brown beef and onions; drain. Stir in the next eight ingredients. Bake meat mixture, uncovered, at 325° for 2 hours, stirring occasionally. Serve on buns. **yield:** 10-12 servings.

nutrition facts: 1 sandwich equals 296 calories, 10 g fat (4 g saturated fat), 46 mg cholesterol, 774 mg sodium, 29 g carbohydrate, 2 g fiber, 20 g protein.

meatball lover's sandwich

prep 45 minutes | **bake** 15 minutes

2 eggs
1/3 cup milk
2 cups soft bread crumbs
1/2 cup finely chopped onion
1-1/2 teaspoons salt
2 pounds ground beef
2 garlic cloves, minced
1 teaspoon butter
1 cup ketchup
2/3 cup chili sauce
1/4 cup packed brown sugar
2 tablespoons Worcestershire sauce
2 tablespoons prepared mustard
2 teaspoons celery seed
1/2 teaspoon salt
1/4 teaspoon hot pepper sauce
8 hoagie buns *or* submarine rolls, split
1 large onion, sliced

In a bowl, beat eggs and milk. Stir in bread crumbs, chopped onion and salt. Add beef; mix well. Shape into 1-in. balls. Place on a greased rack in a shallow baking pan. Bake, uncovered, at 375° for 15-20 minutes or until meat is no longer pink; drain.

In a saucepan, saute garlic in butter. Add ketchup, chili sauce, brown sugar, Worcestershire sauce, mustard, celery seed, salt and hot pepper sauce. Bring to a boil; add meatballs. Reduce heat; cover and simmer for 20 minutes or until heated through, stirring occasionally.

Carefully hollow out buns, leaving a 1/2-in. shell. Spoon meatball mixture into buns; top with sliced onion. **yield:** 8 servings.

kelly gerhardt
council bluffs, iowa

You'll get a big batch of saucy meatballs when you fix this popular recipe. The hollowed-out buns will hold a substantial amount of meat—anyone with a big appetite will be thrilled!

crumb **CLUE**

To make 2 cups of fresh bread crumbs, tear four slices of fresh white, French or whole wheat bread into 1-inch pieces. Place them in a blender or food processor, then cover it and push the pulse button several times for coarse crumbs.

aloha burgers

prep/total time 30 minutes

joi mckim-jones
waikoloa, hawaii

Pineapple and hamburgers are two of my favorite foods, so it just seemed natural for me to combine them. These tangy sandwiches are a nice change of pace.

1 can (8 ounces) sliced pineapple
3/4 cup teriyaki sauce
1 pound ground beef
1 large sweet onion, sliced
1 tablespoon butter
4 lettuce leaves
4 sesame seed *or* onion buns, split and toasted
4 slices Swiss cheese
4 bacon strips, cooked

Drain pineapple juice into a small bowl; add teriyaki sauce. Place 3 tablespoons in a resealable plastic bag. Add pineapple; toss to coat. Set aside. Shape beef into four patties; place in an 8-in. square baking dish. Pour the remaining teriyaki sauce mixture over patties; marinate for 5-10 minutes, turning once.

Drain and discard teriyaki marinade. Grill, covered, over medium heat or broil 4 in. from the heat for 6-9 minutes on each side or until no longer pink. Meanwhile, in a small skillet, saute onion in butter until tender, about 5 minutes; set aside.

Drain and discard pineapple marinade. Place pineapple on grill or under broiler to heat through. Layer lettuce and onion on bottom of buns. Top with burgers, cheese, pineapple and bacon. Replace tops; serve immediately. **yield:** 4 servings.

salsa sloppy joes

prep/total time 30 minutes

- 3 pounds ground beef
- 1 cup chopped onion
- 1 jar (16 ounces) salsa
- 1 can (15 ounces) sloppy joe sauce
- 16 to 20 hamburger buns, split

In a large skillet, cook beef and onion over medium heat until meat is no longer pink; drain. Stir in salsa and sloppy joe sauce; bring to a boil. Reduce heat; cover and simmer for 20 minutes. Spoon about 1/2 cup onto each bun. **yield:** 16-20 servings.

nutrition facts: 1 sandwich equals 225 calories, 8 g fat (3 g saturated fat), 33 mg cholesterol, 470 mg sodium, 21 g carbohydrate, 2 g fiber, 15 g protein.

 This beef recipe is lighter in calories, fat and sodium.

mary banninga

austin, minnesota

When I was looking for a quick-and-easy way to spice up my sloppy joe recipe, I decided to add a little salsa. Everyone who's tried these sandwiches really likes them.

open-faced meatball sandwiches

prep 30 minutes | **cook** 10 minutes

This beef recipe is lighter in calories, fat and sodium.

karen barthel

north canton, ohio

My husband and I love classic meatball subs, but I wanted to create a version that's fast to fix after a long day. This recipe comes together in a snap, and the meatballs are freezer-friendly as well.

- 1/4 cup egg substitute
- 1/2 cup soft bread crumbs
- 1/4 cup finely chopped onion
- 2 garlic cloves, minced
- 1/2 teaspoon onion powder
- 1/2 teaspoon dried oregano
- 1/2 teaspoon dried basil
- 1/4 teaspoon pepper
- Dash salt
- 1-1/4 pounds lean ground beef
- 2 cups garden-style pasta sauce
- 4 hoagie buns, split
- 2 tablespoons shredded part-skim mozzarella cheese
- Shredded Parmesan cheese, optional

In a large bowl, combine the first nine ingredients. Crumble beef over mixture and mix well. Shape into 40 meatballs. In a large skillet coated with nonstick cooking spray, brown meatballs in batches; drain.

Place meatballs in a large saucepan. Add pasta sauce; bring to a boil. Reduce heat; cover and simmer for 10-15 minutes or until meat is no longer pink. Spoon meatballs and sauce onto bun halves; sprinkle with mozzarella and Parmesan cheese if desired. **yield:** 8 servings.

nutrition facts: 1 sandwich equals 277 calories, 10 g fat (4 g saturated fat), 47 mg cholesterol, 506 mg sodium, 28 g carbohydrate, 3 g fiber, 20 g protein.

hamburger salad sandwiches

prep/total time 20 minutes

joyce boriack
georgetown, texas

Mom used to fix these cool salad sandwiches for our family birthdays. Dill pickles, tomato, onion and garlic give the meat mixture great flavor.

1 pound ground beef
1 medium onion, chopped
1 garlic clove, minced
1 medium tomato, chopped
1/2 cup mayonnaise
1/3 cup chopped dill pickles
2 tablespoons prepared mustard
1/2 teaspoon salt
1/2 teaspoon pepper
6 hamburger buns, split
Lettuce leaves

In a large skillet, cook beef, onion and garlic over medium heat until meat is no longer pink; drain. Cool. Add the next six ingredients. Spoon about 1/2 cup onto each bun; top with lettuce. **yield:** 6 servings.

potluck pockets

prep/total time 30 minutes

1 pound ground beef
1/2 cup chopped onion
1/2 cup chopped green pepper
2 tablespoons Worcestershire sauce
2 tablespoons soy sauce
2 teaspoons garlic powder
1 teaspoon ground cumin
1/2 teaspoon Italian seasoning
6 pita breads, halved
2 medium tomatoes, diced
3 cups shredded lettuce

sauce
1/2 cup soy sauce
1/4 cup white vinegar
2 tablespoons Worcestershire sauce
1/2 teaspoon onion powder
1/2 teaspoon Italian seasoning
Dash pepper

debbie jones
california, maryland

My husband showed me how to make these fun and tasty sandwiches. They take little time to prepare and never last long on a buffet table.

In a large skillet, cook beef, onion and green pepper over medium heat until meat is no longer pink; drain. Add Worcestershire sauce, soy sauce, garlic powder, cumin and Italian seasoning; mix well. Simmer for 5-10 minutes.

In a small saucepan, bring all the sauce ingredients to boil. Reduce heat and simmer for 5-10 minutes. Spoon meat mixture into pita halves; top with sauce, tomatoes and lettuce. **yield:** 12 servings.

beef 'n' pork burgers

prep/total time 25 minutes

    4 bacon strips, diced
    1 large onion, finely chopped
    1 garlic clove, minced
1-1/2 cups soft bread crumbs
    1 egg, lightly beaten
  1/2 cup water
    1 tablespoon dried parsley flakes
    2 to 3 teaspoons salt
  1/4 teaspoon dried marjoram
  1/4 teaspoon paprika
  1/4 teaspoon pepper
    1 pound ground beef
    1 pound ground pork
    8 hamburger buns, split and toasted
Mayonnaise, lettuce leaves and tomato slices

In a small skillet, cook bacon, onion and garlic over medium heat until the bacon is crisp; drain and place in a small bowl. Stir in the bread crumbs, egg, water, parsley, salt, marjoram, paprika and pepper. Crumble beef and pork over the mixture and mix well. Shape into eight 3/4-in.-thick patties.

Grill, uncovered, over medium-hot heat for 5-6 minutes on each side or until meat is no longer pink. Serve on buns with mayonnaise, lettuce and tomato. **yield:** 8 servings.

sharon adamczyk
wind lake, wisconsin

Ground pork adds an extra dimension to these juicy grilled burgers. I depend on them time and again for our summer cookouts.

beef stroganoff melt

prep/total time 30 minutes

jerraine barlow

colorado city, arizona

Piled with ground beef, mushrooms, green peppers and more, this open-faced sandwich can feed a crowd. The recipe has been in my collection a long time.

2 pounds ground beef
1 cup sliced fresh mushrooms
1 medium onion, chopped
1 teaspoon salt
1/2 teaspoon garlic powder
1/2 teaspoon pepper
2 cups (16 ounces) sour cream
1 loaf (1 pound) unsliced French bread
3 tablespoons butter, softened
3 cups (12 ounces) shredded Swiss cheese
1 medium green pepper, thinly sliced
2 medium tomatoes, thinly sliced

In a large skillet, cook the beef, mushrooms and onion over medium heat until meat is no longer pink; drain. Stir in the salt, garlic powder and pepper. Remove from the heat; stir in sour cream.

Cut the French bread in half lengthwise. Place on an ungreased baking sheet. Spread butter over cut halves; top with meat mixture and half of the cheese.

Arrange green pepper and tomatoes on top. Sprinkle with remaining cheese. Bake at 375° for 15 minutes or until cheese is melted. **yield:** 8 servings.

coney dogs for a crowd

prep/total time 30 minutes

2 pounds ground beef
2 celery ribs, chopped
1 medium onion, chopped
1/4 cup packed brown sugar
1/4 cup cornstarch
1 teaspoon salt
1/4 teaspoon pepper
1 bottle (32 ounces) ketchup
2 cups tomato juice
4 packages (1 pound *each*) hot dogs
32 to 40 hot dog buns, split

In a large saucepan, cook beef, celery and onion until meat is no longer pink; drain. Combine the brown sugar, cornstarch, salt and pepper; stir into beef mixture. Add ketchup and tomato juice. Bring to a boil; cook and stir for 2 minutes or until thickened. Reduce heat; simmer, uncovered, for 15-20 minutes or until heated through.

Cook the hot dogs according to the package directions; place on buns. Top each hot dog with about 1/4 cup beef mixture. **yield:** 32-40 servings.

nutrition facts: 1 coney dog equals 207 calories, 7 g fat (3 g saturated fat), 17 mg cholesterol, 698 mg sodium, 27 g carbohydrate, 1 g fiber, 9 g protein.

 This beef recipe is lighter in calories, fat and sodium.

betty ann miller
holmesville, ohio

Jazz up plain hot dogs by topping them with this slightly sweet meat sauce. They're a lot more filling, and everyone comments on the great flavor.

---

make-ahead sloppy joes

prep/total time 30 minutes

 This beef recipe is lighter in calories, fat and sodium.

alyne fuller
odessa, texas

When our children were growing up, I frequently made big batches of these stuffed beef-and-sausage buns. Having them in the freezer was such a time-saver on busy weekdays.

1 pound bulk pork sausage
1 pound ground beef
1 medium onion, chopped
14 to 16 sandwich buns, split
2 cans (8 ounces *each*) tomato sauce
2 tablespoons prepared mustard
1 teaspoon dried parsley flakes
1 teaspoon garlic powder
1 teaspoon salt
1/4 teaspoon pepper
1/4 teaspoon dried oregano

In a large skillet, cook sausage, beef and onion over medium heat until meat is no longer pink; drain. Remove the centers from the tops and bottoms of each bun. Tear removed bread into small pieces; add to skillet. Set buns aside.

Stir the remaining ingredients into the sausage mixture. Spoon about 1/3 cupful onto the bottom of each bun; replace tops. Wrap individually in heavy-duty foil. Bake at 350° for 20 minutes or until heated through or freeze for up to 3 months.

TO USE FROZEN SANDWICHES: Bake at 350° for 35 minutes or until heated through. **yield:** 14-16 servings.

nutrition facts: 1 sandwich equals 294 calories, 12 g fat (5 g saturated fat), 24 mg cholesterol, 672 mg sodium, 33 g carbohydrate, 2 g fiber, 14 g protein.

souper joes

prep/total time 15 minutes

erlene cornelius
spring city, tennessee

For this simple spin on sloppy joes, I use mushroom soup, onion soup mix and cheddar. They give the sandwiches fast and satisfying flavor.

1 pound ground beef
1 can (10-3/4 ounces) condensed cream of mushroom soup, undiluted
1 tablespoon onion soup mix
1 cup (4 ounces) shredded cheddar cheese
8 hamburger buns, split

In a large saucepan, cook beef over medium heat until no longer pink; drain. Stir in soup and soup mix; heat through. Stir in cheese until melted. Place about 1/3 cupful on each bun. **yield:** 8 servings.

good-bye GREASE

When making sloppy joes, you can prevent a greasy appearance by thoroughly draining the ground beef in a colander after it's cooked. After draining the meat, you may also want to blot it with paper towels or rinse it with hot water to eliminate any additional fat.

asian-style hamburgers

prep 25 minutes + marinating | **grill** 10 minutes

1-1/2 pounds ground beef
1/4 cup vegetable oil
1/4 cup soy sauce
2 tablespoons ketchup
1 tablespoon white vinegar
2 garlic cloves, minced
1/4 teaspoon pepper
6 hamburger buns, split
Leaf lettuce and tomato slices, optional

myra innes
auburn, kansas

When I'm in the mood for something different, I turn to this recipe. The marinade livens up the beef patties with an Asian-style accent.

Shape meat into six patties; place in a shallow dish. In a bowl, whisk together the oil, soy sauce, ketchup, vinegar, garlic and pepper. Set aside 1/4 cup for basting; cover and refrigerate. Pour remaining marinade over the patties. Cover and refrigerate for at least 3 hours.

Grill burgers, uncovered, over medium heat for 5-6 minutes on each side until meat juices run clear, basting occasionally with reserved marinade. Serve on hamburger buns with lettuce leaves and tomato slices if desired. **yield:** 6 servings.

grilled burgers with horseradish sauce

prep/total time 30 minutes

1/2 cup sour cream
1 tablespoon snipped fresh dill *or*
   1 teaspoon dill weed
1 tablespoon finely chopped onion
1 tablespoon sweet pickle relish
2 teaspoons prepared horseradish

burgers

3/4 cup chopped fresh mushrooms
1/4 cup shredded carrot
1/4 cup finely chopped onion
2 tablespoons minced fresh parsley
1 tablespoon Worcestershire sauce
1/2 teaspoon salt
1/4 teaspoon hot pepper sauce
1/8 teaspoon pepper
1-1/4 pounds lean ground beef
6 whole wheat hamburger buns, split
6 lettuce leaves
12 tomato slices

In a small bowl, combine the sour cream, dill, onion, pickle relish and horseradish; cover and refrigerate. In another bowl, combine the first eight burger ingredients. Crumble beef over mixture and mix well. Shape into six 1/2-in.-thick patties.

Grill patties, covered, over medium-hot heat for 3-4 minutes on each side or until meat is no longer pink. Serve on buns with lettuce, tomato and horseradish sauce. **yield:** 6 servings.

deb anderson
joplin, missouri

For a twist on the traditional grilled burger, try this recipe. The tasty beef-and-veggie patties get extra zip from the homemade sauce.

chili dogs

prep/total time 30 minutes

linda rainey

monahans, texas

With a zippy sauce, these classic chili dogs always make a popular main dish. They're great for a summer picnic, a Super Bowl party… just about any time at all.

1 pound ground beef
1 garlic clove, minced
1 cup tomato juice
1 can (6 ounces) tomato paste
2 tablespoons chili powder
1 teaspoon hot pepper sauce
1 teaspoon salt
1/4 teaspoon pepper
8 hot dogs
8 hot dog buns, split
Chopped onion and shredded cheddar cheese, optional

In a large skillet, cook the beef and garlic over medium heat until the meat is no longer pink; drain. Stir in the tomato juice, tomato paste, chili powder, hot pepper sauce, salt and pepper. Bring to a boil. Reduce heat; simmer, uncovered, for 20 minutes. Keep hot until serving.

Grill or broil hot dogs until heated through. Place on buns; top with chili. Sprinkle with onion and cheese if desired. **yield:** 8 servings.

make it **MINCED**

Minced garlic is commonly available in jars in grocery stores. Typically, 1/2 teaspoon of minced garlic from a jar equals one fresh garlic clove, minced.

You may find jarred garlic to be a bit milder in flavor than fresh garlic…but you may decide that the convenience of using the jarred kind is well worth it.

mushroom pizza burgers

prep/total time 30 minutes

- 1/2 cup sliced fresh mushrooms
- 1/4 cup chopped onion
- 1 garlic clove, minced
- 1/2 teaspoon dried oregano
- 1 cup crushed tomatoes, undrained

burgers

- 1-1/2 cups finely chopped fresh mushrooms
- 1/3 cup minced fresh basil
- 1 egg white, beaten
- 2 tablespoons grated Parmesan cheese
- 2 tablespoons dry bread crumbs
- 1/2 teaspoon salt
- 1/8 teaspoon pepper
- 1 pound lean ground beef
- 6 slices part-skim mozzarella cheese (3 ounces)
- 6 hamburger buns, split and toasted

In a small skillet coated with nonstick cooking spray, saute the sliced mushrooms and onion for 3 minutes. Add the garlic and oregano; saute 1-2 minutes longer or until the onion is tender. Stir in the tomatoes. Cook, uncovered, over medium-low heat for 5 minutes, stirring occasionally. Set aside and keep warm.

In a large bowl, combine the chopped mushrooms, basil, egg white, Parmesan cheese, bread crumbs, salt and pepper. Crumble the beef over the mixture; mix well. Shape into six patties.

Coat grill rack with nonstick cooking spray before starting the grill. Grill patties, covered, over medium-hot heat for 4-5 minutes on each side or until meat juices run clear. Top patties with cheese and tomato sauce. Serve over buns. **yield:** 6 servings.

nutrition facts: 1 burger equals 333 calories, 12 g fat (5 g saturated fat), 36 mg cholesterol, 757 mg sodium, 28 g carbohydrate, 3 g fiber, 25 g protein.

 This beef recipe is lighter in calories, fat and sodium.

harriet stichter
milford, indiana

To me, there's nothing better at a cookout than a good, grilled hamburger. This one definitely fills the bill, and its zesty pizza touch makes it especially tasty.

cheese-stuffed burgers

prep/total time 25 minutes

janet wood
windham, new hampshire

This sandwich does regular cheeseburgers one better— it puts the cheese, ketchup, mustard and onions inside the beef patty. People love biting into a hidden "pocket" of favorite toppings.

- 1/4 cup ketchup
- 1/4 cup finely chopped onion
- 4 teaspoons prepared mustard
- 2 teaspoons salt
- 1 teaspoon pepper
- 4 pounds ground beef
- 1-1/2 cups (6 ounces) shredded cheddar cheese
- 12 hamburger buns, split

In a large bowl, combine the first five ingredients. Crumble beef over mixture; mix well. Shape into 24 thin patties. Sprinkle cheese in the center of 12 patties; top with remaining patties and press edges firmly to seal.

Grill, covered, over medium heat or broil 4 in. from the heat for 6-9 minutes on each side or until no longer pink. Serve on buns. **yield:** 12 servings.

double-decker burgers

prep/total time 25 minutes

marcy schewe
danube, minnesota

Just looking at this "man-sized" sandwich stacked with two burger patties will make your mouth water. I think the special cheese spread is the perfect topping.

2 eggs, lightly beaten
1/4 cup finely chopped onion
2 teaspoons Worcestershire sauce
1 teaspoon salt
1/4 teaspoon pepper
2 pounds ground beef
1-1/2 cups (6 ounces) shredded cheddar cheese
3 tablespoons mayonnaise
4 teaspoons prepared mustard
4 teaspoons dill pickle relish
6 hamburger buns, split
Shredded lettuce
6 onion and tomato slices

In a large bowl, combine the eggs, onion, Worcestershire sauce, salt and pepper. Crumble beef over mixture and mix well. Shape into 12 thin patties. Broil 4 in. from the heat for 7-8 minutes on each side or until no longer pink.

In a small bowl, combine the cheese, mayonnaise, mustard and relish; mix well. Spoon 2 tablespoons on each burger. Return to the broiler just until cheese softens. Serve on buns with lettuce, onion and tomato. **yield:** 6 servings.

saucy pizza burgers

prep 30 minutes + chilling | cook 15 minutes

1 pound ground beef
1/2 teaspoon garlic salt
1 cup (4 ounces) shredded part-skim mozzarella cheese
1 can (8 ounces) pizza sauce
1 can (4 ounces) mushroom stems and pieces, drained
1/2 teaspoon dried oregano
1 medium onion, sliced
1 tablespoon butter
4 hamburger buns, split

In a large bowl, combine beef and garlic salt. Shape into eight patties; top four patties with cheese. Cover with remaining patties; press edges to seal. Refrigerate.

Meanwhile, in a large saucepan, combine the pizza sauce, mushrooms and oregano; cover and simmer for 10 minutes, stirring occasionally. In a small skillet, saute onion in butter until tender; set aside.

Pan-fry, grill or broil burgers until no longer pink. Spread bun bottoms with a little sauce; top with burgers, onion and remaining sauce. Add tops. **yield:** 4 servings.

diane hixon
niceville, florida

Add popular pizza ingredients to plain burgers, and you get these guaranteed-to-please sandwiches. Mozzarella is "hidden" inside the beef.

mexican beef burgers

prep/total time 25 minutes

stanny barta
pisek, north dakota

At dinnertime one night, half of the family said they wanted hamburgers and the other half requested tacos. My daughter-in-law and I hit on a compromise—these burgers wrapped in tortillas.

2 cans (4 ounces *each*) chopped green chilies
2 eggs, lightly beaten
1/3 cup salsa
1/4 cup finely minced onion
1 garlic clove, minced
1 teaspoon salt
1/2 teaspoon pepper
2 pounds ground beef
3/4 cup finely crushed corn chips
8 flour tortillas (10 inches), warmed

toppings
Chopped tomatoes
Chopped ripe olives
Shredded cheddar cheese
Shredded lettuce
Salsa
Sour cream

In a large bowl, combine the first seven ingredients. Crumble beef and chips over mixture; mix well. Shape into eight patties.

Grill, covered, over medium heat or broil 4 in. from the heat for 6-9 minutes on each side or until no longer pink. Wrap burgers and toppings in tortillas. **yield:** 8 servings.

saucy pizza burgers

double-decker burgers

mexican beef burgers

speedy steak sandwiches

prep/total time 15 minutes

4 slices French bread (3/4 inch thick)
Butter, softened
Prepared mustard
1/2 pound uncooked lean ground beef
1/4 cup milk
1 tablespoon minced onion
1 tablespoon steak sauce
1/2 teaspoon garlic salt
1/4 teaspoon pepper

In a broiler, toast one side of the bread. Spread untoasted sides with butter and mustard. In a small bowl, combine remaining ingredients; spread evenly over buttered side of bread. Broil 6 in. from the heat for 5-7 minutes or until beef is no longer pink. **yield:** 2 servings.

ruth page
hillsborough, north carolina

Steak sauce, mustard and seasonings give these ground beef sandwiches great flavor. The recipe is sized for two people but could easily be doubled or tripled.

teriyaki burgers

prep/total time 25 minutes

1 can (8 ounces) water chestnuts, drained and chopped
1/3 cup teriyaki sauce
2 tablespoons chopped green onions
Salt and pepper to taste
1-1/2 pounds ground beef
7 hamburger buns, split
14 tomato slices
7 lettuce leaves

In a large bowl, combine the water chestnuts, teriyaki sauce, onions, salt and pepper. Crumble beef over mixture and mix just until combined. Shape into seven 1/2-in.-thick patties.

Prepare the grill for indirect heat. Grill, covered, over indirect medium heat for 6-8 minutes on each side or until meat is no longer pink. Serve on buns with tomato and lettuce. **yield:** 7 burgers.

nutrition facts: 1 burger with bun (prepared without salt) equals 321 calories, 11 g fat (4 g saturated fat), 35 mg cholesterol, 778 mg sodium, 28 g carbohydrate, 3 g fiber, 25 g protein.

This beef recipe is lighter in calories, fat and sodium.

barb schutz
pandora, ohio

With water chestnuts, these patties have a fun crunch. Top them with additional teriyaki sauce for a flavorful alternative to ketchup.

hawaiian honey burgers

prep/total time 25 minutes

sheryl creech

lancaster, california

These nicely spiced burgers were a favorite of mine when I was growing up. Fresh fruit and corn on the cob are the perfect accompaniments.

1/2 cup honey
1/4 teaspoon ground cinnamon
1/4 teaspoon paprika
1/4 teaspoon curry powder
1/8 teaspoon ground ginger
1/8 teaspoon ground nutmeg
2 pounds ground beef
1/4 cup soy sauce
1 can (20 ounces) sliced pineapple, drained
8 hamburger buns, split and toasted
Lettuce leaves, optional

In a large bowl, combine the first six ingredients. Crumble beef over mixture and mix well. Shape into eight 3/4-in.-thick patties.

Grill, uncovered, over medium-hot heat for 3 minutes on each side. Brush with soy sauce. Continue grilling for 4-6 minutes or until juices run clear, basting and turning several times.

During the last 4 minutes, grill the pineapple slices until browned, turning once. Serve burgers and pineapple on buns with lettuce if desired. **yield:** 8 servings.

speedy sloppy joes

prep/total time 20 minutes

 This beef recipe is lighter in calories, fat and sodium.

nancy lambert

punta gorda, florida

Sweet pickle relish and barbecue sauce jazz up these quick-to-fix sloppy joes. Both children and adults enjoy them.

1 pound ground beef
1 can (10-3/4 ounces) condensed tomato soup, undiluted
2 tablespoons sweet pickle relish
2 tablespoons ketchup
2 tablespoons barbecue sauce
6 to 8 onion rolls *or* hamburger buns, split

In a large skillet, cook beef over medium heat until no longer pink; drain. Add the soup, relish, ketchup and barbecue sauce; cover and simmer for 10 minutes. Serve on buns. **yield:** 6-8 servings.

nutrition facts: 1 sandwich equals 262 calories, 9 g fat (4 g saturated fat), 38 mg cholesterol, 582 mg sodium, 28 g carbohydrate, 2 g fiber, 16 g protein.

ground beef gyros

prep/total time 30 minutes

ruth stahl

shepherd, montana

If you like gyros as much as I do, try this recipe that uses ground beef instead of lamb. The pita sandwiches have a cucumber-yogurt sauce and taste very much like the ones served at a local restaurant.

1 carton (8 ounces) plain yogurt
1/3 cup chopped seeded cucumber
2 tablespoons finely chopped onion
1 garlic clove, minced
1 teaspoon sugar

filling

1-1/2 teaspoons dried oregano
1 teaspoon garlic powder
1 teaspoon onion powder
1 teaspoon salt, optional
3/4 teaspoon pepper
1 pound ground beef
4 pita breads (6 inches), halved, warmed
3 cups shredded lettuce
1 large tomato, chopped
1 small onion, sliced

In a small bowl, combine the first five ingredients. Chill. In a large bowl, combine seasonings; crumble beef over mixture and mix well. Shape into four patties.

Grill, covered, over medium-hot heat for 6-7 minutes on each side or until a meat thermometer reads 160°. Cut patties into thin slices; stuff into pita halves. Add lettuce, tomato and onion. Serve with the yogurt sauce. **yield:** 4 servings.

giant meatball sub

prep 15 minutes | **cook** 30 minutes

deana paul
san dimas, california

Whether you fix it for a party or on a weeknight for your family, this big sub will rise to the top of your list of favorites. Just don't count on having any leftovers!

2 eggs, lightly beaten
1/3 cup milk
1 medium onion, chopped
2 garlic cloves, minced
1 cup soft bread crumbs
1/2 teaspoon salt
1/2 teaspoon Italian seasoning
1-1/4 pounds bulk Italian sausage
3/4 pound ground beef
2 jars (26 ounces *each*) spaghetti sauce
1 loaf (1 pound) unsliced French bread, halved lengthwise
8 slices part-skim mozzarella cheese
Shredded Parmesan cheese, optional

In a large bowl, combine the eggs, milk, onion, garlic, bread crumbs, salt and Italian seasoning. Crumble sausage and beef over mixture; mix well.

Shape the meat mixture into 1-in. balls. Place meatballs on a greased rack in a shallow baking pan. Bake at 425° for 15 minutes or until browned; drain.

In a Dutch oven, heat the spaghetti sauce over medium heat. Add the meatballs; simmer for 15 minutes. Meanwhile, bake the bread at 325° for 10 minutes or until heated through.

Place mozzarella cheese on bottom half of bread; spoon meatballs onto cheese. Replace top. Slice sandwich into serving-size portions; serve with extra spaghetti sauce and Parmesan cheese if desired. **yield:** 8 servings.

cajun burgers

prep/total time 20 minutes

1 large green pepper, chopped
1 large onion, chopped
6 green onions, thinly sliced
6 garlic cloves, minced
1 egg
2 tablespoons Worcestershire sauce
1 tablespoon dry bread crumbs
1 tablespoon soy sauce
1 tablespoon cream cheese, softened
1/4 teaspoon cornstarch
1/4 teaspoon salt
1/4 teaspoon pepper
1/4 teaspoon seasoned salt
1/4 teaspoon dried thyme
1/4 teaspoon ground mustard
1/4 teaspoon hot pepper sauce
2 pounds ground beef
8 hamburger buns, split

ron treadaway
acworth, georgia

You'll get recipe requests for these well-seasoned burgers again and again. The onions, garlic, green pepper and spices make a mouth-watering sandwich that has Cajun flair.

In a large bowl, combine the first 16 ingredients. Crumble beef over mixture and mix well. Shape into eight patties. Grill over medium heat for 5-7 minutes on each side or until no longer pink and juices run clear. Serve on buns. **yield:** 8 servings.

less **MESS**

Want to avoid messy hands when mixing the meat mixture for hamburgers? Put the ingredients in a large resealable plastic bag, then mix them. Or if you do use your bare hands, first dampen them with water, and nothing will stick.

sweet onion bbq burgers

prep 30 minutes + marinating | **grill** 15 minutes

christie gardiner
eagle mountain, utah

Sometimes we don't even bother with a bun for these moist, flavorful hamburgers. Smoked cheese, grilled onions and a special sauce make the beef patties fantastic all by themselves!

1/2 cup dry bread crumbs
2 teaspoons onion salt
2 teaspoons brown sugar
1 egg, lightly beaten
1 pound ground beef
1-1/4 cups barbecue sauce

sauce
1/2 cup mayonnaise
1/2 cup barbecue sauce
1 teaspoon brown sugar

onion topping
2 tablespoons butter
1/4 cup honey
2 large sweet onions, thinly sliced
4 slices smoked cheddar cheese
4 hamburger buns, split

In a large bowl, combine the bread crumbs, onion salt and brown sugar. Add egg. Crumble beef over mixture and mix well. Shape into four patties. Place in a shallow dish; pour barbecue sauce over patties. Cover and refrigerate for 2-4 hours.

In a small bowl, combine the sauce ingredients; cover and refrigerate until serving. For topping, melt butter in a small skillet. Stir in honey until blended. Add onions; saute for 15-20 minutes or until tender and lightly browned. Remove from the heat and keep warm.

Drain and discard barbecue sauce. Grill patties, uncovered, over medium-hot heat for 5-7 minutes on each side or until juices run clear. Top each with a cheese slice; grill 1 minute longer or until cheese is melted. Serve on buns with sauce and onion topping. **yield:** 4 servings.

provolone pepper burgers

prep/total time 30 minutes

1/3 cup finely cubed provolone cheese
1/4 cup diced roasted red peppers
1/4 cup finely chopped onion
Salt and pepper to taste
1 pound ground beef
4 hamburger buns, split

In a bowl, combine the cheese, red peppers, onion, salt and pepper. Add beef and mix well. Shape into four patties.

Grill, covered, over medium-hot heat for 4-5 minutes on each side or until meat is no longer pink. Serve on buns. **yield:** 4 servings.

nick mescia
surprise, arizona

I'm known around the neighborhood as the "grill sergeant." I'm often seen at my grill making these delicious burgers.

hamburger croquettes

prep/total time 20 minutes

lee deneau
lansing, michigan

When I was in the kitchen one day, it occurred to me that a ham-and-cheese combination is often used as a stuffing for chicken but not for other meats. I thought I'd try it with ground beef, and these crumb-coated patties were the tasty result.

1/2 pound lean ground beef
1 thin slice fully cooked ham, halved
2 slices process American cheese, halved
1/4 cup seasoned bread crumbs
1 tablespoon vegetable oil
2 hamburger buns, split
Lettuce leaves and red onion and tomato slices, optional

Shape beef into four thin patties. Place a half slice of ham and two half slices of cheese on two patties. Top with remaining patties; pinch edges to seal. Coat both sides of burgers with bread crumbs.

In a large skillet, cook burgers in oil for 4-5 minutes on each side or until meat is no longer pink. Serve on buns with lettuce, onion and tomato if desired. **yield:** 2 servings.

cabbage sloppy joes

prep 25 minutes | **cook** 10 minutes

1 pound ground beef
1-1/2 cups finely shredded cabbage
1 medium onion, chopped
1 celery rib, chopped
1/4 cup chopped green pepper
1 cup ketchup
3 tablespoons brown sugar
2 tablespoons lemon juice
1 tablespoon white vinegar
1 tablespoon Worcestershire sauce
1 tablespoon prepared mustard
1 teaspoon salt
Dash pepper
8 sandwich rolls, split

darlene brenden
salem, oregon

Many of my guests never realize that these tangy sandwiches contain cabbage. Mixing in that vegetable is a healthy and delicious twist…and it stretches the number of servings, too!

In a large skillet, cook the beef, cabbage, onion, celery and green pepper over medium heat until meat is no longer pink; drain. Stir in the ketchup, brown sugar, lemon juice, vinegar, Worcestershire sauce, mustard, salt and pepper. Cover and simmer for 10 minutes or until cabbage is tender. Spoon 1/2 cup onto each roll. **yield:** 8 servings.

MEAT LOAVES
& meatballs

cranberry kraut meatballs

prep 10 minutes | **bake** 1-1/2 hours

2-1/2 pounds ground beef
1 envelope onion soup mix
1 cup dry bread crumbs
1 can (16 ounces) whole-berry cranberry sauce
1 can (14 ounces) sauerkraut, rinsed and drained
1-1/3 cups water
1 bottle (12 ounces) chili sauce
3/4 cup packed brown sugar
Hot mashed potatoes

In a large bowl, combine the beef, soup mix and bread crumbs. Shape into 18 meatballs. Place in an ungreased 13-in. x 9-in. x 2-in. baking dish.

In a large saucepan, combine the cranberry sauce, sauerkraut, water, chili sauce and brown sugar. Bring to a boil. Pour over the meatballs.

Bake, uncovered, at 350° for 1-1/2 hours or until meat is no longer pink. Serve with mashed potatoes. **yield:** 6 servings.

anne karth
mt. prospect, illinois

The unusual combination of cranberries and sauerkraut gives these meatballs a delightfully different flavor. I always get recipe requests when I take them to potlucks.

prairie meat loaf

prep 15 minutes | **bake** 1-1/4 hours

karen laubman
spruce grove, alberta

When it comes to comfort food, it's hard to beat a big helping of meat loaf with mashed potatoes on the side. This tender, moist loaf with a hint of cheese is a great choice.

2 eggs
1/2 cup ketchup
2 tablespoons prepared mustard
3 cups old-fashioned oats
2 teaspoons salt
1 teaspoon garlic powder
1 teaspoon dried thyme
1 teaspoon dried basil
1-1/2 cups beef broth
1-1/2 cups finely chopped onion
1-1/2 cups finely chopped celery
2-1/2 cups (10 ounces) shredded cheddar cheese, *divided*
4 pounds lean ground beef

In a large bowl, beat eggs; stir in ketchup, mustard, oats, salt, garlic powder, thyme and basil. In a small saucepan, bring broth to a boil; add to oat mixture. Stir in the onion, celery and 2 cups of cheese. Crumble beef over mixture and mix well.

Press into two ungreased 9-in. x 5-in. x 3-in. loaf pans. Bake at 375° for 1-1/4 hours until meat is no longer pink and a meat thermometer reads 160°; drain. Sprinkle with remaining cheese; let stand until melted. **yield:** 2 loaves (6-8 servings each).

green pepper meat loaf

prep 15 minutes | **bake** 1-3/4 hours

2 eggs, lightly beaten
2 medium green peppers, chopped
1 large onion, finely chopped
1/4 cup chopped celery leaves
1/4 cup minced fresh parsley
1 envelope reduced-sodium onion soup mix
2 pounds lean ground beef
1 pound bulk turkey sausage
4 bacon strips, optional

In a large bowl, combine the eggs, green peppers, onion, celery leaves, parsley and soup mix. Crumble beef and sausage over the mixture and mix well. Shape into a 12-in. x 4-in. loaf.

Place on a rack in a shallow baking pan. Bake, uncovered, at 350° for 1 hour. Place the bacon strips over the top if desired. Bake 45-60 minutes longer or until no pink remains and a meat thermometer reads 160°. **yield:** 14 slices.

nutrition facts: 1 slice (prepared with egg substitute equivalent to 2 eggs) equals 193 calories, 10 g fat, 51 mg cholesterol, 398 mg sodium, 5 g carbohydrate, 1 g fiber, 20 g protein.

 This beef recipe is lighter in calories, fat and sodium.

edna lauderdale
milwaukee, wisconsin

My husband and I can't get enough of this classic main dish. Leftover slices are terrific made into sandwiches for lunch the next day.

mom's meat loaf

prep 15 minutes | **bake** 1 hour + standing

michelle beran
claflin, kansas

My mom served this hearty favorite frequently when I was growing up. When I first met my husband, he wasn't fond of meat loaf, but this recipe won him over.

2 eggs
3/4 cup milk
2/3 cup finely crushed saltines
1/2 cup chopped onion
1 teaspoon salt
1/2 teaspoon rubbed sage
Dash pepper
1-1/2 pounds lean ground beef
1 cup ketchup
1/2 cup packed brown sugar
1 teaspoon Worcestershire sauce

In a large bowl, beat eggs. Add milk, saltines, onion, salt, sage and pepper. Crumble beef over mixture and mix well. Shape into an 8-1/2-in. x 4-1/2-in. loaf in an ungreased shallow baking pan.

Combine the remaining ingredients; spread 3/4 cup over the meat loaf. Bake at 350° for 60-65 minutes or until no pink remains; drain. Let stand 10 minutes before slicing. Serve with the remaining sauce. **yield:** 6-8 servings.

country meat loaf

prep 10 minutes | **bake** 1-1/2 hours

jim hopkins
whittier, california

Pork and veal combine with beef to make this tasty loaf a meat-lover's delight. The corn bread stuffing holds it all together and adds flavor.

2 eggs
1 can (10-3/4 ounces) condensed cream of celery soup, undiluted
1/2 teaspoon pepper
1 package (6 ounces) corn bread stuffing mix
1-1/2 pounds ground beef
1/2 pound ground veal
1/4 pound ground pork

In a large bowl, beat the eggs. Add the soup, pepper and stuffing mix. Combine the beef, veal and pork; crumble over the egg mixture and mix well.

Press into a 9-in. x 5-in. x 3-in. loaf pan. Bake at 350° for 1-1/2 hours or until no pink remains. Drain. **yield:** 6-8 servings.

spaghetti 'n' meatballs

prep 20 minutes | **cook** 30 minutes

1 cup chopped onion
1 tablespoon vegetable oil
1 can (28 ounces) stewed tomatoes
2 cans (6 ounces *each*) tomato paste
1 tablespoon sugar
1 teaspoon salt
1/2 teaspoon dried basil
1/4 teaspoon dried oregano
1/8 teaspoon dried marjoram
1/8 teaspoon paprika
Dash pepper
2 eggs
1 garlic clove, minced
2 teaspoons dried parsley flakes
1 pound lean ground beef
1 cup grated Parmesan cheese
1/2 cup dry bread crumbs
Hot cooked spaghetti

ann rath
mankato, minnesota

It's hard to beat this classic main dish. The delectable meatballs are time-savers because you don't need to brown them before adding them to the sauce.

In a soup kettle or Dutch oven, saute onion in oil until tender. Stir in the tomatoes, tomato paste, sugar and seasonings. Bring to a boil.

Meanwhile, in a large bowl, beat the eggs, garlic and parsley. Add the beef and mix well. Sprinkle with the Parmesan cheese and bread crumbs; mix gently. Shape into 1-1/2-in. balls. Add to the sauce; reduce heat. Cover and simmer for 30 minutes or until meat is no longer pink. Serve meatballs and sauce over spaghetti. **yield:** 4 servings.

cranberry meat loaf

prep 15 minutes | **bake** 1-1/4 hours

   2 eggs
 3/4 cup crushed saltines
      (about 22 crackers)
 1/2 cup whole-berry cranberry sauce
 1/4 cup fresh *or* frozen cranberries,
      thawed
 1/4 cup packed brown sugar
   2 tablespoons chopped onion
1-1/2 teaspoons salt
 1/8 teaspoon pepper
1-1/2 pounds ground beef
 1/2 pound ground ham
 1/2 cup barbecue sauce, optional
Bay leaves and fresh cranberries, optional

In a large bowl, combine the first eight ingredients. Crumble beef and ham over mixture and mix well. Pat into a greased 9-in. x 5-in. x 3-in. loaf pan. Bake, uncovered, at 350° for 1-1/4 hours or until a meat thermometer reads 160°.

During the last 15 minutes of baking, baste meat loaf with barbecue sauce if desired. Garnish with bay leaves and cranberries if desired. Discard bay leaves before slicing. **yield:** 4-5 servings.

marcia harris
stevensville, michigan

Everyone in my family loves this unusual recipe, which features both cranberry sauce and cranberries. It's especially nice during fall and the Christmas season.

on a **ROLL**

Festive Meat Loaf Pinwheel is rolled up "jelly-roll style" to create its attractive spiral shape. A jelly roll is a dessert made by spreading jelly, whipped cream or a filling over a cake and rolling it into a log. The jelly-roll style is used when any food is filled and rolled into a log shape.

festive meat loaf pinwheel

prep 20 minutes | **bake** 1-1/4 hours

vera sullivan

amity, oregon

Think meat loaf isn't special enough for a holiday dinner? Think again! The crowd-size pinwheel here features ham, Swiss cheese and a delicious homemade tomato sauce.

- 3 eggs
- 1 cup dry bread crumbs
- 1/2 cup finely chopped onion
- 1/2 cup finely chopped green pepper
- 1/4 cup ketchup
- 2 teaspoons minced fresh parsley
- 1 teaspoon dried basil
- 1 teaspoon dried oregano
- 1 garlic clove, minced
- 2 teaspoons salt
- 1/2 teaspoon pepper
- 5 pounds lean ground beef
- 3/4 pound thinly sliced deli ham
- 3/4 pound thinly sliced Swiss cheese

tomato pepper sauce

- 1/2 cup finely chopped onion
- 2 celery ribs, cut into 1-1/2-in. julienne strips
- 1/2 medium green pepper, cut into 1-1/2-in. julienne strips
- 1 garlic clove, minced
- 1 to 2 teaspoons olive oil
- 2 cups chopped fresh tomatoes
- 1 cup beef broth
- 1 bay leaf
- 1 teaspoon sugar
- 1/4 teaspoon salt
- 1/4 teaspoon dried thyme
- 1 tablespoon cornstarch
- 2 tablespoons cold water

In a large bowl, combine the first 11 ingredients. Crumble beef over mixture and mix well. On a piece of heavy-duty foil, pat beef mixture into a 17-in. x 15-in. rectangle. Cover with ham and cheese slices to within 1/2 in. of edges.

Roll up tightly jelly-roll style, starting with a short side. Place seam side down in a roasting pan. Bake, uncovered, at 350° for 1-1/4 to 1-1/2 hours or until a meat thermometer reads 160°.

In a large saucepan, saute the onion, celery, green pepper and garlic in oil for 3-5 minutes or until tender. Add the tomatoes, broth, bay leaf, sugar, salt and thyme. Simmer, uncovered, for 30 minutes. Discard the bay leaf.

Combine the cornstarch and cold water until smooth; stir into the sauce. Bring to a boil; cook and stir for 2 minutes or until thickened. Drain meat loaf; top with sauce. **yield:** 15-20 servings.

meatballs and beans

prep/total time 30 minutes

- 2/3 cup soft bread crumbs
- 1/2 cup evaporated milk
- 1 teaspoon salt
- 1/4 teaspoon pepper
- 1 pound lean ground beef
- 1 small onion, *divided*
- 1 can (16 ounces) baked beans, undrained
- 2 to 3 tablespoons ketchup
- 1 tablespoon brown sugar
- 1/4 to 1/2 teaspoon ground mustard

Combine bread crumbs, milk, salt and pepper. Crumble beef over mixture and mix well. Shape into 1-1/2-in. balls.

In a large skillet, cook meatballs and onion until meatballs are browned; drain. Add beans, ketchup, brown sugar and mustard. Bring to a boil. Reduce heat; cover and simmer for 20-25 minutes or until meatballs are no longer pink. **yield:** 4-6 servings.

bernice morris
marshfield, missouri

This quick-and-easy dish pairs meatballs with sweet baked beans. I usually serve it with a tossed green salad and dinner rolls for a complete meal.

bavarian meatballs

prep 15 minutes | **bake** 25 minutes

gusty crum
dover, ohio

Gingersnaps and mushrooms give these tender meatballs old-world flavor. The recipe was handed down from my husband's family and is an easy one to double or triple.

- 2 tablespoons chopped onion
- 1 teaspoon butter
- 3/4 cup soft bread crumbs
- 1 tablespoon milk
- 1/2 teaspoon prepared mustard
- 1/2 teaspoon salt
- Dash pepper
- 1/2 pound ground beef
- 1 can (4 ounces) mushroom stems and pieces, undrained
- 2 gingersnaps, coarsely crushed
- 2 tablespoons water
- 1 tablespoon brown sugar
- 1/2 teaspoon beef bouillon granules

In a large skillet, saute onion in butter until tender. Transfer to a large bowl; add the bread crumbs, milk, mustard, salt and pepper. Crumble beef over mixture and mix well. Shape into six meatballs; place in a greased 1-qt. baking dish.

In a small saucepan, combine the mushrooms, gingersnap crumbs, water, brown sugar and bouillon. Cook and stir over low heat for 2-3 minutes or until thickened.

Pour over meatballs. Cover and bake at 350° for 25 minutes or until the meat is no longer pink. **yield:** 2 servings.

meatballs with vegetable sauce

prep 15 minutes | **cook** 25 minutes

dorothy stegall
appleton, wisconsin

This recipe makes terrific meatballs without the mess of frying and turning each one. Served with the tangy, vegetable-rich sauce over pasta, they're sure to please.

1 egg yolk, lightly beaten
1 tablespoon milk
3 tablespoons soft bread crumbs
2 tablespoons finely chopped onion
1/4 teaspoon salt
1/2 pound ground beef

sauce
1/4 cup sliced fresh mushrooms
1/4 cup chopped celery
3 tablespoons chopped onion
3 tablespoons chopped green pepper
1 teaspoon butter
1/2 cup tomato sauce
2 tablespoons brown sugar
2 tablespoons beef broth
4 teaspoons lemon juice
1/8 teaspoon garlic powder
Hot cooked noodles

In a bowl, combine the first five ingredients. Crumble beef over mixture and mix well. Shape into 1-in. balls. Place meatballs on a greased rack in a shallow baking pan. Bake, uncovered, at 425° for 10-12 minutes or until no longer pink. Drain on paper towels.

Meanwhile, in a saucepan, saute the mushrooms, celery, onion and green pepper in butter. Add the tomato sauce, brown sugar, broth, lemon juice and garlic powder. Bring to a boil. Reduce heat; add the meatballs. Cover and simmer for 15 minutes or until heated through. Serve over noodles. **yield:** 2 servings.

taco meatballs

prep 45 minutes | **bake** 15 minutes

1 cup biscuit/baking mix
1 envelope taco seasoning
1 cup (4 ounces) shredded cheddar cheese
1/2 cup water
1 pound lean ground beef
Salsa and taco sauce

In a large bowl, combine the first four ingredients. Crumble beef over mixture and mix well. Shape into 1-in. balls.

Place meatballs on a greased rack in a shallow baking pan. Bake, uncovered, at 350° for 15-20 minutes or until no longer pink; drain. Serve with salsa and taco sauce. **yield:** 3-1/2 dozen.

nutrition facts: 3 meatballs equals 120 calories, 6 g fat (3 g saturated fat), 24 mg cholesterol, 407 mg sodium, 8 g carbohydrate, trace fiber, 9 g protein.

 This beef recipe is lighter in calories, fat and sodium.

jackie hannahs
fountain, michigan

If you and your family like meatballs, try these for something a little different. The oven-baked bites get lots of great flavor from taco seasoning mix.

mashed potato meat loaf

prep 20 minutes | **bake** 50 minutes

dava beck
amarillo, texas

I created this recipe when my children were young and reluctant to eat meat loaf. They loved the potato surprise inside and the zippy topping. Sometimes, I put green beans in the center of the potatoes to make a one-dish meal.

1-1/3 cups water
1/3 cup milk
2 tablespoons butter
1-1/2 teaspoons salt, *divided*
1-1/3 cups mashed potato flakes
1 egg, lightly beaten
1/2 cup quick-cooking oats
1/2 cup chopped green pepper
1/3 cup chopped onion
3/4 teaspoon pepper
1 pound lean ground beef
1 can (11-1/2 ounces) picante V8 juice
1/4 cup ketchup

In a large saucepan, bring water, milk, butter and 1/2 teaspoon salt to a boil. Remove from the heat; stir in potato flakes. Let stand for 30 seconds. Fluff with a fork; set aside.

In a large bowl, combine the egg, oats, green pepper, onion, pepper and remaining salt. Crumble beef over mixture and mix well. On a piece of waxed paper, pat beef mixture into a 12-in. x 8-in. rectangle. Spoon mashed potatoes lengthwise down the center third to within 1 in. of edges. Bring long sides over potatoes to meet in center; seal seam and edges.

Place seam side up in a greased 13-in. x 9-in. x 2-in. baking dish. Bake, uncovered, at 350° for 30 minutes; drain. Pour V8 juice over loaf. Top with ketchup. Bake 18-22 minutes longer or until meat is no longer pink and a meat thermometer reads 160°. Let stand for 5 minutes before slicing. **yield:** 4-6 servings.

microwave meat loaf

prep 10 minutes | **bake** 20 minutes + standing

1 can (8 ounces) tomato sauce
1/4 cup packed brown sugar
1 teaspoon prepared mustard
1 egg, lightly beaten
1 medium onion, chopped
1/4 cup cracker crumbs
   (about 6 crackers)
1 teaspoon salt
1/4 teaspoon pepper
1-1/2 pounds lean ground beef

In a small bowl, combine the tomato sauce, brown sugar and mustard; set aside. In a large bowl, combine the egg, onion, cracker crumbs, salt, pepper and 3/4 cup of the sauce mixture. Crumble beef over mixture and mix well.

Shape into a uniform round loaf in a greased microwave-safe 9-in. pie plate. Cover with waxed paper. Microwave on high for 15-17 minutes or until meat is no longer pink and a meat thermometer reads 160°, turning dish a quarter turn every 5 minutes. Drain; top with remaining sauce mixture. Let stand for 5 minutes before slicing. **yield:** 6 servings.

nutrition facts: 1 piece equals 256 calories, 10 g fat (4 g saturated fat), 91 mg cholesterol, 696 mg sodium, 16 g carbohydrate, 1 g fiber, 24 g protein.

editor's note: This recipe was tested in a 1,100-watt microwave.

This beef recipe is lighter in calories, fat and sodium.

becky cain
hutchinson, kansas

This is a super summer recipe because you don't have to turn on your oven and heat up the kitchen on a hot day. With the saucy topping, this loaf never fails to please.

tamale loaf

prep 15 minutes | **bake** 1-1/2 hours

letha smith
amarillo, texas

If you like Southwest-style food, you're sure to enjoy this delicious loaf. I've prepared it for large groups and have received many compliments.

1 pound lean ground beef
1 cup chopped celery
1 cup chopped green pepper
1/2 cup chopped onion
2 cans (8 ounces *each*) tomato sauce
1 cup yellow cornmeal
1 can (14-3/4 ounces) cream-style corn
1 can (4-1/4 ounces) chopped ripe olives, drained
2 eggs, lightly beaten
1 tablespoon chili powder
2 teaspoons salt
1/2 teaspoon pepper
Taco sauce, optional

In a large saucepan, cook beef, celery, green pepper and onion over medium heat until meat is no longer pink; drain. Stir in the tomato sauce, cornmeal, corn, olives, eggs, chili powder, salt and pepper.

Pour into a well-greased 9-in. x 5-in. x 3-in. loaf pan. Bake, uncovered, at 350° for 1-1/2 hours until a meat thermometer reaches 160°. Serve meat loaf with taco sauce if desired. **yield:** 8-10 servings.

complete **COOKING**

Ground beef should always be cooked until it is medium (160°) and no longer pink. The most accurate way to determine doneness in meat loaves, meatballs and thick patties is to use an instant-read thermometer. Insert the thermometer far enough in the loaf, meatball or patty to read the temperature in the center.

fiesta meatballs

prep 25 minutes | **bake** 30 minutes

1 egg
1-1/2 teaspoons Worcestershire sauce
1/4 cup finely chopped onion
1/4 cup finely chopped celery
2-1/2 teaspoons garlic salt, *divided*
1/4 teaspoon pepper
1 pound ground beef
1 cup soft bread crumbs
1 tablespoon cornstarch
1 cup beef broth
1 can (14-1/2 ounces) stewed tomatoes
2 cups sliced zucchini
1 teaspoon dried oregano
1/2 teaspoon sugar
1/2 teaspoon dried basil

In a large bowl, combine the egg, Worcestershire sauce, onion, celery, 1-1/2 teaspoons garlic salt and pepper. Add beef and mix well. Sprinkle with bread crumbs; mix just until combined. Shape into 2-in. balls. Place on a greased rack in a shallow baking pan. Bake, uncovered, at 375° for 20 minutes or until meat is no longer pink.

Meanwhile, in a saucepan, combine the cornstarch and broth until smooth. Stir in the stewed tomatoes, zucchini, oregano, sugar, basil and remaining garlic salt. Bring to a boil; cook and stir for 2 minutes or until thickened.

Drain the meatballs; top with the tomato mixture. Bake 10 minutes longer or until heated through. **yield:** 4 servings.

patricia archie
geldo, wyoming

My husband is crazy about rice, not about zucchini. But when I serve them together in these flavorful meatballs, he always comes back for more.

italian meatball mix

prep 15 minutes | **bake** 20 minutes

This beef recipe is lighter in calories, fat and sodium.

lois crissman

mansfield, ohio

I keep this blend for moist meatballs in the fridge so I can whip up an Italian dinner in a snap. Sometimes when my daughter stops by, a cupful of the mix will be missing and I'll find a note on the refrigerator door!

2-1/2 cups dry bread crumbs
2/3 cup dried minced onion
2/3 cup grated Parmesan cheese
1/3 cup dried parsley flakes
1 tablespoon garlic powder
1 tablespoon garlic salt

additional ingredients (for each batch):
1 egg, lightly beaten
1 pound ground beef

In a large bowl, combine the first six ingredients. Store the mix in the refrigerator for up to 2 months. **yield:** 4 batches (about 4 cups total).

TO PREPARE MEATBALLS: In a large bowl, combine the egg and 1 cup meatball mix. Crumble beef over mixture and mix well. Shape into 1-1/2-in. balls.

In a skillet, brown the meatballs; drain. Transfer to a 13-in. x 9-in. x 2-in. baking dish. Bake at 400° for 20-25 minutes or until meat is no longer pink. **yield:** 16 meatballs per batch.

nutrition facts: 4 meatballs equals 83 calories, 4 g fat (2 g saturated fat), 33 mg cholesterol, 155 mg sodium, 4 g carbohydrate, trace fiber, 7 g protein.

---

pinwheel pizza loaf

prep 15 minutes | **bake** 1-1/4 hours + standing

2 eggs
Salt and pepper to taste
3 pounds lean ground beef
6 thin slices deli ham
2 cups (8 ounces) shredded part-skim mozzarella cheese
1 jar (14 ounces) pizza sauce

rhonda touchet

jennings, louisiana

This fun, pizza-flavored loaf is especially popular with kids. Many neighbors have called me to get the recipe after their children tried it at my house.

In a large bowl, beat the eggs, salt and pepper. Crumble beef over eggs and mix well. On a piece of heavy-duty foil, pat beef mixture into a 12-in. x 10-in. rectangle. Cover with ham and cheese to within 1/2 in. of edges. Roll up jelly-roll style, starting with a short side and peeling away foil while rolling. Seal seam and ends.

Place meat loaf seam side down in a greased 13-in. x 9-in. x 2-in. baking dish. Top with pizza sauce. Bake, uncovered, at 350° for 1-1/4 hours or until meat is no longer pink and a meat thermometer reads 160°. Let stand for 10 minutes before slicing. **yield:** 12 servings.

picante cranberry meatballs

prep 20 minutes | **bake** 30 minutes

marge wyse
winfield, british columbia

Cranberry, chili and picante sauces may seem like an unusual combination, but they're delicious together in these zippy meatballs. Even our grandkids enjoy them.

2 eggs, lightly beaten
1/3 cup ketchup
1/3 cup minced fresh parsley
2 tablespoons soy sauce
2 tablespoons dried minced onion
1/2 teaspoon garlic powder
1/4 teaspoon pepper
1 cup crushed saltines (about 30 crackers)
2 pounds lean ground beef

sauce

1 can (16 ounces) jellied cranberry sauce
1 cup chili sauce
1/4 cup picante sauce
2 tablespoons brown sugar
1 tablespoon lemon juice
Hot cooked noodles, optional

In a bowl, combine the eggs, ketchup, parsley, soy sauce, onion, garlic powder and pepper. Add cracker crumbs. Crumble beef over mixture; mix well. Shape into 1-1/2-in. balls. In a skillet, brown meatballs over medium heat. Transfer to a greased 13-in. x 9-in. x 2-in. baking dish.

In a saucepan, combine the cranberry sauce, chili sauce, picante sauce, brown sugar and lemon juice. Cook and stir until cranberry sauce is melted and mixture is heated through. Pour over meatballs. Cover and bake at 350° for 30-35 minutes or until meat is no longer pink. Serve over noodles if desired. **yield:** 8 servings.

cottage cheese meat loaf

prep 10 minutes | **bake** 30 minutes + standing

1 cup 4% cottage cheese
1 egg, lightly beaten
1/4 cup ketchup
2 tablespoons chopped onion
1 tablespoon prepared mustard
1/2 cup quick-cooking oats
1 teaspoon salt
1/8 teaspoon pepper
1 pound lean ground beef
1/3 cup grated Parmesan cheese

In a large bowl, combine the first eight ingredients. Crumble beef over mixture and mix well. Press into an ungreased 8-in. square baking pan.

Bake at 350° for 20 minutes. Sprinkle with the Parmesan cheese; bake 10-15 minutes longer or until the meat is no longer pink. Drain; let stand 10 minutes before cutting. **yield:** 4 servings.

maggie slocum
lindon, utah

Putting cottage cheese in this meat loaf makes it wonderfully moist. Plus, the recipe couldn't be much easier to prepare.

swedish meatballs

prep 30 minutes | **bake** 1 hour

4 eggs
1 cup milk
8 slices white bread, torn
2 pounds ground beef
1/4 cup finely chopped onion
4 teaspoons baking powder
1 to 2 teaspoons salt
1 teaspoon pepper
2 tablespoons shortening
2 cans (10-3/4 ounces *each*) condensed cream of chicken soup, undiluted
2 cans (10-3/4 ounces *each*) condensed cream of mushroom soup, undiluted
1 can (12 ounces) evaporated milk
Minced fresh parsley

In a large bowl, beat eggs and milk. Add bread; mix gently and let stand for 5 minutes. Add beef, onion, baking powder, salt and pepper; mix well (mixture will be soft). Shape into 1-in. balls.

In a large skillet, brown meatballs, a few at a time, in shortening. Place in an ungreased 3-qt. baking dish. In a bowl, stir soups and milk until smooth; pour over meatballs. Bake, uncovered, at 350° for 1 hour. Sprinkle with parsley. **yield:** 8-10 servings.

donna hanson
lusk, wyoming

My parents were ranchers all of their lives, and most of our dinners featured beef. This is Mom's recipe for tender Swedish meatballs with a thick, savory gravy.

south dakota meat loaf

prep 10 minutes | **bake** 1-1/4 hours

This beef recipe is lighter in calories, fat and sodium.

lauree buus
rapid city, south dakota

I've tried other versions of meat loaf, but I always end up coming back to this one. It's based on my mother's traditional recipe.

1 egg
1/3 cup fat-free evaporated milk
3/4 cup quick-cooking oats
1/4 cup chopped onion
2 tablespoons Worcestershire sauce
1 teaspoon salt
1/2 teaspoon rubbed sage
1/8 teaspoon pepper
1-1/2 pounds lean ground beef
1/4 cup ketchup

In a large bowl, combine the first eight ingredients. Crumble beef over mixture and mix well. Press into an ungreased 8-in. x 4-in. x 2-in. loaf pan. Bake, uncovered, at 350° for 1-1/4 hours; drain.

Drizzle meat loaf with ketchup; bake 10 minutes longer or until meat is no longer

pink and a meat thermometer reads 160°. **yield:** 6 servings.

nutrition facts: 1 serving equals 272 calories, 12 g fat (4 g saturated fat), 77 mg cholesterol, 683 mg sodium, 13 g carbohydrate, 1 g fiber, 27 g protein.

potato-topped chili loaf

prep 15 minutes | **bake** 40 minutes

3/4 cup diced onion
1/3 cup saltine crumbs
1 egg
3 tablespoons milk
1 tablespoon chili powder
1/2 teaspoon salt
1-1/2 pounds lean ground beef

topping
3 cups hot mashed potatoes (with milk and butter)
1 can (11 ounces) Mexicorn, drained
1 can (16 ounces) kidney beans, rinsed and drained
1/4 cup thinly sliced green onions
1 cup (4 ounces) shredded cheddar *or* taco cheese, *divided*

Combine the first six ingredients; crumble beef over mixture and mix well. Press into an ungreased 9-in. square baking pan. Bake at 375° for 25 minutes or until a meat thermometer reaches 160°; drain.

Combine the potatoes, corn, beans, onions and 1/2 cup of cheese; spread over meat loaf. Sprinkle with the remaining cheese. Bake 15 minutes longer or until the potato layer is lightly browned and heated through. **yield:** 6 servings.

quick CRUMBS

For cracker crumbs, place the crackers in a heavy-duty resealable plastic bag. Seal the bag, pushing out as much of the air as possible. Then press a rolling pin over it, crushing the crackers into fine crumbs.

glenn schildknecht
savannah, missouri

This all-in-one main dish packed with beef, potatoes, beans and corn makes a complete meal. Even the heartiest of appetites are sure to be satisfied!

meatballs monte carlo

prep 20 minutes | **cook** 40 minutes

1/3 cup evaporated milk
1/4 cup dry bread crumbs
1 small onion, chopped
1/4 teaspoon salt
Dash pepper
1 pound ground beef
1 envelope spaghetti sauce mix
4 cans (11-1/2 ounces *each*) tomato juice
1 cup water
5 cups uncooked wide egg noodles
1 can (2-1/4 ounces) sliced ripe olives, drained

In a large bowl, combine the milk, bread crumbs, onion, salt and pepper. Crumble beef over mixture and mix well. Shape into 1-1/2-in. balls.

In a large skillet over medium-high heat, brown the meatballs; drain. Combine the spaghetti sauce mix, tomato juice and water; pour over the meatballs. Bring to a boil. Stir in the noodles and olives. Reduce heat; cover and simmer for 20-25 minutes or until noodles are tender, stirring occasionally. **yield:** 6 servings.

margaret wilson
hemet, california

I need just one pan to prepare this simple entree. After I've browned the meatballs, the noodles cook in the tomatoey sauce right along with them.

deluxe meat loaf

prep 15 minutes | **bake** 70 minutes

patricia zwerk
tucson, arizona

When I make meat loaf, I usually just mix together whatever I have on hand. One time, I added leftover kidney beans I had in the fridge. The result was a soft texture…and a new family-favorite recipe!

2 eggs, lightly beaten
1-1/2 cups ketchup, *divided*
1 can (16 ounces) kidney beans, rinsed, drained and mashed
1 cup seasoned bread crumbs
1 large onion, chopped
1 celery rib, chopped
2 teaspoons Worcestershire sauce
1 teaspoon salt-free lemon-pepper seasoning
1/2 teaspoon seasoned salt
2-1/2 pounds lean ground beef
1/2 cup water

In a large bowl, combine the eggs, 1 cup ketchup, beans, bread crumbs, onion, celery, Worcestershire sauce, lemon-pepper and seasoned salt; crumble beef over mixture and mix well.

Shape into two loaves. Place in a 13-in. x 9-in. x 2-in. baking dish coated with non-stick cooking spray.

In a bowl, combine water and remaining ketchup; pour over meat loaves. Bake, uncovered, at 325° for 70 minutes or until meat is no longer pink and a meat thermometer reads 160°. **yield:** 12 servings.

best TEXTURE

When shaping meat loaves and meatballs, handle the mixture as little as possible to keep the final product light in texture. Combine all meat loaf or meatball ingredients except the ground beef. Then crumble the ground beef over the mixture and mix it well.

sweet 'n' sour meatballs

prep/total time 30 minutes

 This beef recipe is lighter in calories, fat and sodium.

andrea busch
brackenridge, pennsylvania

This Oriental dinner served over rice is a welcome change of pace from routine menus. My husband isn't normally a big fan of stir-fries, and our children can be picky eaters, but I never have leftovers when I serve this dish.

  1 egg
1/4 cup seasoned bread crumbs
1/2 teaspoon salt
1/4 teaspoon ground ginger
Dash pepper
  1 pound ground beef
  1 can (20 ounces) pineapple chunks
1/4 cup cider vinegar
1/4 cup packed brown sugar
  2 tablespoons soy sauce
  1 cup sliced carrots
  1 medium green pepper, julienned
  1 tablespoon cornstarch
  2 tablespoons cold water
Hot cooked rice

In a bowl, combine the first five ingredients. Add beef and mix well. Shape into 1-in. balls. In a skillet, cook meatballs over medium heat until no longer pink; drain.

Drain pineapple, reserving juice; set pineapple aside. Add water to juice to measure 1 cup. Stir in vinegar, brown sugar and soy sauce; pour over meatballs. Add carrots. Bring to a boil. Reduce heat; cover and simmer for 5-8 minutes or until carrots are crisp-tender. Stir in green pepper and pineapple; cover and simmer 5 minutes longer or until pepper is crisp-tender.

Combine the cornstarch and cold water until smooth; stir into the meatball mixture. Bring to a boil; cook and stir for 2 minutes or until thickened. Serve over rice. **yield:** 4-6 servings.

nutrition facts: 1 cup equals 264 calories, 8 g fat (3 g saturated fat), 72 mg cholesterol, 648 mg sodium, 32 g carbohydrate, 2 g fiber, 16 g protein.

mexican meat loaf

prep 10 minutes | **bake** 65 minutes + standing

  4 cups cooked shredded hash brown potatoes
1/4 cup salsa
  1 egg, lightly beaten
  2 tablespoons vegetable soup mix
  2 tablespoons taco seasoning
  2 cups (8 ounces) shredded cheddar cheese, *divided*
  2 pounds ground beef

In a large bowl, combine the hash browns, salsa, egg, soup mix, taco seasoning and 1 cup cheese. Crumble beef over mixture and mix well. Shape into a 12-in. loaf. Place in a 13-in. x 9-in. x 2-in. baking dish.

Bake meat loaf, uncovered, at 350° for 1 hour or until a meat thermometer reads 160°. Sprinkle with remaining cheese; bake 5 minutes longer or until the cheese is melted. Let stand for 10 minutes before slicing. **yield:** 6-8 servings.

alice mccauley
beaumont, texas

Being a working mother with a small budget and little time, I often rely on ground beef. When our son was getting bored with meat loaf, I made this taco-seasoned version. Everyone loves it with sour cream and extra salsa.

reuben meatballs

prep 15 minutes | **bake** 1 hour

irlana waggoner

hays, kansas

Fans of the classic Reuben sandwich are sure to savor these distinctive meatballs. The recipe came from a good friend of mine who is from Germany and a great cook.

1 egg
1 small onion, finely chopped
2/3 cup soft bread crumbs
1/4 cup minced fresh parsley
1/2 teaspoon salt
1/2 teaspoon pepper
1 cup cooked rice
1-1/2 pounds lean ground beef
2 cups sauerkraut, rinsed and well drained
1 to 2 teaspoons caraway seeds
1 can (10-3/4 ounces) condensed cream of mushroom soup, undiluted
1/2 cup Thousand Island salad dressing
1/4 cup shredded Swiss cheese
Rye bread, optional

In a bowl, combine the egg, onion, bread crumbs, parsley, salt and pepper. Stir in rice. Crumble beef over the mixture and mix well. Shape into 15 balls. Place meatballs on a greased rack in a shallow baking pan. Bake, uncovered, at 350° for 15-20 minutes or until browned; drain.

Transfer meatballs to an ungreased 13-in. x 9-in. x 2-in. baking dish. Arrange sauerkraut over meatballs; sprinkle with caraway seeds. Combine soup and salad dressing; spread over the top.

Cover and bake for 35-45 minutes or until meat is no longer pink. Uncover; sprinkle with Swiss cheese. Bake 10 minutes longer or until cheese is melted. Serve with rye bread if desired. **yield:** 5 servings.

eat one-freeze one meat loaf

prep 15 minutes | **bake** 45 minutes

 This beef recipe is lighter in calories, fat and sodium.

bonnie baumgardner
sylva, north carolina

This convenient recipe yields a pair of delicious ground beef loaves—one to serve right away and one to keep in the freezer for a busy night. All I have to do is thaw the frozen loaf and reheat it.

1 egg, beaten
2/3 cup milk
1 tablespoon ketchup
1 tablespoon soy sauce
1/2 cup herb-seasoned stuffing mix, crushed
1 small onion, minced
2 tablespoons finely chopped sweet red pepper
1 garlic clove, minced
1/2 teaspoon salt
1/4 teaspoon pepper
1 pound lean ground beef
Additional ketchup, optional

In a large bowl, combine the first 10 ingredients. Crumble beef over mixture and mix well. Shape into two loaves; place in an ungreased shallow baking pan.

Bake, uncovered, at 350° for 45-50 minutes. If desired, top loaf with ketchup before serving. Cool and freeze the other loaf. **yield:** 2 loaves (4 servings).

nutrition facts: 1 piece equals 252 calories, 11 g fat (5 g saturated fat), 114 mg cholesterol, 768 mg sodium, 10 g carbohydrate, 1 g fiber, 26 g protein.

saucy microwave meatballs

prep/total time 30 minutes

1 egg
1/4 cup finely chopped onion
1 teaspoon salt
1 pound ground beef
1 can (8 ounces) tomato sauce
1/3 cup packed brown sugar
3 tablespoons lemon juice
1/8 teaspoon garlic salt
Hot cooked spaghetti

In a large bowl, combine the egg, onion and salt. Crumble beef over the mixture and mix well. Shape into 1-1/2-in. balls.

Place half of meatballs in a microwave-safe 2-qt. dish. Cover and microwave on high for 2 to 2-1/2 minutes or until meatballs are firm and no longer pink; drain. Repeat with remaining meatballs.

In a microwave-safe bowl, combine the tomato sauce, brown sugar, lemon juice and garlic salt. Cook, uncovered, on high for 30-60 seconds or until sugar is dissolved, stirring every 15 seconds. Pour over meatballs. Cover and microwave at 50% power for 3-4 minutes or until heated through. Serve with spaghetti. **yield:** 4 servings.

editor's note: This recipe was tested in a 1,100-watt microwave.

edna denny
pine island, minnesota

For a speedy Italian meal, these moist meatballs are a terrific choice. They're ready in just 30 minutes and are perfect with spaghetti.

my mom's meat loaf wellington

prep 20 minutes | **bake** 1 hour

**taste of home
test kitchen**
greendale, wisconsin

Meat loaf doesn't get much fancier than this! The ground beef, veal and pork mixture is covered with puff pastry and draped with an elegant sauce.

3 eggs
1/2 cup ketchup
2-1/2 teaspoons seasoned salt
2 teaspoons Worcestershire sauce
1/4 teaspoon ground mustard
1/8 teaspoon pepper
3/4 pound lean ground beef
3/4 pound ground veal
3/4 pound ground pork
1/3 cup chopped onion
3/4 cup dry bread crumbs
1 package (17.30 ounces) frozen puff pastry, thawed

madeira sauce

1/4 cup butter, cubed
5 tablespoons all-purpose flour
2 cups condensed beef consomme, undiluted
1 tablespoon tomato paste
1/4 teaspoon dried thyme
1/4 teaspoon dried rosemary, crushed
1/4 teaspoon browning sauce, optional
Dash cloves
1/2 cup Madeira wine *or* beef broth
2 cups sliced fresh mushrooms
2 tablespoons olive oil

In a large bowl, beat 2 eggs, ketchup, seasoned salt, Worcestershire sauce, mustard and pepper. Crumble meat over mixture and mix well. Sprinkle with onion and bread crumbs; mix gently. Shape into two loaves, about 9 in. x 3 in.

On a lightly floured surface, roll out each pastry sheet into an 18-in. x 16-in. rectangle. Invert meat loaves and place in center of each pastry; fold short sides of pastry over loaf. Fold long sides over loaf and pastry; seal seams.

Place seam side down on a rack in a 15-in. x 10-in. x 1-in. baking pan. Beat remaining egg; brush over pastry. Bake at 350° for 60-70 minutes or until a meat thermometer reads 160°-170°.

Meanwhile, for the sauce, in a small saucepan, melt butter. Whisk in flour until smooth. Stir in the consomme, tomato paste, thyme, rosemary, browning sauce if desired and cloves. Bring to a boil; cook and stir for 2 minutes or until thickened. Stir in wine or broth.

In a small skillet, saute mushrooms in oil until tender. Serve the mushrooms and sauce with meat loaf slices. **yield:** 2 meat loaves (5-6 servings each) and about 2-1/2 cups sauce.

pepper jack meat loaf

prep 20 minutes | **bake** 50 minutes

debra hartze
zeeland, north dakota

Want an easy entree that looks impressive? Try this colorful loaf. It's stuffed with pepper Jack cheese and has even more melted on top.

1 egg
1 cup seasoned bread crumbs
1/4 cup chopped onion
1/2 to 1 teaspoon salt
1/2 teaspoon pepper
1-1/2 pounds lean ground beef
1 cup (4 ounces) pepper Jack cheese, *divided*

In a large bowl, combine the egg, bread crumbs, onion, salt and pepper. Crumble beef over mixture and mix well. Press half of the beef mixture onto the bottom and halfway up the sides of a greased 8-in. x 4-in. x 2-in. loaf pan. Sprinkle 3/4 cup cheese over meat to within 1/2 in. of sides. Pat re-

maining beef mixture over cheese.

Bake, uncovered, at 350° for 50-55 minutes or until meat is no longer pink and a meat thermometer reads 160°. Sprinkle with remaining cheese. Bake 5 minutes longer or until cheese is melted. Let stand for 10 minutes before slicing. **yield:** 6 servings.

meatball hash brown bake

prep 25 minutes | **bake** 1 hour

- 2 eggs
- 3/4 cup crushed saltines (about 20 crackers)
- 6 to 8 garlic cloves, minced
- 2 teaspoons salt, *divided*
- 1-1/2 teaspoons pepper, *divided*
- 1 pound lean ground beef
- 1 can (10-3/4 ounces) condensed cream of chicken soup, undiluted
- 1 cup (8 ounces) sour cream
- 1 cup (4 ounces) shredded cheddar cheese
- 1 large onion, chopped
- 1 package (30 ounces) frozen shredded hash brown potatoes, thawed

In a bowl, lightly beat eggs. Stir in cracker crumbs, garlic, 1 teaspoon salt and 1/2 teaspoon pepper. Crumble beef over mixture; mix well. Shape into 1-in. balls.

In a covered skillet over low heat, cook meatballs in a small amount of water until browned; drain. In a bowl, combine the soup, sour cream, cheese, onion and remaining salt and pepper. With paper towels, pat hash browns dry. Stir into the soup mixture.

Transfer to a greased 13-in. x 9-in. x 2-in. baking dish. Arrange the meatballs over the top, pressing lightly into the mixture. Cover and bake at 350° for 45 minutes. Uncover and bake 15 minutes longer or until the meat is no longer pink and the potatoes are tender. **yield:** 8 servings.

joann fritzler
belen, new mexico

For a seniors' potluck at church, I wanted to bring something that was a main dish and side dish all in one. This creamy casserole proved to be a real crowd-pleaser.

tomato meat loaf

prep 10 minutes | **bake** 1-1/2 hours

linda begley
stoutsville, missouri

Topped with slices of tomato, this tender beef loaf looks fancy but is actually easy to fix. It's one of my husband's all-time favorite dinners.

1 egg, lightly beaten
1/2 cup fat-free milk
1/4 cup ketchup
1 cup quick-cooking oats
1 slice white bread, crumbled
4 saltines, crushed
1/2 teaspoon salt
1/4 teaspoon pepper
2 pounds lean ground beef
1 medium tomato, sliced

In a large bowl, combine the first eight ingredients. Crumble beef over mixture and mix well. Shape into a loaf in a greased 13-in. x 9-in. x 2-in. baking dish. Bake, uncovered, at 350° for 1 hour.

Arrange tomato slices over loaf. Bake 30 minutes longer or until meat is no longer pink and a meat thermometer reads 160°. Using two large spatulas, carefully transfer loaf to a serving platter. **yield:** 8 servings.

pizza meat loaf cups

prep/total time 30 minutes

 This beef recipe is lighter in calories, fat and sodium.

susan wollin
marshall, wisconsin

I fix these little pizza-flavored loaves ahead of time and pop them in the freezer. They're convenient to reheat as an after-school snack or quick dinner. We like to drizzle extra pizza sauce on top.

1   egg, beaten
1/2   cup pizza sauce
1/4   cup seasoned bread crumbs
1/2   teaspoon Italian seasoning
1-1/2   pounds ground beef
1-1/2   cups (6 ounces *each*) shredded part-skim mozzarella cheese
Additional pizza sauce, optional

In a large bowl, combine the egg, pizza sauce, bread crumbs and Italian seasoning. Crumble beef over mixture and mix well. Divide between 12 greased muffin cups; press onto the bottom and up the sides. Fill center with cheese.

Bake at 375° for 15-18 minutes or until meat is no longer pink. Serve immediately with additional pizza sauce if desired. Or cool, place in freezer bags and freeze for up to 3 months. **yield:** 1 dozen.

TO USE FROZEN PIZZA CUPS: Thaw in the refrigerator for 24 hours. Heat on a microwave-safe plate on high for 2-3 minutes or until heated through.

nutrition facts: 1 serving equals 167 calories, 10 g fat (4 g saturated fat), 63 mg cholesterol, 177 mg sodium, 3 g carbohydrate, trace fiber, 16 g protein.

meatball potato supper

prep 30 minutes | **bake** 60 minutes

2   eggs
1/2   cup dry bread crumbs
1   envelope onion soup mix
1-1/2   pounds lean ground beef
2   tablespoons all-purpose flour
6   medium potatoes, peeled and thinly sliced
1   can (10-3/4 ounces) condensed cream of celery soup, undiluted
1   cup milk
Paprika, optional

In a bowl, combine the eggs, bread crumbs and soup mix. Crumble beef over mixture and mix well. Shape into 1-in. balls. In a large skillet, brown the meatballs in small batches over medium heat; drain. Sprinkle with flour; gently roll to coat.

Place half of the potatoes in a greased 2-1/2-qt. baking dish. Top with the meatballs and remaining potatoes. In a bowl, combine the soup and milk until blended; pour over the potatoes. Sprinkle with paprika if desired. Cover and bake at 350° for 60-65 minutes or until the potatoes are tender. **yield:** 6-8 servings.

nutrition facts: 1 cup equals 361 calories, 11 g fat (4 g saturated fat), 100 mg cholesterol, 739 mg sodium, 42 g carbohydrate, 3 g fiber, 24 g protein.

 This beef recipe is lighter in calories, fat and sodium.

sonya morton
molena, georgia

I'm often asked to bring this creamy casserole to potluck suppers. People must enjoy it, because I never have any leftovers to take home!

south-of-the-border meat loaf

prep 10 minutes | **bake** 1 hour + cooling

 This beef recipe is lighter in calories, fat and sodium.

ruth bogdanski

grants pass, oregon

This zesty recipe uses black beans, chopped jalapeno, green peppers and crushed taco shells. It's a tasty twist on a classic comfort food.

- 1 can (15 ounces) black beans, rinsed and drained
- 4 taco shells, crushed
- 1/2 cup chopped onion
- 1/2 cup chopped green pepper
- 1/3 cup minced fresh cilantro
- 2 egg whites
- 2 tablespoons chopped jalapeno pepper
- 2 teaspoons ground cumin
- 2 teaspoons chili powder
- 3 garlic cloves, minced
- 1 teaspoon salt
- 1/2 teaspoon pepper
- 2 pounds lean ground beef

Salsa, optional

In a large bowl, combine the first 12 ingredients. Crumble beef over mixture and mix well. Press into a 9-in. x 5-in. x 3-in. loaf pan coated with nonstick cooking spray. Bake, uncovered, at 375° for 1 hour or until meat is no longer pink and a meat thermometer reads 160°.

Cool for 10 minutes before removing from pan. Drizzle with salsa if desired. **yield:** 6-8 servings.

nutrition facts: 1 serving equals 253 calories, 10 g fat (4 g saturated fat), 56 mg cholesterol, 514 mg sodium, 13 g carbohydrate, 3 g fiber, 26 g protein.

editor's note: When cutting or seeding hot peppers, use rubber or plastic gloves to protect your hands. Avoid touching your face.

pesto meat loaf

prep 15 minutes | **bake** 50 minutes + standing

pesto
- 2 garlic cloves
- 1/3 cup olive oil
- 1 cup fresh basil leaves
- 3/4 cup cooked long grain rice
- 1/4 cup chopped walnuts
- 1/4 cup shredded sharp cheddar cheese
- 1/4 teaspoon salt

meat loaf
- 1/2 cup quick-cooking oats
- 1/2 cup finely chopped green onions
- 1 egg, lightly beaten
- 1/4 cup salsa
- 2 garlic cloves, minced
- 1/2 teaspoon salt
- 2 pounds lean ground beef

margaret pache

mesa, arizona

The homemade pesto in this recipe transforms ordinary meat loaf into something extra special. Salsa provides an added burst of flavor.

Place pesto ingredients in the order listed in a food processor; cover and process on low speed until a paste forms.

In a large bowl, combine the first six meat loaf ingredients; add pesto. Crumble beef over mixture and mix well. Press into a greased 9-in. x 5-in. x 3-in. loaf pan.

Bake at 350° for 50-60 minutes or until a meat thermometer reads 160°, draining off fat when necessary. Let stand in pan for 10 minutes before slicing. **yield:** 8 servings.

beef stroganoff meatballs

prep 30 minutes | **bake** 15 minutes

1	egg
1/4	cup milk
1/4	cup finely chopped onion
2	teaspoons Worcestershire sauce
1-1/2	cups soft bread crumbs
1	teaspoon salt
1/4	teaspoon pepper
1-1/2	pounds ground beef

sauce

1-1/2	cups sliced fresh mushrooms
1/2	cup chopped onion
1/4	cup butter
4	tablespoons all-purpose flour, *divided*
1/4	teaspoon salt
1-1/2	cups beef broth
1	cup (8 ounces) sour cream

Hot cooked noodles

Paprika, optional

In a large bowl, combine the egg, milk, onion and Worcestershire sauce. Stir in bread crumbs, salt and pepper. Add beef; mix well. Shape into 1-1/4-in. balls. Place on a greased rack in a shallow baking pan. Bake, uncovered, at 350° for 15-20 minutes or until meat is no longer pink; drain.

In a large saucepan, saute mushrooms and onion in butter until tender. Stir in 3 tablespoons flour and salt until blended. Gradually add broth. Bring to a boil over medium heat. Cook and stir for 2 minutes or until thickened.

Combine the sour cream and remaining flour until smooth; stir into the mushroom mixture. Add the meatballs. Simmer, uncovered, for 4-5 minutes or until heated through, stirring occasionally. Serve over noodles. Sprinkle with paprika if desired. **yield:** 6 servings.

chris duncan
ellensburg, washington

With a rich sour cream and mushroom sauce, these meatballs are delicious. Served over pasta, they're a great choice for any occasion.

spicy meat loaves

prep 15 minutes | **bake** 35 minutes

melanie ellis
marion, north carolina

Here's a fun spin on a ground beef classic. I top the taco-flavored, single-serving loaves with zesty tomato sauce and shredded cheese.

2 eggs, lightly beaten
1/2 cup seasoned bread crumbs
2 tablespoons taco seasoning
2 tablespoons onion mushroom soup mix
1 tablespoon Italian seasoning
1 tablespoon Worcestershire sauce
1/2 teaspoon pepper
1 can (15 ounces) Italian tomato sauce, *divided*
2 pounds lean ground beef
1/2 cup shredded Colby-Monterey Jack cheese

In a large bowl, combine the first seven ingredients. Stir in 3/4 cup tomato sauce. Crumble beef over mixture and mix well. Shape into six loaves.

Place in an ungreased 13-in. x 9-in. x 2-in. baking dish. Top each with 1 tablespoon of tomato sauce (save remaining sauce for another use). Sprinkle with cheese.

Bake, uncovered, at 350° for 35-40 minutes or until meat is no longer pink and a meat thermometer reads 160°; drain. Let the loaves stand for 5 minutes before serving. **yield:** 6 servings.

sweet 'n' sour meat loaf

prep 15 minutes | **bake** 50 minutes + standing

2 cups water
5 tablespoons brown sugar
5 tablespoons white vinegar
2 tablespoons cornstarch
2 tablespoons corn syrup
2 tablespoons soy sauce
1 teaspoon salt

meat loaf

2 eggs
2 teaspoons Worcestershire sauce
1 cup dry bread crumbs
1/2 cup chopped onion
2 teaspoons salt
1/2 teaspoon pepper
2 pounds lean ground beef
1/2 pound ground pork

In a saucepan, combine the first seven ingredients; bring to a boil. Cook and stir for 2 minutes or until thickened; set aside.

In a large bowl, combine the first six meat loaf ingredients; add 2/3 cup of the reserved sauce. Crumble beef and pork over mixture and mix well.

Pat into two greased 8-in. x 4-in. x 2-in. loaf pans. Pour the remaining sauce over the meat loaves. Bake, uncovered, at 350° for 50 minutes or until the meat is no longer pink and a meat thermometer reads 160°. Let stand for 10 minutes before slicing. **yield:** 2 loaves (5 servings each).

tia yeatts

tappahannock, pennsylvania

This recipe was in a cookbook published by friends of the small independent school where I teach. The two tangy meat loaves feature both ground beef and pork.

surprise meatball skewers

prep 30 minutes | **grill** 20 minutes

kristen wondra

hudson, kansas

I still remember the first time I served these colorful kabobs— my family was thrilled with the mushroom-and-cheese center inside each meatball. Sometimes I use different vegetables or cheeses for a change of pace.

1/3 cup honey
3 tablespoons Dijon mustard
2 tablespoons finely chopped onion
2 tablespoons apple juice
Dash cayenne pepper
1 egg
1/4 cup dry bread crumbs
1 tablespoon minced fresh parsley
1 teaspoon Italian seasoning
1/4 teaspoon salt
Pepper to taste
1 pound ground beef
1 block (1-1/2 ounces) Monterey Jack cheese, cut into 12 cubes
12 small mushrooms, stems removed
1 medium green pepper, cut into pieces
1 medium sweet yellow *or* red pepper, cut into pieces
1 medium onion, cut into wedges

In a saucepan, combine the first five ingredients. Bring to a boil. Reduce heat; simmer, uncovered, for 5-7 minutes or until onion is tender and sauce is slightly thickened. Remove from the heat; set aside.

In a large bowl, combine the egg, bread crumbs, parsley, Italian seasoning, salt and pepper. Add beef and mix well. Divide into 12 portions. Place a cube of cheese in each mushroom cap; shape each meat portion around a mushroom.

On six metal or soaked wooden skewers, alternate meatballs, peppers and onion wedges. Grill, uncovered, over medium heat for 3 minutes on each side.

Grill 10-12 minutes longer or until meat juices run clear, turning occasionally. Brush with reserved glaze during the last 2 minutes. **yield:** 6 servings.

scandinavian meatballs with dill sauce

prep 15 minutes | **bake** 25 minutes

linda swanson

riverside, washington

This saucy dish comes from a cookbook that has been used so often, I have to hold it together with rubber bands! But with timeless recipes like this, it's a keeper.

- 2 eggs
- 1 cup heavy whipping cream
- 1/2 cup shredded peeled apple
- 1/2 cup chopped raisins
- 1/2 cup cubed rye bread (1/4-inch cubes)
- 1/4 cup thinly sliced green onions
- 1/4 cup chopped almonds, optional
- 1 teaspoon salt
- 1 teaspoon pepper
- 2 pounds ground beef

sauce
- 1/4 cup butter, cubed
- 1/4 cup all-purpose flour
- 2 cups beef broth
- 2 teaspoons snipped fresh dill *or* 1/2 to 1 teaspoon dill weed
- 1 cup (8 ounces) plain yogurt
- 1 can (8 ounces) sliced water chestnuts, drained

In a large bowl, combine the eggs, cream, apple, raisins, bread, onions, almonds if desired, salt and pepper. Crumble meat over mixture and mix well.

Shape into 2-in. balls. Place on a greased rack in a shallow baking pan. Bake, uncovered, at 400° for 25-30 minutes or until meat is no longer pink; drain.

Meanwhile, in a small saucepan, melt butter. Stir in flour until smooth; gradually add the broth and dill. Bring to a boil over medium heat; cook and stir for 2 minutes or until thickened. Remove from the heat; stir in yogurt and water chestnuts. Serve with meatballs. **yield:** 8-10 servings.

bacon swiss meat loaf

prep 10 minutes | **bake** 65 minutes + standing

- 1 egg
- 1/4 cup evaporated milk
- 1-1/2 cups (6 ounces) shredded Swiss cheese, *divided*
- 1 cup crumbled cooked bacon (about 12 bacon strips), *divided*
- 1/2 cup soft bread crumbs
- 1/2 teaspoon garlic powder
- 1/2 teaspoon onion powder
- 1-1/2 pounds ground beef

kimberly lund

park city, kansas

On busy weekdays, I rely on this fuss-free meat loaf. I keep packages of cooked bacon in the freezer for added convenience.

In a large bowl, combine the egg, milk, 1 cup Swiss cheese, 3/4 cup bacon, bread crumbs, garlic powder and onion powder. Crumble beef over mixture and mix well. Shape into a loaf in a greased 11-in. x 7-in. x 2-in. baking dish.

Bake, uncovered, at 350° for 1 hour or until meat is no longer pink and a meat thermometer reads 160°. Drain. Sprinkle with remaining cheese and bacon. Bake 3-5 minutes longer or until cheese is melted. Let stand for 10 minutes before slicing. **yield:** 6 servings.

zesty meatballs

prep/total time 30 minutes

1/3 cup finely chopped onion
2 egg whites, lightly beaten
1/4 cup fat-free milk
2 teaspoons prepared mustard
1/2 teaspoon salt
3/4 cup graham cracker crumbs
3/4 pound lean ground beef
3/4 pound lean ground turkey

barbecue sauce

1/2 cup packed brown sugar
3 tablespoons cornstarch
1/2 cup cider vinegar
1/2 cup ketchup
1/2 cup molasses
1/4 cup orange juice concentrate
2 tablespoons Dijon mustard
2 tablespoons reduced-sodium soy sauce
1/4 teaspoon hot pepper sauce
6 cups hot cooked yolk-free noodles

Place the onion in a small microwave-safe bowl; cover and microwave on high for 1-1/2 minutes or until tender. In a large bowl, combine the egg whites, milk, mustard, salt, cracker crumbs and onion. Crumble beef and turkey over mixture and mix well.

Shape into 1-1/4-in. balls. Place meatballs on a rack coated with nonstick cooking spray in a shallow baking pan. Bake at 375° for 15 -18 minutes or until meat is no longer pink; drain.

Meanwhile, in a large saucepan, combine brown sugar and cornstarch. Stir in vinegar until smooth. Add the ketchup, molasses, orange juice concentrate, mustard, soy sauce and hot pepper sauce. Bring to a boil; cook and stir for 2 minutes or until thickened. Add meatballs; heat through. Serve over noodles. **yield:** 6 servings.

editor's note: This recipe was tested in a 1,100-watt microwave.

debbie segate
grande prairie, alberta

Molasses adds a touch of sweetness to the tangy sauce that covers these moist meatballs. Serve them over egg noodles for a flavorful, family-pleasing meal.

broccoli meat roll

prep 25 minutes | **bake** 1-1/4 hours

diane burling
pingree, north dakota

*Most people are surprised to
see what's inside this rolled-up
loaf. But the broccoli combines
wonderfully with the ham
and mozzarella cheese.*

2 eggs
1/4 cup milk
1/4 cup ketchup
3/4 cup soft bread crumbs
1-1/2 teaspoons salt, *divided*
1/4 teaspoon pepper
1/4 teaspoon dried oregano
2 pounds lean ground beef
3 cups frozen chopped broccoli,
thawed and drained
1 package (2-1/2 ounces) thinly sliced
deli ham
1/3 cup shredded part-skim mozzarella
cheese

In a large bowl, combine the eggs, milk,
ketchup, bread crumbs, 1/2 teaspoon salt,
pepper and oregano. Crumble beef over
mixture and mix well.

On a piece of heavy-duty foil, pat beef
mixture into a 12-in. x 10-in. rectangle. Top
with broccoli to within 1/2 in. of edges.
Sprinkle with remaining salt. Top with ham.
Roll up jelly-roll style, starting with a short
side and peeling foil away while rolling. Seal
seam and ends. Place in a greased 13-in. x
9-in. x 2-in. baking dish.

Bake, uncovered, at 350° for 1-1/4 hours
or until meat is no longer pink and a meat
thermometer reads 160°; drain. Sprinkle
with cheese. Bake 1 minute longer or until
the cheese is melted. **yield:** 8 servings.

honey barbecue meat loaf

prep 10 minutes | **bake** 65 minutes + standing

1 teaspoon beef bouillon granules
1 tablespoon hot water
1 egg
1/2 cup quick-cooking oats
1/3 cup honey barbecue sauce
1/4 cup chopped onion
2 tablespoons brown sugar
1 tablespoon Worcestershire sauce
1 tablespoon prepared mustard
1/2 teaspoon garlic powder
1/4 teaspoon salt
1/4 teaspoon pepper
1/4 teaspoon chili powder
1 pound ground beef
Ketchup

In a large bowl, dissolve bouillon in water. Stir in the egg, oats, barbecue sauce, onion, brown sugar, Worcestershire sauce, mustard, garlic powder, salt, pepper and chili powder. Crumble beef over mixture and mix well.

Press beef mixture into an ungreased 8-in. x 4-in. x 2-in. loaf pan. Bake at 350° for 1 hour. Top with ketchup. Bake 5-10 minutes longer or until a meat thermometer reads 160°. Let stand 10 minutes before serving. **yield:** 4-6 servings.

nutrition facts: 1 slice equals 238 calories, 11 g fat (4 g saturated fat), 86 mg cholesterol, 495 mg sodium, 16 g carbohydrate, 1 g fiber, 17 g protein.

 This beef recipe is lighter in calories, fat and sodium.

jeff gill
valdosta, georgia

Mixing honey barbecue sauce with the ground beef gives this loaf a sweet, smoky flavor. It's a taste twist that never disappoints my guests.

mini meat loaves

prep 20 minutes | **bake** 40 minutes

janet hyson
pasadena, maryland

This main course can be made ahead of time and is one of my favorites for church suppers. The individual loaves get a boost from chili sauce, ketchup and horseradish.

2 eggs, lightly beaten
1/2 cup dry bread crumbs
1/4 cup chopped onion
1/4 cup prepared horseradish
2 tablespoons dried parsley flakes
2 teaspoons salt
1/4 teaspoon pepper
2 pounds lean ground beef

sauce

1 cup chili sauce
1/3 cup ketchup
2 teaspoons Worcestershire sauce
1 teaspoon ground mustard
Dash hot pepper sauce

In a large bowl, combine the first seven ingredients. Crumble beef over mixture and mix well. Shape into six loaves, about 5 in. x 2 in. x 1-1/2 in. Place in a greased 13-in. x 9-in. x 2-in. baking dish.

In a large bowl, combine the sauce ingredients. Spoon half over the top and sides of loaves. Bake, uncovered, at 350° for 20 minutes. Spread with remaining sauce.

Bake 20-30 minutes longer or until the meat is no longer pink and a meat thermometer reads 160°. Serve meat loaves immediately; or cool, wrap individually and freeze for up to 3 months. **yield:** 6 meat loaves (1-2 servings each).

TO USE FROZEN MEAT LOAVES: Thaw in the refrigerator. Unwrap loaves and place in a greased baking dish. Cover and bake at 350° for 30-35 minutes or until heated through.

no-fuss meat loaf

prep 15 minutes | **bake** 1 hour 35 minutes

betty braswell
elgin, pennsylvania

Instant stuffing mix makes this meat loaf simple enough for even novice cooks to fix. I often combine the mixture in a resealable plastic bag instead of a bowl, then just toss the bag for easy cleanup.

2 eggs
1/2 cup water
1 package (6 ounces) instant stuffing mix
2 pounds ground beef
Ketchup

In a large bowl, beat eggs and water. Stir in the stuffing mix and the contents of the seasoning packet. Crumble the beef over the mixture and mix well.

Press into an ungreased 9-in. x 5-in. x 3-in. loaf pan. Top with ketchup. Bake, uncovered, at 350° for 1-1/4 to 1-1/2 hours or until no pink remains and a meat thermometer reads 160°. **yield:** 6-8 servings.

meal on a stick

prep 25 minutes | **grill** 10 minutes

8 small red potatoes
2 eggs, lightly beaten
2 teaspoons Worcestershire sauce
1-1/4 cups seasoned bread crumbs
1 teaspoon curry powder
1-1/2 pounds ground beef
24 stuffed olives
8 plum tomatoes, halved
2 medium green peppers, cut into quarters
8 large fresh mushrooms
1/4 cup barbecue sauce

sundra hauck
bogalusa, louisiana

My husband and I were thrilled to receive a gas grill as a wedding gift. We love these meatball-and-veggie kabobs, which get sweetness from the barbecue sauce.

Scrub and pierce potatoes; place on a microwave-safe plate. Microwave, uncovered, on high for 3-5 minutes or until potatoes are slightly tender.

Meanwhile, in a large bowl, combine the eggs, Worcestershire sauce, bread crumbs and curry powder. Crumble beef over mixture and mix well. Divide into 24 portions; shape each portion around an olive. Alternately thread meatballs and vegetables onto metal or soaked wooden skewers.

Grill kabobs, covered, over medium-hot heat for 5 minutes. Turn; brush with barbecue sauce. Cook 5 minutes longer or until meatballs are no longer pink, basting once. **yield:** 6-8 servings.

editor's note: This recipe was tested in a 1,100-watt microwave.

sized **RIGHT**

To make 24 beef portions of equal size for the meatballs in Meal on a Stick, try this method. Lightly pat the meat mixture into a 1-inch-thick rectangle, then use a knife to cut it into 24 portions. This idea can come in handy almost any time you want meatballs of equal size.

cool-kitchen meat loaf

prep 10 minutes | **grill** 30 minutes

1 cup soft bread crumbs
1 medium onion, chopped
1/2 cup tomato sauce
1 egg
1-1/2 teaspoons salt
1/4 teaspoon pepper
1-1/2 pounds lean ground beef

sauce

1/2 cup ketchup
3 tablespoons brown sugar
3 tablespoons Worcestershire sauce
2 tablespoons white vinegar
2 tablespoons prepared mustard

In a large bowl, combine the first six ingredients. Crumble beef over mixture and mix well. Shape into two loaves; place each loaf in a disposable 8-in. x 4-in. x 2-in. loaf pan. Cover with foil.

Prepare grill for indirect heat. Grill, covered, over medium heat for 30 minutes or until the meat is no longer pink and a meat thermometer reads 160°.

Meanwhile, in a small saucepan, combine the sauce ingredients. Cook and stir over low heat until the sugar is dissolved. Spoon the sauce over meat loaves before serving. **yield:** 2 loaves (3 servings each).

susan taul
birmingham, alabama

Juicy slices of this tender meat loaf are great alone, but they're even better with the sweet-and-sour sauce. Using the grill lets me keep the oven off on hot days.

SLOW COOKER
specialties

hearty italian sandwiches

prep 20 minutes | **cook** 6 hours

elaine krupsky
las vegas, nevada

I've been making this sweet and spicy sandwich filling for many years. The Italian-flavored meat mixture smells just as good as it tastes!

1-1/2 pounds lean ground beef
1-1/2 pounds bulk Italian sausage
2 large onions, sliced
2 large green peppers, sliced
2 large sweet red peppers, sliced
1 teaspoon salt
1 teaspoon pepper
1/4 teaspoon crushed red pepper flakes
8 sandwich rolls, split
Shredded Monterey Jack cheese, optional

In a Dutch oven, cook beef and sausage over medium heat until no longer pink; drain. Place a third of the onions and peppers in a 5-qt. slow cooker; top with half of the meat mixture. Repeat layers; top with remaining vegetables. Sprinkle with salt, pepper and pepper flakes.

Cover and cook on low for 6 hours or until vegetables are tender. With a slotted spoon, serve about 1 cup of meat and vegetables on each roll. Top with cheese if desired. Use pan juices for dipping if desired. **yield:** 8 servings.

egg noodle lasagna

prep 15 minutes | **cook** 4 hours

6-1/2 cups uncooked wide egg noodles
   3 tablespoons butter
1-1/2 pounds ground beef
2-1/4 cups spaghetti sauce
   6 ounces process cheese (Velveeta), cubed
   3 cups (12 ounces) part-skim shredded mozzarella cheese

Cook noodles according to package directions; drain. Add butter; toss to coat.

In a large skillet, cook beef over medium heat until no longer pink; drain. Spread a fourth of the spaghetti sauce into an ungreased 5-qt. slow cooker. Layer with a third of the noodles, a third of the beef, a third of the remaining sauce and a third of the cheeses. Repeat layers twice.

Cover and cook on low for 4 hours or until cheese is melted and lasagna is heated through. **yield:** 12-16 servings.

mary oberlin
selinsgrove, pennsylvania

Here's a great take-along dish for church potlucks and other get-togethers. Plus, it requires just five ingredients in addition to the ground beef.

slow-cooked cabbage rolls

prep 20 minutes | **cook** 6 hours

rosemary jarvis
sparta, tennessee

This recipe takes a home-style supper and adds the convenience of slow cooking. The aroma when I walk in the door at dinnertime is heavenly!

   1 large head cabbage
   1 egg, beaten
   1 can (8 ounces) tomato sauce
3/4 cup quick-cooking rice
1/2 cup chopped green pepper
1/2 cup crushed saltines (about 15 crackers)
   1 ounce onion soup mix
1-1/2 pounds lean ground beef
   1 can (46 ounces) V8 juice
Salt to taste
Grated Parmesan cheese, optional

Cook cabbage in boiling water just until leaves fall off head. Set aside 12 large leaves for rolls; drain well. (Refrigerate remaining cabbage for another use.) Cut out the thick vein from the bottom of each reserved leaf, making a V-shaped cut; set aside.

In a large bowl, combine the egg, tomato sauce, rice, green pepper, cracker crumbs and soup mix. Crumble beef over mixture and mix well. Place about 1/3 cup meat mixture on each cabbage leaf; overlap cut ends of leaf. Fold in sides, beginning from the cut end. Roll up completely to enclose filling. Secure with toothpicks if desired.

Place cabbage rolls in a 3-qt. slow cooker. Pour V8 juice over rolls. Cover and cook on low for 6-7 hours or until filling reaches 160°. Just before serving, sprinkle with salt and Parmesan if desired. **yield:** 6 servings.

peppered meatballs

prep 35 minutes | **cook** 2 hours

darla schroeder

stanley, north dakota

Plenty of ground pepper gives these saucy appetizers their irresistible zest. They're so hearty, I sometimes serve them over hot noodles as a main course.

- 1/2 cup sour cream
- 2 teaspoons grated Parmesan *or* Romano cheese
- 2 to 3 teaspoons pepper
- 1 teaspoon salt
- 1 teaspoon dry bread crumbs
- 1/2 teaspoon garlic powder
- 1-1/2 pounds ground beef

sauce

- 1 cup (8 ounces) sour cream
- 1 can (10-3/4 ounces) condensed cream of mushroom soup, undiluted
- 2 teaspoons dill weed
- 1/2 teaspoon sugar
- 1/2 teaspoon pepper
- 1/4 teaspoon garlic powder

In a large bowl, combine the sour cream and Parmesan cheese. Add pepper, salt, bread crumbs and garlic powder. Crumble meat over mixture and mix well. Shape into 1-in. balls. Place on a greased rack in a shallow baking pan. Bake at 350° for 20-25 minutes or until no longer pink; drain.

Transfer meatballs to a 1-1/2-qt. slow cooker. Combine the sauce ingredients; pour over meatballs. Cover and cook on high for 2 hours or until heated through. **yield:** 1-1/2 dozen (2 cups sauce).

---

italian bow tie supper

prep 10 minutes | **cook** 7-1/4 hours

- 1-1/2 pounds ground beef
- 1 medium onion, chopped
- 1 garlic clove, minced
- 2 cans (8 ounces *each*) tomato sauce
- 1 can (14-1/2 ounces) stewed tomatoes, chopped
- 1 teaspoon dried oregano
- 1 teaspoon Italian seasoning
- Salt and pepper to taste
- 1 package (16 ounces) bow tie pasta, cooked and drained
- 1 package (10 ounces) frozen chopped spinach, thawed and squeezed dry
- 1-1/2 cups (6 ounces) part-skim shredded mozzarella cheese
- 1/2 cup grated Parmesan cheese

In a large skillet, cook beef, onion and garlic over medium heat until meat is no longer pink; drain. Transfer to a 3-qt. slow cooker. Stir in the tomato sauce, tomatoes and seasonings. Cover and cook on low for 7-8 hours or until bubbly.

Increase heat to high; stir in pasta, spinach and cheeses. Cover and cook 10 minutes longer or until heated through and cheese is melted. **yield:** 6 servings.

joy frey

kelso, missouri

For a family-pleasing Italian dinner, you can't go wrong with this all-in-one meal featuring bow tie pasta. Any leftovers taste just as good the next day.

under **COVER**

When using your slow cooker, do not lift the lid during cooking unless the recipe instructs you to stir in or add ingredients. The loss of steam can mean an additional 15 to 30 minutes of cooking each time you lift the lid. Also, be sure that the lid is sealed properly—not tilted or askew. The steam creates a seal.

slow cooker enchiladas

prep 30 minutes | **cook** 5 hours

- 1 pound ground beef
- 1 cup chopped onion
- 1/2 cup chopped green pepper
- 1 can (16 ounces) pinto *or* kidney beans, rinsed and drained
- 1 can (15 ounces) black beans, rinsed and drained
- 1 can (10 ounces) diced tomatoes and green chilies, undrained
- 1/3 cup water
- 1 teaspoon chili powder
- 1/2 teaspoon ground cumin
- 1/2 teaspoon salt
- 1/4 teaspoon pepper
- 1 cup (4 ounces) shredded sharp cheddar cheese
- 1 cup (4 ounces) shredded Monterey Jack cheese
- 6 flour tortillas (6 inches)

In a skillet, cook beef, onion and green pepper until beef is browned and vegetables are tender; drain. Add the next eight ingredients; bring to a boil. Reduce heat; cover and simmer for 10 minutes.

Combine cheeses. In a 5-qt. slow cooker, layer about 3/4 cup beef mixture, one tortilla and about 1/3 cup cheese. Repeat layers. Cover and cook on low for 5-7 hours or until heated through. **yield:** 4 servings.

mary luebbert
benton, kansas

When you're craving Southwestern food but won't have time to prepare it in the evening, rely on this recipe. I simply fill the slow cooker in the morning, then come home to a sensational supper.

slow-cooked spaghetti sauce

prep 15 minutes | **cook** 6 hours

This beef recipe is lighter in calories, fat and sodium.

david shields

barberton, ohio

When I wanted a versatile tomato sauce that could be used for different types of dishes, I tried making my own. The result was this thick sauce that's great not only with pasta, but also on pizza.

 1 pound ground beef
 4 cans (14-1/2 ounces *each*) diced tomatoes, undrained
 6 cans (6 ounces *each*) tomato paste
 1 cup beef broth
 1/4 cup packed brown sugar
 3 tablespoons minced fresh marjoram *or* 1 tablespoon dried marjoram
 2 tablespoons garlic powder
 2 tablespoons minced fresh basil *or* 2 teaspoons dried basil
 2 tablespoons minced fresh oregano *or* 2 teaspoons dried oregano
 2 tablespoons minced fresh parsley
 1 teaspoon salt
 1 bay leaf
Hot cooked spaghetti

In a large skillet, cook beef over medium heat until no longer pink; drain. Transfer to a 5-qt. slow cooker. Stir in the tomatoes, tomato paste, broth, brown sugar and seasonings. Cover and cook on low for 6-8 hours or until bubbly. Discard bay leaf. Serve with spaghetti. **yield:** 12-14 servings.

nutrition facts: 1 serving equals 89 calories, 3 g fat (1 g saturated fat), 16 mg cholesterol, 297 mg sodium, 9 g carbohydrate, 1 g fiber, 7 g protein.

hearty pork 'n' beans

prep 15 minutes | **cook** 4 hours

janice toms
saline, louisiana

Sweet and chunky, this mixture goes over big as a side dish at barbecues and potlucks. The meaty beans can also make a satisfying main course served with French bread or corn bread.

1 pound ground beef
1 medium green pepper, chopped
1 small onion, chopped
1 package (16 ounces) smoked sausage, halved lengthwise and thinly sliced
1 can (16 ounces) pork and beans, undrained
1 can (15-1/4 ounces) lima beans, rinsed and drained
1 can (15 ounces) pinto beans, rinsed and drained
1 cup ketchup
1/2 cup packed brown sugar
1 teaspoon salt
1/2 teaspoon garlic powder
1/4 teaspoon pepper

In a large skillet, cook beef, green pepper and onion over medium heat until meat is no longer pink; drain.

In a 5-qt. slow cooker, combine the remaining ingredients. Stir in beef mixture. Cover and cook on high for 4-5 hours or until heated through. **yield:** 8 main-dish servings or 12 side-dish servings.

potluck **PLEASER**

Consider dishes such as Hearty Pork 'n' Beans for your next barbecue, potluck or other get-together. The slow cooker is a great way to keep the beans hot while they're on the buffet table.

melt-in-your-mouth meat loaf

prep 15 minutes | **cook** 5-1/4 hours + standing

suzanne codner
starbuck, minnesota

When my husband and I were newlyweds, he said he never ate meat loaf because it was bland and dry. Then I tried this version, and he changed his mind. In fact, it became his favorite dinner!

2 eggs
3/4 cup milk
2/3 cup seasoned bread crumbs
2 teaspoons dried minced onion
1 teaspoon salt
1/2 teaspoon rubbed sage
1-1/2 pounds ground beef
1/4 cup ketchup
2 tablespoons brown sugar
1 teaspoon ground mustard
1/2 teaspoon Worcestershire sauce

In a large bowl, combine the first six ingredients. Crumble beef over mixture and mix well (mixture will be moist.) Shape into a round loaf; place in a 5-qt. slow cooker. Cover and cook on low for 5-6 hours or until a meat thermometer reads 160°.

In a small bowl, whisk the ketchup, brown sugar, mustard and Worcestershire sauce. Spoon over the meat loaf. Cook 15 minutes longer or until heated through. Let stand for 10-15 minutes before cutting. **yield:** 6 servings.

spicy beef vegetable stew

prep 10 minutes | **cook** 8 hours

lynnette davis
tullahoma, tennessee

This zesty beef stew is packed with flavor and goes together quickly. Try pairing it with warm corn bread, sourdough bread or French bread for a memorable meal.

1 pound ground beef
1 cup chopped onion
1 jar (30 ounces) meatless spaghetti sauce
3-1/2 cups water
1 package (16 ounces) frozen mixed vegetables
1 can (10 ounces) diced tomatoes and green chilies
1 cup sliced celery
1 teaspoon beef bouillon granules
1 teaspoon pepper

In a large skillet, cook beef and onion over medium heat until meat is no longer pink; drain. Transfer to a 5-qt. slow cooker. Stir in the remaining ingredients. Cover and cook on low for 8 hours or until the vegetables are tender. **yield:** 12 servings.

party-pleasing beef dish

prep 15 minutes | **cook** 4 hours 10 minutes

1 pound ground beef
1 medium onion, chopped
3/4 cup water
1 can (8 ounces) tomato sauce
1 can (6 ounces) tomato paste
2 teaspoons sugar
1 garlic clove, minced
1 teaspoon chili powder
1 teaspoon ground cumin
1 teaspoon dried oregano
1 cup cooked rice
Tortilla chips
Shredded cheddar cheese, chopped green onions, sliced ripe olives, sour cream, chopped tomatoes and taco sauce

 This beef recipe is lighter in calories, fat and sodium.

glee witzke
crete, nebraska

Mild and saucy, this mixture is served over tortilla chips and topped with popular taco ingredients. My guests can't get enough of it!

In a large skillet, cook beef and onion over medium heat until meat is no longer pink; drain. Transfer to a 3-qt. slow cooker. Add the next eight ingredients; mix well.

Cover and cook on low for 4 hours or until heated through. Add rice; cover and cook 10 minutes longer. Serve over tortilla chips with the toppings of your choice. **yield:** 6-8 servings.

nutrition facts: 1 serving equals 155 calories, 5 g fat (2 g saturated fat), 28 mg cholesterol, 188 mg sodium, 15 g carbohydrate, 2 g fiber, 12 g protein.

italian meatball subs

prep 25 minutes | **cook** 4 hours

2 eggs, beaten
1/4 cup milk
1/2 cup dry bread crumbs
2 tablespoons grated Parmesan cheese
1 teaspoon salt
1/4 teaspoon pepper
1/8 teaspoon garlic powder
1 pound ground beef
1/2 pound bulk Italian sausage

sauce

1 can (15 ounces) tomato sauce
1 can (6 ounces) tomato paste
1 small onion, chopped
1/2 cup chopped green pepper
1/2 cup dry red wine *or* beef broth
1/3 cup water
2 garlic cloves, minced
1 teaspoon dried oregano
1 teaspoon salt
1/2 teaspoon sugar
1/2 teaspoon pepper
6 to 7 Italian rolls, split
Shredded Parmesan cheese, optional

In a large bowl, combine eggs and milk; add the bread crumbs, Parmesan cheese, salt, pepper and garlic powder. Add beef and sausage; mix well. Shape into 1-in. balls. Broil 4 in. from the heat for 4 minutes; turn and broil 3 minutes longer.

Transfer to a 5-qt. slow cooker. Combine the tomato sauce and paste, onion, green pepper, wine or broth, water and seasonings; pour over meatballs. Cover and cook on low for 4-5 hours. Serve on rolls. Sprinkle with shredded Parmesan cheese if desired. **yield:** 6-7 servings.

jean glacken
elkton, maryland

This is one of those recipes you always come back to. The flavorful tomato sauce and nicely spiced meatballs make a hearty sandwich filling…and could even be served over pasta.

beef 'n' bean torta

prep 30 minutes | **cook** 4 hours

joan hallford

north richland hills, texas

This layered main dish is a top choice of mine because it not only has family-pleasing Southwestern taste, it's easy to prepare. I fix it on days when we have only a few minutes to eat before running off to meetings or sports events.

1 pound ground beef
1 small onion, chopped
1 can (15 ounces) pinto *or* black beans, rinsed and drained
1 can (10 ounces) diced tomatoes and green chilies, undrained
1 can (2-1/4 ounces) sliced ripe olives, drained
1-1/2 teaspoons chili powder
1/2 teaspoon salt
1/8 teaspoon pepper
3 drops hot pepper sauce
4 flour tortillas (8 inches)
1 cup (4 ounces) shredded cheddar cheese
Minced fresh cilantro, optional
Salsa, sour cream, shredded lettuce and chopped tomatoes, optional

Cut four 20-in. x 3-in. strips of heavy-duty foil; crisscross so they resemble spokes of a wheel. Place strips on the bottom and up the sides of a 5-qt. slow cooker. Coat strips with nonstick cooking spray.

In a large skillet, cook beef and onion over medium heat until meat is no longer pink; drain. Stir in the beans, tomatoes, olives, chili powder, salt, pepper and hot pepper sauce. Spoon about 1-2/3 cups into prepared slow cooker; top with one tortilla and 1/4 cup cheddar cheese. Repeat layers three times.

Cover and cook on low for 4-5 hours or until heated through. Using foil strips as handles, remove the tortilla stack to a platter. Sprinkle with cilantro. Serve with salsa, sour cream, lettuce and tomatoes if desired. **yield:** 4 servings.

lots-a-veggies stew

prep 10 minutes | **cook** 5 hours

- 1 pound ground beef
- 1 medium onion, diced
- 2 garlic cloves, minced
- 1 can (16 ounces) baked beans, undrained
- 1 can (16 ounces) kidney beans, rinsed and drained
- 1 can (15 ounces) butter beans, rinsed and drained
- 1 can (14-1/2 ounces) beef broth
- 1 can (11 ounces) whole kernel corn, undrained
- 1 can (10-1/2 ounces) condensed vegetable soup, undiluted
- 1 can (6 ounces) tomato paste
- 1 medium green pepper, diced
- 1 cup sliced carrots
- 1 cup sliced celery
- 2 tablespoons chili powder
- 1 teaspoon dried oregano
- 1 teaspoon dried thyme
- 1 teaspoon salt, optional
- 1/2 teaspoon dried marjoram
- 1/2 teaspoon pepper

In a large skillet, cook beef, onion and garlic over medium heat until meat is no longer pink; drain. Transfer to a 5-qt. slow cooker. Stir in the remaining ingredients. Cover and cook on low for 5 hours or until vegetables are tender. **yield:** 10 servings.

judy page
edenville, michigan

When I needed a no-fuss dinner, I went through my pantry and refrigerator to gather whatever ingredients I had on hand. This nicely seasoned stew packed with vegetables was the result.

zippy slow-cooked chili

prep 10 minutes | **cook** 6 hours

travis skrock
stratford, wisconsin

Serve up steaming bowls of this spiced-up chili to warm your family on a cold winter's day. You'll get plenty of compliments!

- 1 pound lean ground beef
- 1 can (28 ounces) diced tomatoes, undrained
- 1 medium onion, chopped
- 1 medium green pepper, chopped
- 1 can (15 ounces) fat-free vegetarian chili
- 1 can (8 ounces) tomato sauce
- 2 tablespoons chili powder
- 2 tablespoons minced fresh parsley
- 1 tablespoon dried basil
- 2 teaspoons ground cumin
- 4 garlic cloves, minced
- 1 teaspoon dried oregano
- 3/4 teaspoon pepper
- 1/8 teaspoon hot pepper sauce
- 6 tablespoons shredded reduced-fat cheddar cheese
- 1 tablespoon minced chives

In a nonstick skillet, cook beef over medium heat until no longer pink; drain. Transfer to a 3-qt. slow cooker. Add the tomatoes, onion, green pepper, chili, tomato sauce, chili powder, parsley, basil, cumin, garlic, oregano, pepper and hot pepper sauce. Cover and cook on low for 6-8 hours or until the vegetables are tender. Sprinkle with cheese and chives before serving. **yield:** 6 servings.

stuffed cabbage casserole

prep 20 minutes | **cook** 4 hours

joann alexander
center, texas

I love cabbage rolls but don't always have time to prepare them, so I created this easy recipe. It uses the traditional ingredients and delivers the same great taste.

1 pound ground beef
1/3 cup chopped onion
4 cups chopped cabbage
1 medium green pepper, chopped
1 cup uncooked instant rice
1 cup water
1 can (6 ounces) tomato paste
1 can (14-1/2 ounces) diced tomatoes, undrained
1/2 cup ketchup
2 tablespoons cider vinegar
1 to 2 tablespoons sugar, optional
1 tablespoon Worcestershire sauce
1 teaspoon salt
1/2 teaspoon pepper
1/4 teaspoon garlic powder

In a large skillet, cook beef and onion over medium heat until meat is no longer pink; drain. Transfer to a 5-qt. slow cooker; add cabbage, green pepper and rice.

In a large bowl, combine water and tomato paste. Stir in remaining ingredients. Pour over beef mixture; mix well. Cover; cook on low for 4-5 hours or until rice and vegetables are tender. **yield:** 6 servings.

picking **CABBAGE**

When purchasing cabbage, look for heads with crisp-looking leaves that are firmly packed. The head should feel heavy for its size.

To store cabbage, tightly wrap it and place it in a plastic bag in the refrigerator for up to 2 weeks. Remove the core, rinse the cabbage and blot it dry just before you are ready to use it.

slow cooker chili

prep 15 minutes | **cook** 6 hours

2 pounds ground beef
4 cans (16 ounces *each*) kidney beans, rinsed and drained
1 can (28 ounces) stewed tomatoes, undrained
1 can (15 ounces) pizza sauce
1 can (4 ounces) chopped green chilies
1/4 cup chopped onion
4 to 5 teaspoons chili powder
2 garlic cloves, minced
1 teaspoon dried basil
1/2 teaspoon salt
1/8 teaspoon pepper

 This beef recipe is lighter in calories, fat and sodium.

sandra mckenzie
braham, minnesota

For low-fuss chili with the classic flavor you crave, this slow cooker recipe is hard to beat. You'll want to make it regularly for your family.

In a large skillet, cook beef over medium heat until no longer pink; drain. Transfer to a 5-qt. slow cooker. Stir in the remaining ingredients. Cover and cook on low for 6 hours or until vegetables are tender. **yield:** 12 servings.

nutrition facts: 1 cup equals 188 calories, 7 g fat (3 g saturated fat), 37 mg cholesterol, 473 mg sodium, 15 g carbohydrate, 3 g fiber, 17 g protein.

beef barley lentil soup

prep 5 minutes | **cook** 8 hours

1 pound lean ground beef
1 medium onion, chopped
2 cups cubed red potatoes (1/4-inch pieces)
1 cup chopped celery
1 cup chopped carrot
1 cup dried lentils, rinsed
1/2 cup medium pearl barley
8 cups water
2 teaspoons beef bouillon granules
1 teaspoon salt
1/2 teaspoon lemon-pepper seasoning
2 cans (14-1/2 ounces *each*) stewed tomatoes

In a nonstick skillet, cook beef and onion over medium heat until meat is no longer pink; drain.

Transfer to a 5-qt. slow cooker. Layer with the potatoes, celery, carrots, lentils and barley. Combine the water, bouillon, salt and lemon-pepper; pour over vegetables. Cover and cook on low for 6 hours or until vegetables and barley are tender.

Add the tomatoes; cook 2 hours longer. **yield:** 10 servings.

judy metzentine
the dalles, oregon

You can fill your slow cooker with this soup and forget about supper…until the kitchen is filled with a wonderful aroma, that is! I like to serve each bowlful with a roll and salad.

mushroom salsa chili

prep 10 minutes | **cook** 8 hours

richard rundels
waverly, ohio

I often make this tasty, colorful chili for my grandsons. I use a mild variety of salsa, but feel free to use whatever kind suits your family best.

1 pound ground beef
1 pound bulk pork sausage
2 cans (16 ounces *each*) kidney beans, rinsed and drained
1 jar (24 ounces) chunky salsa
1 can (14-1/2 ounces) diced tomatoes, undrained
1 large onion, chopped
1 can (8 ounces) tomato sauce
1 can (4 ounces) mushroom stems and pieces, drained
1/2 cup *each* chopped green pepper, sweet red and yellow pepper
1/2 teaspoon dried oregano
1/4 teaspoon garlic powder
1/8 teaspoon dried thyme
1/8 teaspoon dried marjoram

In a large skillet, cook beef and sausage over medium heat until meat is no longer pink; drain. Transfer meat to a 5-qt. slow cooker. Stir in the remaining ingredients. Cover and cook on low for 8-9 hours or until vegetables are tender. **yield:** 8 servings.

meal-in-one casserole

prep 15 minutes | **cook** 4 hours

- 1 pound ground beef
- 1 medium onion, chopped
- 1 medium green pepper, chopped
- 1 can (15-1/4 ounces) whole kernel corn, drained
- 1 can (4 ounces) mushroom stems and pieces, drained
- 1 teaspoon salt
- 1/4 teaspoon pepper
- 1 jar (11 ounces) salsa
- 5 cups cooked medium egg noodles
- 1 can (28 ounces) diced tomatoes, undrained
- 1 cup water
- 1 cup (4 ounces) shredded cheddar cheese *or* blend of cheddar, Monterey Jack and American cheese

In a skillet, cook beef and onion over medium heat until meat is no longer pink; drain.

Transfer to a 5-qt. slow cooker. Top with the green pepper, corn and mushrooms. Sprinkle with salt and pepper. Pour salsa over mushrooms. Top with noodles. Pour tomatoes and water over all. Sprinkle with cheese. Cover and cook on low for 4 hours or until heated through. **yield:** 4-6 servings.

dorothy pritchett
wills point, texas

This pasta dish is truly a fix-and-forget-it meal. I simply cook the beef in a skillet, then toss everything into the slow cooker.

hearty broccoli dip

prep 10 minutes | **cook** 2 hours

sue call
beech grove, indiana

You'll need just five ingredients to stir up this no-fuss appetizer. People often ask me to bring this creamy dip to potlucks.

- 1 pound ground beef
- 1 pound process cheese (Velveeta), cubed
- 1 can (10-3/4 ounces) condensed cream of mushroom soup, undiluted
- 1 package (10 ounces) frozen chopped broccoli, thawed
- 2 tablespoons salsa

Tortilla chips

In a large skillet, cook beef over medium heat until no longer pink; drain. Transfer to a 3-qt. slow cooker. Add cheese, soup, broccoli and salsa; mix well. Cover and cook on low for 2-3 hours or until heated through, stirring after 1 hour. Serve with tortilla chips. **yield:** 5-1/2 cups.

hearty beans with beef

prep 5 minutes | **cook** 3 hours

- 1 pound ground beef
- 1 medium onion, chopped
- 1 can (16 ounces) baked beans, undrained
- 1 can (15-1/2 ounces) butter beans, rinsed and drained
- 1/2 cup ketchup
- 1/3 cup packed brown sugar
- 1 tablespoon barbecue sauce
- 1/4 teaspoon Worcestershire sauce

In a large skillet, cook beef and onion over medium heat until meat is no longer pink; drain. Transfer to a 5-qt. slow cooker. Stir in the remaining ingredients. Cover and cook on high for 3-4 hours or until heated through. **yield:** 8-10 servings.

nutrition facts: 1 cup equals 209 calories, 6 g fat (2 g saturated fat), 33 mg cholesterol, 525 mg sodium, 27 g carbohydrate, 5 g fiber, 14 g protein.

 This beef recipe is lighter in calories, fat and sodium.

jan biehl
leesburg, indiana

My husband raved about this sweet bean dish after tasting it at a party, so I knew I had to get the recipe. It's perfect for busy cooks because you can mix it up a day early and toss it in the slow cooker a few hours before guests arrive.

pizza casserole

prep 25 minutes | **cook** 1 hour

julie sterchi

harrisburg, illinois

A friend from church gave me the recipe for this crowd-pleasing casserole. The pizza-flavored dish is always one of the first to disappear at potlucks.

3 pounds ground beef
1/2 cup chopped onion
1 jar (28 ounces) spaghetti sauce
2 jars (4-1/2 ounces *each*) sliced mushrooms, drained
1 teaspoon salt
1/2 teaspoon garlic powder
1/2 teaspoon dried oregano
Dash pepper
1 package (16 ounces) wide egg noodles, cooked and drained
2 packages (3-1/2 ounces *each*) sliced pepperoni
2 cups (8 ounces) shredded cheddar cheese
2 cups (8 ounces) shredded part-skim mozzarella cheese

In a Dutch oven, cook beef and onion over medium heat until meat is no longer pink; drain. Add spaghetti sauce, mushrooms, salt, garlic powder, oregano and pepper; heat through.

Spoon 4 cups into a 6-qt. slow cooker. Top with half of the noodles, pepperoni and cheeses. Repeat layers. Cover and cook on high for 1 hour or until cheese is melted. **yield:** 12 servings.

editor's note: This recipe can be halved to use in a 3-qt. slow cooker.

corny chili

prep 20 minutes | **cook** 3 hours

1 pound ground beef
1 small onion, chopped
1 can (16 ounces) kidney beans, rinsed and drained
2 cans (14-1/2 ounces *each*) diced tomatoes, undrained
1 can (11 ounces) whole kernel corn, drained
3/4 cup picante sauce
1 tablespoon chili powder
1/4 to 1/2 teaspoon garlic powder
Corn chips, sour cream and shredded cheddar cheese, optional

marlene olson

hoople, north dakota

This Southwestern chili full of corn is so delicious and fuss-free, I love to share the recipe. Busy moms really appreciate its simplicity.

In a large skillet, cook beef and onion over medium heat until the meat is no longer pink; drain.

Transfer to a 3-qt. slow cooker. Stir in the beans, tomatoes, corn, picante sauce, chili powder and garlic powder. Cover and cook on low for 3-4 hours or until heated through. Serve with corn chips, sour cream and cheese if desired. **yield:** 4-6 servings.

beef vegetable soup

prep 15 minutes | **cook** 9 hours

 This beef recipe is lighter in calories, fat and sodium.

jean hutzell
dubuque, iowa

This nicely seasoned soup tastes so good, especially on a chilly day. I like the convenience of doing the prep work in the morning and then letting my slow cooker do the rest.

1 pound lean ground beef
1 medium onion, chopped
1/2 teaspoon salt
1/4 teaspoon pepper
3 cups water
3 medium potatoes, peeled and cut into 3/4-inch cubes
1 can (14-1/2 ounces) Italian diced tomatoes, undrained
1 can (11-1/2 ounces) V8 juice
1 cup chopped celery
1 cup sliced carrots
2 tablespoons sugar
1 tablespoon dried parsley flakes
2 teaspoons dried basil
1 bay leaf

In a nonstick skillet, cook beef and onion over medium heat until meat is no longer pink; drain. Stir in salt and pepper. Transfer to a 5-qt. slow cooker.

Add the remaining ingredients. Cover and cook on low for 9-11 hours or until vegetables are tender. Discard the bay leaf before serving. **yield:** 7 servings.

nutrition facts: 1-1/3 cups equals 210 calories, 5 g fat (2 g saturated fat), 32 mg cholesterol, 537 mg sodium, 26 g carbohydrate, 3 g fiber, 15 g protein.

hamburger vegetable soup

prep 15 minutes | **cook** 8 hours

1 pound lean ground beef
1 medium onion, chopped
2 garlic cloves, minced
4 cups V8 juice
1 can (14-1/2 ounces) stewed tomatoes
2 cups coleslaw mix
2 cups frozen green beans
2 cups frozen corn
2 tablespoons Worcestershire sauce
1 teaspoon dried basil
1/2 teaspoon salt
1/4 teaspoon pepper

In a large saucepan, cook beef, onion and garlic over medium heat until meat is no longer pink; drain. In a 5-qt. slow cooker, combine the remaining ingredients. Stir in beef mixture. Cover and cook on low for 8-9 hours or until the vegetables are tender. **yield:** 10 servings.

nutrition facts: 1 cup equals 159 calories, 4 g fat (2 g saturated fat), 17 mg cholesterol, 511 mg sodium, 19 g carbohydrate, 3 g fiber, 12 g protein.

 This beef recipe is lighter in calories, fat and sodium.

theresa jackson
cicero, new york

I work full-time, but my family sits down to a home-cooked meal just about every night—thanks in part to my slow cooker. This hearty soup is always a popular choice.

CASSEROLES &
oven entrees

beefy tomatoes

prep 20 minutes | bake 20 minutes

- 6 medium tomatoes
- 1 pound lean ground beef
- 1 medium onion, chopped
- 2 teaspoons dried basil
- 1 teaspoon salt
- 1/4 teaspoon pepper
- 1/2 cup cooked rice
- 1/2 cup shredded reduced-fat cheddar cheese
- 1 egg, lightly beaten

This beef recipe is lighter in calories, fat and sodium.

liz gallagher
gilbertsville, pennsylvania

My husband loves to garden, and I often fix this entree at the end of summer using the harvest from our backyard. The hollowed-out tomatoes are filled with a delicious beef-and-rice mixture.

Cut a thin slice off the top of each tomato and discard; remove core. Carefully scoop out pulp, leaving a 1/2-in. shell. Reserve 1 cup pulp (discard remaining pulp or save for another use). Invert tomatoes onto paper towels to drain.

In a nonstick skillet, cook beef and onion over medium heat until meat is no longer pink; drain. Stir in the basil, salt, pepper and reserved tomato pulp; bring to a boil. Reduce heat; simmer, uncovered, for 10-12 minutes or until the liquid has evaporated.

Stir in the rice, cheese and egg; heat through. Spoon into tomato shells. Place in a shallow 2-qt. baking dish coated with nonstick cooking spray. Bake, uncovered, at 350° for 20-25 minutes or until heated through. **yield:** 6 servings.

nutrition facts: 1 stuffed tomato equals 215 calories, 10 g fat (4 g saturated fat), 68 mg cholesterol, 525 mg sodium, 12 g carbohydrate, 2 g fiber, 21 g protein.

beef stuffing bake

prep 10 minutes | bake 30 minutes

denise goedeken
platte center, nebraska

I work full-time, so I'm always looking for quick and easy dishes that taste great. This one features ground beef, stuffing and veggies for a satisfying meal-in-one.

- 1 pound ground beef
- 1 small onion, chopped
- 1 package (10 ounces) beef- *or* pork-flavored stuffing mix
- 1 can (10-3/4 ounces) condensed cream of celery soup, undiluted
- 1 can (10-3/4 ounces) condensed cream of mushroom soup, undiluted
- 1 jar (4-1/2 ounces) sliced mushrooms, drained
- 1 cup water
- 1 cup frozen mixed vegetables

In a skillet, cook beef and onion over medium heat until meat is no longer pink; drain. Transfer to an ungreased 13-in. x 9-in. x 2-in. baking dish.

In a bowl, combine contents of stuffing seasoning packet, soups, mushrooms, water and vegetables. Sprinkle stuffing over beef mixture; top with soup mixture. Bake, uncovered, at 350° for 30 minutes or until heated through. **yield:** 6-8 servings.

pizza pasta casserole

prep 20 minutes + freezing | **bake** 25 minutes

nancy scarlett
graham, north carolina

Kids will line up for this zippy, pizza-flavored dish. The recipe makes two casseroles, so you can serve one to your family right away and keep one in the freezer for another night.

2 pounds ground beef
1 large onion, chopped
2 jars (28 ounces *each*) spaghetti sauce
1 package (16 ounces) spiral pasta, cooked and drained
4 cups (16 ounces) shredded part-skim mozzarella cheese
8 ounces sliced pepperoni

In a large skillet, cook beef and onion over medium heat until meat is no longer pink; drain. Stir in spaghetti sauce and pasta. Transfer to two greased 13-in. x 9-in. x 2-in. baking dishes. Sprinkle with cheese. Arrange pepperoni over the top.

Cover and freeze one casserole for up to 3 months. Bake the second casserole, uncovered, at 350° for 25-30 minutes or until heated through.

TO USE FROZEN CASSEROLE: Thaw in the refrigerator overnight. Bake at 350° for 35-40 minutes or until heated through. **yield:** 2 casseroles (8-10 servings each).

breakfast supreme

prep 20 minutes + chilling | **bake** 35 minutes + standing

1 pound bulk pork sausage
1 pound ground beef
1 small onion, chopped
3/4 cup sliced fresh mushrooms
1/2 cup chopped green pepper
1 to 1-1/2 teaspoons salt
1/4 to 1/2 teaspoon pepper
2 tablespoons butter, melted
2 cups (8 ounces) shredded cheddar cheese, *divided*
12 eggs
2/3 cup heavy whipping cream

In a large skillet, cook the sausage, beef, onion, mushrooms and green pepper over medium heat until meat is no longer pink; drain. Stir in salt and pepper; set aside.

Pour butter into an ungreased 13-in. x 9-in. x 2-in. baking dish. Sprinkle with 1 cup cheese. Beat eggs; pour over cheese. Top with sausage mixture.

Pour the cream over sausage mixture. Sprinkle with remaining cheese. Cover and refrigerate for 8 hours or overnight.

Remove from the refrigerator 30 minutes before baking. Bake, uncovered, at 325° for 35-40 minutes or until set. Let stand for 10 minutes before cutting. **yield:** 12 servings.

laurie harms
grinnell, iowa

Friends shared this recipe with me many years ago, when we spent the night at their home. After one taste, you'll understand why this breakfast is "supreme." It's really that good!

biscuit pizza bake

prep 15 minutes | **bake** 25 minutes

emma hageman
waucoma, iowa

You'll get all of the flavor of traditional pizza in this convenient casserole. It's chock-full of ground beef, pepperoni, veggies and two kinds of cheese.

1 pound ground beef
2 tubes (12 ounces *each*) refrigerated buttermilk biscuits
1 can (15 ounces) pizza sauce
1 cup chopped green pepper
1/2 cup chopped onion
1 can (4 ounces) mushroom stems and pieces, drained
1 package (3-1/2 ounces) sliced pepperoni
1 cup (4 ounces) shredded part-skim mozzarella cheese
1 cup (4 ounces) shredded cheddar cheese

In a large skillet, cook beef over medium heat until no longer pink. Meanwhile, quarter the biscuits; place in a greased shallow 3-qt. baking dish. Top with pizza sauce. Drain beef; sprinkle over biscuits and sauce.

Layer with green pepper, onion, mushrooms, pepperoni and cheeses. Bake, uncovered, at 350° for 25-30 minutes or until cheese is melted. Let stand for 5-10 minutes before serving. **yield:** 6-8 servings.

buying **BEEF**

When purchasing ground beef, look for meat that is bright red in color and is in a tightly sealed package. Buy ground beef before the "sell by" date that is listed on the package. Keep in mind that 1 pound of ground beef serves 3 to 4 people.

zesty stuffed peppers

prep 20 minutes | **bake** 30 minutes

6 medium green peppers, tops and seeds removed
1 pound ground beef
1/4 cup chopped onion
1 can (11 ounces) whole kernel corn, drained
1 can (8 ounces) tomato sauce
1 cup cooked rice
1/4 cup steak sauce
1/4 teaspoon *each* salt and pepper

This beef recipe is lighter in calories, fat and sodium.

margery bryan
royal city, washington

People are pleasantly surprised to find corn in the stuffing of these hearty peppers. They're colorful and always go over well.

In a large kettle over medium-high heat, cook peppers in boiling salted water for 3-5 minutes. Drain and rinse in cold water; set aside.

In a large skillet, cook beef and onion over medium heat until meat is no longer pink; drain. Add remaining ingredients and mix well. Loosely stuff into peppers. Place in a 9-in. square baking dish. Bake, uncovered, at 350° for 30-35 minutes or until peppers are done and filling is hot. **yield:** 6 servings.

nutrition facts: 1 serving equals 244 calories, 8 g fat (3 g saturated fat), 37 mg cholesterol, 653 mg sodium, 25 g carbohydrate, 4 g fiber, 17 g protein.

fake steak

prep 15 minutes + chilling | **bake** 35 minutes

fran wolfley
st. mary, jamaica

My husband and I are hosts at a mission house and cook for 30 to 60 people each week. This simple but tasty beef entree is one we can always rely on.

2 cups milk, *divided*
1-3/4 cups dry bread crumbs
2 medium onions, finely chopped
4 teaspoons salt
3/4 teaspoon pepper
5 pounds ground beef
2 cans (26 ounces *each*) condensed cream of mushroom soup, undiluted

In a large bowl, combine 1-3/4 cups milk, bread crumbs, onions, salt and pepper. Crumble beef over mixture and mix well. Shape into 24 oval patties, about 4 in. x 2-1/2 in. Place in two greased 15-in. x 10-in. x 1-in. baking pans. Cover and refrigerate for 8 hours or overnight.

Bake, uncovered, at 350° for 15 minutes; drain. Combine soup and remaining milk; pour over patties. Cover and bake 20-30 minutes longer or until a meat thermometer reads 160° (the patties will remain pink inside). **yield:** 24 servings.

beef spinach hot dish

prep 30 minutes | **bake** 20 minutes

1   pound ground beef
1   medium onion, chopped
2   garlic cloves, minced
1   can (4 ounces) mushroom stems and pieces, drained
1   teaspoon salt
1   teaspoon dried oregano
1/4 teaspoon pepper
2   packages (10 ounces *each*) frozen chopped spinach, thawed and squeezed dry
1   can (10-3/4 ounces) condensed cream of celery soup, undiluted
1   cup (8 ounces) sour cream
2   cups (8 ounces) shredded part-skim mozzarella cheese, *divided*

rachel jones
roland, arkansas

Everyone in my family loves this recipe. Even people who say they usually don't care for spinach enjoy the flavor of this home-style bake.

In a large skillet, cook beef, onion and garlic over medium heat until the meat is no longer pink; drain. Stir in the mushrooms, salt, oregano and pepper. Add the spinach, soup and sour cream. Stir in half of the mozzarella cheese.

Transfer to a greased 2-qt. baking dish. Bake, uncovered, at 350° for 15 minutes. Sprinkle with the remaining cheese; bake 5 minutes longer or until cheese is melted. **yield:** 6-8 servings.

deep-dish beef bake

prep 15 minutes | **bake** 35 minutes

karen owen
rising sun, indiana

You'll need just 15 minutes to assemble this before popping it in the oven. The golden crust is topped with beef, tomatoes and a creamy cheese layer.

1   pound ground beef
2   cups biscuit/baking mix
1/2 cup cold water
3   medium tomatoes, thinly sliced
1   medium green pepper, chopped
2   large onions, chopped
1   cup (4 ounces) shredded cheddar cheese, *divided*
1   cup (8 ounces) sour cream
2/3 cup mayonnaise

In a large skillet, cook beef over medium heat until no longer pink; drain.

Meanwhile, in a large bowl, combine the biscuit mix and water until a soft dough forms. Spread into a greased 13-in. x 9-in. x 2-in. baking dish. Layer with the beef, tomatoes and green pepper.

In a large bowl, combine the onions, 1/2 cup cheese, sour cream and mayonnaise; spread over top. Bake, uncovered, at 375° for 30-35 minutes or until edges are browned. Sprinkle with remaining cheese. Bake 5 minutes longer or until the cheese is melted. **yield:** 12 servings.

editor's note: Reduced-fat or fat-free mayonnaise is not recommended for this recipe.

unstuffed cabbage

prep 20 minutes | **bake** 45 minutes

6 cups chopped cabbage
1/2 pound lean ground beef
1 small onion, chopped
1 cup uncooked instant rice
1/2 teaspoon salt, optional
1/4 teaspoon pepper
2 cans (10-3/4 ounces *each*) condensed reduced-fat reduced-sodium tomato soup, undiluted
1 cup water
1/3 cup shredded reduced-fat cheddar cheese

Place the cabbage in a greased 2-1/2-qt. baking dish. In a skillet, cook beef and onion over medium heat until meat is no longer pink; drain. Stir in the rice, salt if desired and pepper; spoon over cabbage.

Combine soup and water; pour over beef mixture. Cover and bake at 350° for 40-50 minutes or until rice and cabbage are tender. Uncover; sprinkle with cheese. Bake 5-10 minutes longer or until the cheese is melted. **yield:** 4 servings.

nutrition facts: 1 serving (prepared without salt) equals 342 calories, 8 g fat (3 g saturated fat), 23 mg cholesterol, 690 mg sodium, 48 g carbohydrate, 5 g fiber, 19 g protein.

 This beef recipe is lighter in calories, fat and sodium.

judy thorn
mars, pennsylvania

A teacher at the preschool where I work shared the recipe for this delicious ground beef and cabbage casserole. It's a nutritious and economical meal for busy families.

chili-stuffed peppers

prep 40 minutes | **bake** 20 minutes

This beef recipe is lighter in calories, fat and sodium.

verna redman
dade city, florida

For a new take on chili, I decided to try stuffing green peppers with it. They taste terrific and require little more effort than ordinary chili.

6 medium green peppers
1 pound lean ground beef
1/2 cup chopped onion
1 can (15 ounces) chili beans, undrained
1 can (10 ounces) diced tomatoes and green chilies, undrained
1 teaspoon chili powder
1/2 teaspoon salt, optional
1/4 teaspoon pepper
1/4 teaspoon cayenne pepper
3/4 cup shredded reduced-fat cheddar cheese

Cut tops off peppers and remove seeds. Place peppers in a large kettle and cover with water. Bring to a boil; cook until crisp-tender, about 3 minutes. Drain and rinse in cold water; set aside.

In a large skillet, cook beef and onion over medium heat until meat is no longer pink; drain. Add the beans, tomatoes, chili powder, salt if desired, pepper and cayenne. Bring to a boil. Reduce heat; cover and simmer for 5 minutes.

Spoon meat mixture into peppers; place in an ungreased 3-qt. baking dish. Cover and bake at 350° for 20-25 minutes or until heated through. Sprinkle with cheese. **yield:** 6 servings.

nutrition facts: 1 serving (prepared without salt) equals 259 calories, 9 g fat (0 saturated fat), 31 mg cholesterol, 656 mg sodium, 24 g carbohydrate, 6 g fiber, 24 g protein.

italian noodle casserole

prep 15 minutes | **bake** 35 minutes

joann hosbach

las cruces, new mexico

Canned beans and other convenience products make it a snap to assemble this cheesy pasta dish. Everyone loves the Italian flavor.

1 pound ground beef

1 package (8 ounces) wide egg noodles

1 tablespoon olive oil

2 cups (8 ounces) shredded Colby cheese, *divided*

2 cans (15 ounces *each*) tomato sauce

1 can (15-1/2 ounces) great northern beans, rinsed and drained

1 can (14-1/2 ounces) Italian stewed tomatoes

1 can (10-3/4 ounces) condensed tomato soup, undiluted

2 teaspoons Italian seasoning

2 teaspoons dried parsley flakes

1/8 teaspoon *each* onion salt, garlic salt and pepper

2 tablespoons grated Parmesan cheese

In a large skillet, cook beef over medium heat until no longer pink; drain. Meanwhile, cook noodles according to package directions; drain. In a large bowl, combine the beef, noodles, oil, 1-1/2 cups Colby cheese, tomato sauce, beans, tomatoes, soup and seasonings.

Transfer to a greased 13-in. x 9-in. x 2-in. baking dish. Cover and bake at 350° for 30 minutes. Sprinkle with Parmesan cheese and remaining Colby cheese. Bake, uncovered, for 5-10 minutes longer or until cheese is melted. **yield:** 6-8 servings.

curried beef-stuffed squash

prep 35 minutes | **bake** 20 minutes

This beef recipe is lighter in calories, fat and sodium.

edna lee
greeley, colorado

My husband and I often make a meal of this deliciously different entree. Filled with savory beef, the acorn squash halves are especially nice during the fall season.

3 medium acorn squash (about 1 pound *each*), halved and seeded
1 pound ground beef
1/2 cup chopped onion
2 garlic cloves, minced
1 teaspoon beef bouillon granules
1/2 cup hot water
1/2 cup cooked rice
2 tablespoons chopped fresh parsley
1 tablespoon orange juice concentrate
1 teaspoon brown sugar
1 teaspoon curry powder
1/2 teaspoon ground ginger
1/4 teaspoon salt

Invert squash in a greased 15-in. x 10-in. x 1-in. baking pan. Bake, uncovered, at 350° for 35-45 minutes or until almost tender.

Meanwhile, in a skillet, cook beef, onion and garlic over medium heat until meat is no longer pink and onion is tender; drain.

Dissolve bouillon in water; add to skillet. Stir in remaining ingredients; mix well. Turn squash cut side up in pan and fill with meat mixture.

Fill pan with hot water to a depth of 1/4 in.; cover loosely with foil. Bake at 350° for 20-30 minutes or until heated through. **yield:** 6 servings.

nutrition facts: 1/2 stuffed squash equals 209 calories, 10 g fat (4 g saturated fat), 50 mg cholesterol, 270 mg sodium, 15 g carbohydrate, 2 g fiber, 16 g protein.

beans and biscuits

prep/total time 30 minutes

1 pound ground beef
2 green onions, chopped
1 garlic clove, minced
1 can (28 ounces) baked beans, drained
1/2 cup barbecue sauce
1/4 cup packed brown sugar
1/4 cup ketchup
1 tablespoon prepared mustard
1 tube (4-1/2 ounces) refrigerated buttermilk biscuits
1/2 cup shredded cheddar cheese

In a large skillet, cook the ground beef, onions and garlic over medium heat until meat is no longer pink; drain. Add the beans, barbecue sauce, brown sugar, ketchup and mustard. Simmer for 5 minutes or until heated through.

Transfer to a greased 11-in. x 7-in. x 2-in. baking dish. Separate biscuits and cut in half; arrange over beef mixture. Bake, uncovered, at 400° for 18 minutes or until biscuits are golden brown. Sprinkle with cheese; bake 2-3 minutes longer or until cheese is melted. **yield:** 4-6 servings.

sandra mckenzie
braham, minnesota

When there's a chill in the air, you can't beat a big helping of this stick-to-your-ribs casserole. It's also great for days when you don't have a lot of time to cook.

super supper

prep 20 minutes | **bake** 30 minutes

jane hartery

sarasota, florida

My children really like the combination of beef, pasta and cheesy sauce in this family-friendly dish. I can assemble it in no time.

1 pound ground beef
1 small onion, chopped
3/4 cup water
1 can (6 ounces) tomato paste
1 teaspoon salt
1/2 teaspoon garlic powder
1 package (8 ounces) cream cheese, cubed
3/4 cup milk
1/2 cup grated Parmesan cheese
7 cups cooked egg noodles

In a large skillet, cook beef and onion over medium heat until meat is no longer pink; drain. Add the water, tomato paste, salt and garlic powder. Bring to a boil. Reduce heat; cover and simmer for 5-7 minutes or until heated through.

In a small saucepan, melt cream cheese over low heat, stirring constantly. Gradually stir in milk and Parmesan cheese until blended.

Place noodles in a greased 13-in. x 9-in. x 2-in. baking dish. Spread meat sauce over noodles. Spoon cream cheese mixture evenly over top. Bake, uncovered, at 350° for 30-35 minutes or until heated through. **yield:** 6 servings.

italian beef roll-ups

prep 20 minutes | **bake** 50 minutes

2 pounds lean ground beef
2 eggs, lightly beaten
1 cup Italian-seasoned bread crumbs
1/2 cup milk
5 teaspoons dried minced onion
1-1/2 teaspoons salt
1/4 teaspoon pepper
3 to 3-1/2 pounds boneless beef top round steak
2 tablespoons vegetable oil
4 cups spaghetti sauce, *divided*
Hot cooked spaghetti, optional

joanne gruff

james creek, pennsylvania

Meat lovers will be thrilled with these saucy rolls of ground beef wrapped with pieces of round steak. For a complete meal, serve them over hot spaghetti.

In a large bowl, combine ground beef, eggs, crumbs, milk, onion, salt and pepper; mix thoroughly. Shape into twelve 3-in. rolls.

Cut steak into twelve 6-1/2-in. x 3-1/2-in. pieces. Wrap each roll in a piece of steak; secure with toothpicks. In a large skillet, brown roll-ups in oil over medium heat.

Spread 2 cups of spaghetti sauce into a 13-in. x 9-in. x 2-in. baking dish. Place roll-ups over sauce; cover with remaining sauce. Cover and bake at 350° for 50-55 minutes or until steak is tender. Remove toothpicks. Serve over pasta if desired. **yield:** 12 servings.

beefy eggplant parmigiana

prep 1 hour 10 minutes | **bake** 35 minutes + standing

1/3 cup chopped onion
1/4 cup finely chopped celery
1 teaspoon dried parsley flakes
1/8 teaspoon garlic powder
2 tablespoons vegetable oil
1 can (14-1/2 ounces) Italian stewed tomatoes
1/4 cup tomato paste
1/2 teaspoon dried oregano
1-1/4 teaspoons salt, *divided*
1/2 teaspoon pepper, *divided*
1 bay leaf
3/4 cup all-purpose flour
1 cup buttermilk
1 medium eggplant, peeled and cut into 3/8-inch slices
Additional vegetable oil
1/2 cup grated Parmesan cheese
1 pound ground beef, cooked and drained
2 cups (8 ounces) shredded part-skim mozzarella cheese, *divided*
1-1/2 teaspoons minced fresh parsley

In a large saucepan, saute onion, celery, parsley and garlic powder in oil until tender. Stir in the tomatoes, tomato paste, oregano, 1/2 teaspoon salt, 1/4 teaspoon pepper and bay leaf. Bring to a boil. Reduce heat; cover and simmer for 1 hour. Discard bay leaf.

In a shallow dish, combine flour and remaining salt and pepper. Place buttermilk in another shallow dish. Dip eggplant in buttermilk, then in flour mixture.

In a large skillet, cook eggplant in batches in 1 in. of hot oil until golden brown on each side; drain.

Place half of eggplant in a greased 13-in. x 9-in. x 2-in. baking dish. Top with half of Parmesan cheese, beef and tomato mixture. Sprinkle with 1 cup mozzarella cheese. Top with remaining eggplant, Parmesan cheese, beef and tomato mixture.

Bake, uncovered, at 350° for 30 minutes or until heated through. Sprinkle with the remaining mozzarella cheese. Bake 5-10 minutes longer or until cheese is melted. Let stand for 10 minutes before serving. Sprinkle with parsley. **yield:** 8 servings.

celeste copper
baton rouge, louisiana

I created this cheesy bake one summer when my husband planted eggplant and tomatoes. The recipe won high honors in a national beef contest.

beef cabbage roll-ups

prep 30 minutes | **bake** 30 minutes

This beef recipe is lighter in calories, fat and sodium.

irma finely
lockwood, missouri

Cooking up new recipes is a hobby of mine, and this is my version of classic cabbage rolls. I like them best served with rice or noodles.

1   head cabbage
1   large potato, peeled and shredded
1   large carrot, shredded
1/2 cup finely chopped celery
1/2 cup finely chopped green pepper
1/2 cup finely chopped onion
2   eggs, beaten
2   garlic cloves, minced
3/4 teaspoon salt
1/2 teaspoon pepper
1   pound lean ground beef
2   cans (8 ounces *each*) tomato sauce
1/2 teaspoon dried basil
1/2 teaspoon dried parsley flakes

Cook cabbage in boiling water just until the leaves fall off head. Cut out the thick vein from the bottom of 12 large leaves, making a V-shaped cut; set aside. (Refrigerate remaining cabbage for another use.)

In a large bowl, combine the potato, carrot, celery, green pepper, onion, eggs, garlic, salt and pepper. Crumble beef over mixture; mix well. Shape into 12 logs. Place one log on each cabbage leaf; overlap cut ends of leaf. Fold in sides, beginning from the cut end. Roll up completely to enclose filling. Secure with a toothpick.

Place in a greased 13-in. x 9-in. x 2-in. baking dish. Pour tomato sauce over roll-ups. Sprinkle with basil and parsley. Cover and bake at 350° for 30-35 minutes or until a meat thermometer reads 160° and cabbage is tender. **yield:** 6 servings.

nutrition facts: 2 roll-ups equals 251 calories, 8 g fat (3 g saturated fat), 108 mg cholesterol, 584 mg sodium, 25 g carbohydrate, 6 g fiber, 21 g protein.

zippy beef supper

prep 15 minutes | **bake** 35 minutes

2 pounds ground beef
1 medium onion, chopped
1 cup cubed cooked potatoes
1 can (11 ounces) condensed nacho cheese soup, undiluted
1 can (10-3/4 ounces) condensed cream of onion soup, undiluted
1 can (10 ounces) diced tomatoes and green chilies, undrained
2 to 3 teaspoons ground cumin
1/2 to 1 teaspoon garlic powder
3 cups crushed tortilla chips
1 cup (4 ounces) shredded cheddar cheese

In a large saucepan, cook beef and onion over medium heat until meat is no longer pink; drain. Add potatoes; cook and stir until heated through. Stir in the soups, tomatoes, cumin and garlic powder.

Transfer to a greased 13-in. x 9-in. x 2-in. baking dish. Cover and bake at 350° for 30 minutes. Uncover; sprinkle with the tortilla chips and cheddar cheese. Bake, uncovered, 5-10 minutes longer or until cheese is melted. **yield:** 6-8 servings.

ruth foster
crooksville, ohio

I rely on canned soup and canned tomatoes with chilies to make this spicy, satisfying casserole. Shredded cheddar cheese and crushed tortilla chips create the tasty topping.

spinach beef biscuit bake

prep 15 minutes | **bake** 25 minutes

bonnie bootz
scottsdale, arizona

My family is from Greece, and I grew up eating Greek food. I also love casseroles, so I combined the two and came up with this deliciously different main dish.

2 tubes (6 ounces *each*) refrigerated buttermilk biscuits
1-1/2 pounds ground beef
1/2 cup finely chopped onion
2 eggs
1 package (10 ounces) frozen chopped spinach, thawed and squeezed dry
1 can (4 ounces) mushroom stems and pieces, drained
4 ounces crumbled feta *or* shredded Monterey Jack cheese
1/4 cup grated Parmesan cheese
1-1/2 teaspoons garlic powder
Salt and pepper to taste
1 to 2 tablespoons butter, melted

Press and flatten biscuits onto the bottom and up the sides of a greased 11-in. x 7-in. x 2-in. baking dish; set aside.

In a skillet over medium heat, cook the ground beef and onion until the meat is no longer pink; drain.

In a bowl, beat eggs. Add spinach and mushrooms; mix well. Stir in the cheeses, garlic powder, salt, pepper and beef mixture; mix well. Spoon into prepared crust. Drizzle with butter.

Bake, uncovered, at 375° for 25-30 minutes or until crust is lightly browned. **yield:** 6 servings.

mushroom beef patties

prep 20 minutes | **bake** 30 minutes

janice miller
creston, iowa

*My husband and I work
full-time off of the farm, so
I'm always looking for quick,
fuss-free recipes. Our three
girls really like this beef
and mushroom sauce.*

1 egg
1-3/4 cups milk, *divided*
2 cups crushed cornflakes
1 medium onion, chopped
2 pounds ground beef
1 can (10-3/4 ounces) condensed
   cream of mushroom soup, undiluted

In a large bowl, combine egg, 1/2 cup milk,
cornflakes and onion. Crumble beef over
mixture and mix well. Shape beef mixture
into eight patties.

In a large skillet, cook patties over medium heat until meat is no longer pink; drain.
Transfer to a greased 13-in. x 9-in. x 2-in.
baking dish.

In a small bowl, combine soup and remaining milk until blended. Pour over patties. Bake, uncovered, at 350° for 30 minutes
or until hot and bubbly. **yield:** 8 servings.

beef noodle casserole

prep 20 minutes | **bake** 45 minutes

2 pounds ground beef
1 large onion, chopped
1 medium green pepper, chopped
1 can (14-3/4 ounces) cream-style corn
1 can (10-3/4 ounces) condensed
   tomato soup, undiluted
1 can (8 ounces) tomato sauce
1 jar (2 ounces) sliced pimientos,
   drained
2 tablespoons chopped jalapeno
   pepper
1-1/2 teaspoons salt
1/2 teaspoon chili powder
1/4 teaspoon ground mustard
1/4 teaspoon pepper
1 package (8 ounces) medium egg
   noodles, cooked and drained
1 jar (4-1/2 ounces) sliced mushrooms,
   drained
1-1/2 cups (6 ounces) shredded cheddar
   cheese

grace lema
winton, california

*This cheese-topped casserole
is ideal for a potluck, church
supper or family gathering.
The flavors blend to create
a delicious combination.*

In a large skillet, cook beef, onion and green
pepper over medium heat until the meat is
no longer pink and vegetables are tender;
drain. Add the next nine ingredients. Stir in
noodles and mushrooms.

Transfer to a greased 13-in. x 9-in. x 2-in.
baking dish. Sprinkle with cheese. Bake, uncovered, at 350° for 45 minutes or until
heated through. **yield:** 8-10 servings.

editor's note: When cutting or seeding hot peppers,
use rubber or plastic gloves to protect your hands.
Avoid touching your face.

greek pasta bake

prep 40 minutes | **bake** 60 minutes

1/2 pound ground beef
1/2 pound ground lamb
1 large onion, chopped
4 garlic cloves, minced
3 teaspoons dried oregano
1 teaspoon dried basil
1/2 teaspoon salt
1/4 teaspoon pepper
1/4 teaspoon dried thyme
1 can (15 ounces) tomato sauce
1 can (14-1/2 ounces) diced tomatoes, undrained
1 tablespoon lemon juice
1 teaspoon sugar
1/4 teaspoon ground cinnamon
2 cups uncooked rigatoni *or* large tube pasta
4 ounces feta cheese, crumbled

In a large skillet, cook beef and lamb over medium heat until no longer pink; drain. Stir in onion, garlic, oregano, basil, salt, pepper and thyme; mix well. Add the tomato sauce, tomatoes and lemon juice. Bring to a boil. Reduce heat; simmer, uncovered, for 20 minutes, stirring occasionally. Stir in the sugar and cinnamon. Simmer, uncovered, 15 minutes longer.

Meanwhile, cook the pasta according to the package directions; drain. Stir into the meat mixture.

Transfer to a greased 2-qt. baking dish. Sprinkle with feta cheese. Cover and bake at 325° for 45 minutes. Uncover; bake 15 minutes longer or until heated through. **yield:** 6 servings.

carol stevens
basye, virginia

My mom taught me to coo' and I love creating new recipes. I came up with th beef-and-lamb cassero   a wintry afternoon mar   ars ago. The tangy lemo'   d herbs are complem   d by the subtle cinnam

baked mostaccioli

prep 10 minutes | **bake** 50 minutes

andrea warneke
st. paul, minnesota

I created this simple recipe when I had a group to feed and only a few ingredients on hand. With cheddar, salsa, pasta and spaghetti sauce, it's a sure-to-please dinner.

1 package (16 ounces) mostaccioli
1-1/2 pounds ground beef
1 jar (28 ounces) spaghetti sauce
1 jar (24 ounces) salsa
1-1/2 cups (6 ounces) shredded cheddar cheese

Cook pasta according to package directions. Meanwhile, in a Dutch oven, cook beef over medium heat until no longer pink; drain. Stir in spaghetti sauce and salsa. Drain pasta; stir into meat mixture.

Transfer to a greased 13-in. x 9-in. x 2-in. baking dish (dish will be full). Cover and bake at 350° for 40 minutes. Uncover; sprinkle with cheese. Bake 8-12 minutes longer or until heated through and cheese is melted. **yield:** 6-8 servings.

potluck **PLAN**

Are you going to a potluck? Casseroles and meat dishes can be wrapped in an insulated carrying case that keeps food warm for short periods of time. To keep your food safe, make sure to follow the directions for recommended maximum holding times for these carriers.

If there will be a stove available at your destination, cook, chill and transport your food in a cooler for safe traveling, then reheat the food upon arrival.

inside-out stuffed peppers

prep 15 minutes | **bake** 65 minutes

1 pound ground beef
1/2 cup chopped onion
1 can (14-1/2 ounces) stewed tomatoes, cut up
1 large green pepper, chopped
1/2 cup uncooked long grain rice
1/2 cup water
2 teaspoons Worcestershire sauce
1/2 teaspoon salt
1/4 teaspoon pepper
1 cup (4 ounces) shredded cheddar cheese

In a large skillet, cook beef over medium heat until no longer pink; drain. Transfer to a greased 2-qt. casserole. Add the next eight ingredients.

Cover and bake at 350° for 1 hour or until the rice is tender. Uncover and sprinkle with cheese; cook 5 minutes longer or until cheese is melted. **yield:** 4-6 servings.

darlene brenden
salem, oregon

My daughters don't care for the usual hollowed-out green peppers stuffed with a meat-and-rice mixture, so one of the girls dreamed up this alternative. The peppers are simply chopped and combined with the other ingredients in a casserole.

zesty beef corn bread dinner

prep 25 minutes | **bake** 30 minutes

edith lawler
clinton, missouri

These Southwest-inspired squares are delicious all by themselves, but the accompanying sauce gives them an extra "zing" of zesty flavor. I never make the beefy bread without it!

1 pound ground beef
1/3 cup chopped onion
1 garlic clove, minced
1/4 cup ketchup
1 teaspoon salt
1 package (8-1/2 ounces) corn bread/muffin mix
1 cup (4 ounces) shredded cheddar cheese

tangy tomato sauce
2 tablespoons cold water
2 teaspoons cornstarch
1 can (8 ounces) diced tomatoes, undrained
1/4 teaspoon chili powder
1/4 teaspoon ground cumin
1/4 teaspoon garlic powder
1 teaspoon sugar
2 tablespoons chopped chili peppers
2 tablespoons chopped green pepper
1 teaspoon Worcestershire sauce

In a large skillet, cook beef, onion and garlic over medium heat until meat is no longer pink; drain. Stir in ketchup and salt.

Prepare muffin mix according to package directions. Spread half of batter into a greased 8-in. square baking dish. Spoon beef mixture over batter; sprinkle with cheese. Spread remaining batter over cheese.

Bake at 350° for 30 to 35 minutes or until golden brown. Meanwhile, in a small saucepan, combine sauce ingredients. Cook and stir over medium heat until thickened. Let bread stand for 5 minutes after removing from oven; cut into squares and spoon sauce over. **yield:** 6-8 servings.

baked salisbury steak

prep 20 minutes | **bake** 30 minutes

elsie epp

newton, kansas

I bake ground beef patties in a mushroom-soup gravy to make this mild, moist entree. The recipe is easy to prepare and always brings compliments.

2 eggs, lightly beaten
1 cup quick-cooking oats
1/2 cup *each* chopped green pepper, celery and onion
1/2 teaspoon salt
2 pounds ground beef
1 can (10-3/4 ounces) condensed golden mushroom *or* cream of mushroom soup, undiluted
3/4 cup water
1/4 teaspoon pepper

In a large bowl, combine the eggs, oats, green pepper, celery, onion and salt. Crumble beef over mixture and mix well. Shape into eight oval patties. In a large skillet, brown patties on both sides; drain.

Place patties in an ungreased 13-in. x 9-in. x 2-in. baking dish. Combine the soup, water and pepper; pour over beef. Cover and bake at 350° for 30-35 minutes or until the meat is no longer pink. **yield:** 8 servings.

crowned beef bake

prep 20 minutes | **bake** 25 minutes

1 pound ground beef
1 can (4 ounces) mushroom stems and pieces, drained
1 can (2.8 ounces) french-fried onions, crumbled, *divided*
2 cups frozen mixed vegetables
1 can (10-3/4 ounces) condensed cream of celery soup, undiluted
1 cup (8 ounces) sour cream, *divided*
1 tube (7-1/2 ounces) refrigerated buttermilk biscuits
1 egg, lightly beaten
1 teaspoon celery seed
1/2 teaspoon salt

linda parker

covington, georgia

Because this comforting casserole looks so special, it's often my first choice when I'm having dinner guests or attending a church supper. Using refrigerated biscuits is a real time-saver.

In a large skillet, cook beef over medium heat until no longer pink; drain. Place half of beef in a greased 2-qt. baking dish. Layer with the mushrooms, two-thirds of the onions and all of the vegetables. Top with the remaining beef.

In a large saucepan, combine soup and 1/2 cup sour cream; cook over low heat until heated through. Pour over beef. Cut each biscuit in half; arrange cut side down around edge of dish. Sprinkle remaining onions in center of casserole.

In a small bowl, combine the egg, celery seed, salt and remaining sour cream; drizzle over biscuits. Bake, uncovered, at 375° for 25-30 minutes or until golden brown. **yield:** 4-6 servings.

mashed potato hot dish

prep 15 minutes | **bake** 20 minutes

- 1 pound ground beef
- 1 can (10-3/4 ounces) condensed cream of chicken soup, undiluted
- 2 cups frozen French-style green beans
- 2 cups hot mashed potatoes (prepared with milk and butter)
- 1/2 cup shredded cheddar cheese

In a large skillet, cook beef over medium heat until no longer pink; drain. Stir in soup and beans.

Transfer to a greased 2-qt. baking dish. Top with mashed potatoes; sprinkle with cheese. Bake, uncovered, at 350° for 20-25 minutes or until bubbly and cheese is melted. **yield:** 4 servings.

tanya abernathy
yacolt, washington

My cousin gave me this simple but delicious recipe. Whenever I'm making homemade mashed potatoes, I throw in a few extra spuds so I can fix this dish for supper the next night.

potato **POINTERS**

When purchasing potatoes, select firm, well-shaped ones that are free from decay, cuts, blemishes or green discoloration under the skin. Avoid sprouted or shriveled potatoes.

Store potatoes in a dry, cool, dark and well-ventilated area for up to 2 months. Do not store them with onions or in the refrigerator.

To prepare potatoes, scrub them with a vegetable brush under cold water and remove any sprouts or eyes.

crescent-topped casserole

zucchini beef bake

crescent-topped casserole

prep 15 minutes | **bake** 25 minutes

- 2 pounds ground beef
- 1/4 cup chopped onion
- 2 cans (8 ounces *each*) tomato sauce
- 1 envelope spaghetti sauce mix
- 3/4 cup sour cream
- 2 cups (8 ounces) shredded part-skim mozzarella cheese
- 1 tube (8 ounces) refrigerated crescent rolls
- 2 tablespoons butter, melted
- 1/3 cup grated Parmesan cheese

In a large skillet, cook beef and onion over medium heat until meat is no longer pink; drain. Stir in tomato sauce and spaghetti sauce mix. Reduce heat; simmer, uncovered, for 5 minutes. Remove from the heat; stir in sour cream. Spoon into a greased 13-in. x 9-in. x 2-in. baking dish. Sprinkle with mozzarella cheese.

Unroll crescent dough into one rectangle; seal seams and perforations. Place over cheese. Brush with butter and sprinkle with Parmesan cheese. Bake, uncovered, at 375° for 25-30 minutes or until golden brown. **yield:** 6-8 servings.

trann foley
columbia, missouri

My husband is a fairly picky eater, but he requests this rich and creamy dish for dinner at least once a month. I like to keep the ingredients on hand for last-minute preparation.

zucchini beef bake

prep 20 minutes | **bake** 25 minutes

christy saniga
tacoma, washington

I think zucchini is a great vegetable for cooks because it's so versatile. I combined it with beef, rice and cheddar for this meal-in-one casserole.

- 6 cups water
- 4 cups sliced zucchini
- 1 pound ground beef
- 1 large onion, chopped
- 1 garlic clove, minced
- 2 cups cooked rice
- 1 can (8 ounces) tomato sauce
- 1 cup small-curd cottage cheese
- 1 egg, lightly beaten
- 1-1/2 teaspoons minced fresh oregano *or* 1/2 teaspoon dried oregano
- 1 teaspoon minced fresh basil *or* 1/4 teaspoon dried basil
- 1/2 teaspoon salt
- 1 cup (4 ounces) shredded cheddar cheese

In a large saucepan, bring water to a boil. Add the zucchini. Return to a boil. Reduce heat; cover and simmer for 3 minutes or just until tender. Drain and immediately place zucchini in ice water. Drain; pat dry.

In a skillet, cook the beef, onion and garlic over medium heat until meat is no longer pink; drain. Stir in the rice, tomato sauce, cottage cheese, egg, oregano, basil and salt.

Arrange half of the zucchini in a greased 13-in. x 9-in. x 2-in. baking dish. Top with meat mixture. Arrange remaining zucchini over top; sprinkle with cheddar cheese. Bake, uncovered, at 350° for 25-30 minutes or until bubbly and cheese is melted. **yield:** 6-8 servings.

barbecue beef patties

prep 10 minutes | **bake** 25 minutes

- 1 egg
- 1/2 cup barbecue sauce, *divided*
- 3/4 cup crushed cornflakes
- 1/2 to 1 teaspoon salt
- 1 pound ground beef

In a bowl, combine egg, 1/4 cup barbecue sauce, cornflake crumbs and salt. Add beef and mix well. Shape into four oval patties, about 3/4 in. thick.

Place in a greased 11-in. x 7-in. x 2-in. baking pan. Spread with remaining barbecue sauce. Bake, uncovered, at 375° for 25-30 minutes or until meat is no longer pink and meat thermometer reads 160°; drain. **yield:** 4 servings.

marlene harguth
maynard, minnesota

These easy, family-pleasing patties taste like individual meat loaves. Purchased barbecue sauce brushed on top gives them fast flavor.

onion-topped hot dish

prep 10 minutes | **bake** 50 minutes

1-1/2 pounds ground beef
1 package (16 ounces) frozen California-blend vegetables, thawed
1 can (10-3/4 ounces) condensed cheddar cheese soup, undiluted
1 cup (4 ounces) shredded part-skim mozzarella cheese
1/2 cup milk
1/2 teaspoon salt
1/4 teaspoon pepper
1 package (32 ounces) frozen shredded hash brown potatoes, thawed
1/4 cup butter, melted
1/2 teaspoon seasoned salt
20 frozen large onion rings
1 cup (4 ounces) shredded cheddar cheese

In a large skillet, cook beef over medium heat until no longer pink; drain. Stir in the vegetables, soup, mozzarella cheese, milk, salt and pepper. Transfer to a greased 13-in. x 9-in. x 2-in. baking dish. Sprinkle with potatoes; drizzle with butter. Top with seasoned salt and onion rings.

Cover and bake at 350° for 45-50 minutes or until heated through. Uncover; sprinkle with cheddar cheese. Bake 3-5 minutes longer or until cheese is melted. **yield:** 6-8 servings.

marilisa fagerlind
glidden, iowa

With ground beef, hash browns, veggies and onion rings, one hearty serving of this dish satisfies hunger in a hurry. Be prepared to get many requests for it!

potato sloppy joe bake

prep 15 minutes | **bake** 30 minutes

This beef recipe is lighter in calories, fat and sodium.

ruth chiarenza
la vale, maryland

I created this family-friendly casserole one night when I was racing against the clock. The quick recipe requires just five ingredients.

1 pound ground beef
1 can (15-1/2 ounces) sloppy joe sauce
1 can (10-3/4 ounces) condensed cream of potato soup, undiluted
1 package (32 ounces) frozen cubed hash brown potatoes, thawed
1 cup (4 ounces) shredded cheddar cheese

In a large skillet, cook beef over medium heat until no longer pink; drain. Add sloppy joe sauce and soup. Place hash browns in a greased 13-in. x 9-in. x 2-in. baking dish. Top with beef mixture.

Cover and bake at 450° for 20 minutes. Uncover; bake 10 minutes longer or until heated through. Sprinkle with cheese. **yield:** 6-8 servings.

nutrition facts: 1 cup equals 290 calories, 11 g fat (6 g saturated fat), 47 mg cholesterol, 763 mg sodium, 30 g carbohydrate, 3 g fiber, 18 g protein.

baked spaghetti

prep 20 minutes | **bake** 30 minutes + standing

8 ounces uncooked spaghetti, broken into thirds
1 egg
1/2 cup milk
1/2 teaspoon salt
1/2 pound ground beef
1/2 pound bulk Italian sausage
1 small onion, chopped
1/4 cup chopped green pepper
1 jar (14 ounces) meatless spaghetti sauce
1 can (8 ounces) tomato sauce
1 to 2 cups (4 to 8 ounces) shredded part-skim mozzarella cheese

Cook spaghetti according to package directions; drain. In a large bowl, beat the egg, milk and salt. Add spaghetti; toss to coat. Transfer to a greased 13-in. x 9-in. x 2-in. baking dish.

In a large skillet, cook the beef, sausage, onion and green pepper over medium heat until meat is no longer pink; drain. Stir in spaghetti sauce and tomato sauce. Spoon over the spaghetti mixture.

Bake, uncovered, at 350° for 20 minutes. Sprinkle with the mozzarella cheese. Bake 10 minutes longer or until cheese is melted. Let stand for 10 minutes before cutting.
yield: 6-8 servings.

nutrition facts: 1 serving equals 286 calories, 11 g fat (5 g saturated fat), 65 mg cholesterol, 718 mg sodium, 29 g carbohydrate, 2 g fiber, 17 g protein.

 This beef recipe is lighter in calories, fat and sodium.

betty rabe
mahtomedi, minnesota

This satisfying pasta bake pleases young and old, family and friends...everyone! Add a tossed green salad and breadsticks to round out a memorable menu.

cheeseburger pepper cups

prep 15 minutes | **bake** 35 minutes

betty winscher

royalton, minnesota

I always like to serve my grandchildren something special, and this supper is one of their favorites. The kids prefer red and yellow peppers because they're sweeter.

4 medium sweet red, yellow *or* green peppers
1/2 pound ground beef
1/4 cup finely chopped onion
2 cups cooked brown rice
1 can (6 ounces) tomato paste
2 tablespoons ketchup
1 tablespoon Worcestershire sauce
1 tablespoon spicy brown mustard
1/2 teaspoon garlic salt
1/4 teaspoon pepper
1 cup vegetable broth
1 cup (4 ounces) shredded cheddar cheese

Cut the peppers in half lengthwise and remove the seeds; set aside. In a skillet, cook the beef and onion over medium heat until meat is no longer pink; drain. Stir in the rice, tomato paste, ketchup, Worcestershire sauce, mustard, garlic salt and pepper. Spoon into the peppers.

Place in a greased 13-in. x 9-in. x 2-in. baking dish; pour broth around the peppers. Cover and bake at 350° for 30 minutes. Sprinkle with cheese. Bake, uncovered, 5 minutes longer or until heated through. **yield:** 4 servings.

sauerkraut beef supper

prep 10 minutes | **bake** 65 minutes

2/3 cup finely chopped fully cooked ham
2 cups cooked long grain rice
1-1/4 cups finely chopped onions, *divided*
1-1/4 teaspoons salt, *divided*
1/4 teaspoon pepper, *divided*
1 pound lean ground beef
1 can (14 ounces) sauerkraut, rinsed and drained
1/2 teaspoon sugar
1 bacon strip, diced

In a large bowl, combine the ham, rice, 3/4 cup onions, 1 teaspoon salt and 1/8 teaspoon pepper; crumble beef over mixture and mix gently.

In a greased 2-1/2-qt. baking dish, place half of sauerkraut; sprinkle with half of the remaining onions. Top with meat mixture, remaining sauerkraut and onions. Sprinkle with sugar and remaining salt and pepper. Top with bacon.

Cover and bake at 375° for 65-70 minutes or until hot and bubbly. **yield:** 6 servings.

carol ann cassaday
st. louis, missouri

When I was growing up, my mother prepared this old-fashioned dish in fall. Made-from-scratch rolls and custard raisin pie were wonderful accompaniments.

four-pasta beef bake

prep 15 minutes | **bake** 25 minutes

This beef recipe is lighter in calories, fat and sodium.

harriet stichter
milford, indiana

This crowd-pleasing bake tastes a lot like lasagna but is quicker to assemble because you don't layer the ingredients. Pair it with bread or a salad, and you'll have a complete supper.

8 cups uncooked pasta (four assorted pasta shapes of your choice)
2 pounds ground beef
2 medium green peppers, chopped
2 medium onions, chopped
2 cups sliced fresh mushrooms
4 jars (26 ounces *each*) meatless spaghetti sauce
2 eggs, lightly beaten
4 cups (16 ounces) shredded part-skim mozzarella cheese

Cook pasta according to package directions. Meanwhile, in a large skillet, cook the beef, green peppers, onions and mushrooms over medium heat until meat is no longer pink; drain.

Drain pasta and place in a large bowl; stir in the beef mixture, two jars of spaghetti sauce and eggs.

Transfer to two greased 13-in. x 9-in. x 2-in. baking dishes. Top with remaining sauce; sprinkle with cheese. Bake, uncovered, at 350° for 25-30 minutes or until heated through. **yield:** 2 casseroles (8-10 servings each).

nutrition facts: 1 serving equals 265 calories, 9 g fat (4 g saturated fat), 57 mg cholesterol, 306 mg sodium, 27 g carbohydrate, 2 g fiber, 19 g protein.

beef 'n' rice bake

prep 15 minutes | **bake** 30 minutes

- 1 pound ground beef
- 3 celery ribs, thinly sliced
- 1 medium onion, chopped
- 2 cups cooked rice
- 1/2 cup chopped green pepper
- 1/2 cup chopped sweet red pepper
- 1 jar (4-1/2 ounces) sliced mushrooms, drained
- 1/2 cup soy sauce
- 2 tablespoons butter
- 1 tablespoon brown sugar
- 1 can (3 ounces) chow mein noodles

In a large skillet, cook the beef, celery and onion over medium heat until meat is no longer pink; drain. Stir in the rice, peppers, mushrooms, soy sauce, butter and brown sugar; heat through.

Transfer to a greased 2-qt. baking dish. Cover and bake at 350° for 25-30 minutes. Sprinkle with chow mein noodles. Bake, uncovered, 5-10 minutes longer or until the noodles are crisp. **yield:** 4-6 servings.

deborah schermerhorn
colorado springs, colorado

A friend of mine who's a missionary in the Phillipines shared this Oriental casserole recipe with me. Chow mein noodles add a nice crunch.

---

peppy potato casserole

prep 10 minutes | **bake** 35 minutes

joanna goodman
conway, arkansas

Packaged potatoes give me a head start on this pizza-like main dish. It truly is "peppy" because it gets great flavor from pepperoni, Italian seasoning and cheese.

- 2 cans (8 ounces *each*) tomato sauce
- 1-1/2 cups water
- 1-1/2 teaspoons Italian seasoning
- 1 package (5 ounces) scalloped potato mix
- 1/2 pound ground beef
- 24 pepperoni slices
- 4 ounces sliced provolone cheese
- 1/2 cup shredded part-skim mozzarella cheese
- 1 tablespoon grated Parmesan cheese

In a large saucepan, combine the tomato sauce, water and Italian seasoning; bring to a boil. Add potatoes with contents of sauce mix. Transfer to an ungreased 2-qt. baking dish.

In a large skillet, cook beef over medium heat until no longer pink; drain. Spoon over potatoes; top with pepperoni. Bake, uncovered, at 400° for 20 minutes. Top with cheeses. Bake 15-20 minutes longer or until potatoes are tender. **yield:** 4 servings.

---

hobo dinner

prep 5 minutes | **bake** 45 minutes

- 1/4 pound ground beef
- 1 potato, sliced
- 1 carrot, sliced
- 2 tablespoons chopped onion
- 1 sheet heavy-duty aluminum foil (18 inches x 13 inches)

Salt and pepper to taste, optional

Shape beef into a patty; place in the center of foil with potato, carrot and onion. Sprinkle with salt and pepper if desired. Fold foil over and seal well; place on a baking sheet. Bake at 350° for 45 minutes. Open foil carefully. **yield:** 1 serving.

pat walter
pine island, minnesota

The meat and vegetables in this effortless dinner are all wrapped in a piece of foil and cooked together. The recipe yields a single serving, but you could make as many of the meal-in-one packets as you need.

pizza rice casserole

prep 25 minutes | **bake** 30 minutes

christine reimer
niverville, manitoba

Anyone who likes pizza and lasagna is sure to like this Italian-style bake. I usually prepare two or three of the casseroles at one time and freeze some for quick dinners on busy nights.

3/4 pound ground beef
1 medium onion, chopped
2 cans (8 ounces *each*) tomato sauce
1 teaspoon sugar
1 teaspoon salt
1 teaspoon dried parsley flakes
1/4 teaspoon garlic powder
1/4 teaspoon oregano
Dash pepper
2 cups cooked rice
1/2 cup small-curd cottage cheese
1/2 cup shredded part-skim mozzarella cheese

In a large skillet, cook beef and onion over medium heat until meat is no longer pink; drain. Add the tomato sauce, sugar, salt, parsley, garlic powder, oregano and pepper. Bring to a boil. Reduce heat; cover and simmer for 15 minutes.

Combine the rice and cottage cheese; spoon half into a greased 11-in. x 7-in. x 2-in. baking dish. Top with half of the meat mixture. Repeat layers. Sprinkle with mozzarella cheese.

Bake, uncovered, at 325° for 30-35 minutes or until heated through and bubbly. **yield:** 4 servings.

rapid **RICE**

Cooking 2 cups of rice to use for Pizza Rice Casserole is easy and takes just a few minutes.

Bring 1 cup of water and, if desired, 1/4 teaspoon of salt to a boil in a saucepan. Stir in 1 cup of instant white rice and return the water to a boil. Cover and reduce the heat to a simmer. Cook the rice for 5 minutes or until tender.

mom's ground beef casserole

prep 15 minutes | **bake** 45 minutes

julie gillespie
kirklin, indiana

This family-favorite recipe was passed down from my mom. It makes two casseroles, so it's perfect for a crowd. Just add a green vegetable for a complete meal.

2 pounds ground beef
1 medium green pepper, chopped
1 medium onion, chopped
9 cups cooked wide egg noodles
1 pound process cheese (Velveeta)
1 can (15-1/4 ounces) whole kernel corn, drained
1 can (11-1/2 ounces) condensed chicken with rice soup, undiluted
1 can (10-3/4 ounces) condensed cream of mushroom soup, undiluted
1/2 cup milk
1 teaspoon salt
1/4 teaspoon pepper

In a Dutch oven, cook beef, green pepper and onion over medium heat until meat is no longer pink; drain. Remove from heat; stir in remaining ingredients.

Transfer to two greased 2-1/2-qt. baking dishes. Cover; bake at 350° for 45-50 minutes or until bubbly. **yield:** 16-18 servings.

meat bun bake

prep 20 minutes | **bake** 20 minutes

taste of home test kitchen

greendale, wisconsin

Biscuit mix really speeds up the preparation of this can't-miss casserole. You just pour the batter over the beef mixture and pop the dish into the oven.

1-1/2 pounds ground beef
2 cups chopped cabbage
1/4 cup chopped onion
1/2 teaspoon salt
1/4 teaspoon pepper
1/2 to 1 cup shredded cheddar cheese
1-1/2 cups biscuit/baking mix
1 cup milk
2 eggs

In a large skillet, cook beef over medium heat until no longer pink; drain. Add the cabbage, onion, salt and pepper; cook over medium heat for 15 minutes or until the cabbage and onion are tender. Stir in the cheddar cheese.

Spoon into a greased 13-in. x 9-in. x 2-in. baking dish. In a large bowl, blend biscuit mix, milk and eggs. Pour over beef mixture. Bake, uncovered, at 400° for 20-25 minutes or until golden brown. **yield:** 6 servings.

veggie beef bundles

prep 20 minutes | **bake** 25 minutes

2 cups julienned uncooked potatoes
1 pound lean ground beef
1 envelope onion soup mix
1/4 cup water
1 cup sliced fresh mushrooms
1 package (9 ounces) frozen cut green beans, thawed

Coat four pieces of heavy-duty foil (about 12 in. square) with nonstick cooking spray. Place 1/2 cup potatoes on each square. Shape the beef into four patties; place over potatoes. Combine the onion soup mix and water; spoon half over patties. Top with the mushrooms, green beans and remaining soup mixture.

Fold foil around meat and vegetables and seal tightly. Place on a baking sheet. Bake at 375° for 25-30 minutes or until meat is no longer pink and potatoes are tender. **yield:** 4 servings.

carolyn dixon
wilmar, arkansas

These individual foil packets of meat and veggies were a mainstay for my husband and me when we were building a log home. The meal-in-one bundles make cleanup a snap.

lasagna casserole

prep 15 minutes | **bake** 1 hour

deb morrison
skiatook, oklahoma

When I was growing up, this lasagna-like dish was my favorite dinner. We had it every year for my birthday, and I enjoy the casserole just as much today.

1 pound ground beef
1/4 cup chopped onion
1/2 teaspoon salt
1/2 teaspoon pepper, *divided*
1 pound medium pasta shells, cooked and drained
4 cups (24 ounces) shredded part-skim mozzarella cheese
3 cups (24 ounces) 4% cottage cheese
2 eggs, lightly beaten
1/3 cup grated Parmesan cheese
2 tablespoons dried parsley flakes
1 jar (26 ounces) meatless spaghetti sauce

In a large skillet, cook beef and onion over medium heat until meat is no longer pink; drain. Sprinkle with salt and 1/4 teaspoon pepper; set aside. In a large bowl, combine pasta, 3 cups of mozzarella cheese, cottage cheese, eggs, Parmesan cheese, parsley and remaining pepper; stir gently.

Pour into a greased 13-in. x 9-in. x 2-in. or shallow 3-qt. baking dish. Top with beef mixture and spaghetti sauce (dish will be full).

Cover and bake at 350° for 45 minutes. Sprinkle with remaining mozzarella. Bake, uncovered, 15 minutes longer or until the cheese is melted and bubbly. Let stand 10 minutes before serving. **yield:** 6-8 servings.

more **MOZZARELLA**

Will you be shredding the mozzarella for Lasagna Casserole? An opened block of cheese should be wrapped with waxed paper, then wrapped again with a tight seal of plastic wrap or foil. Mozzarella cheese stored this way in the refrigerator at a temperature of 34° to 38° will keep for several weeks.

If mold appears, trim off the mold plus 1/2 inch of extra cheese and discard it. The rest of the cheese may be eaten.

SKILLET &
stovetop dishes

pepper patties

prep/total time 25 minutes

 This beef recipe is lighter in calories, fat and sodium.

taste of home test kitchen

greendale, wisconsin

Red and green peppers dress up these beef burgers. Try serving the patties on hot cooked noodles for a hearty dinner…alone for a lighter meal…or on bread as an open-faced sandwich.

2 tablespoons soy sauce
1/4 teaspoon garlic powder
1/4 teaspoon pepper
1 pound ground beef
1 small onion, sliced
1 small green pepper, julienned
1 small sweet red pepper, julienned
1 teaspoon vegetable oil
Hot cooked noodles, optional

In a large bowl, combine the soy sauce, garlic powder and pepper; reserve 1 tablespoon and set aside. Crumble beef over the remaining soy sauce mixture; mix well. Shape into four 1/2-in.-thick patties.

In a large skillet, saute onion and peppers in oil and reserved soy sauce mixture for 3-4 minutes or until crisp-tender. Remove and set aside.

Add patties to skillet; cook, uncovered, for 4-5 minutes on each side or until a meat thermometer reaches 160°; drain. Top patties with peppers and onion; cook until heated through. Serve over noodles if desired. **yield:** 4 servings.

nutrition facts: 1 serving equals 209 calories, 11 g fat (5 g saturated fat), 56 mg cholesterol, 536 mg sodium, 4 g carbohydrate, 1 g fiber, 22 g protein.

creamy bean goulash

prep/total time 25 minutes

- 1 pound ground beef
- 1 medium onion, chopped
- 1 garlic clove, minced
- 2 cans (15 ounces *each*) butter beans, rinsed and drained
- 1 can (10-3/4 ounces) condensed tomato soup, undiluted
- 1 teaspoon salt
- 1 teaspoon Worcestershire sauce
- 1/4 teaspoon pepper
- 1/2 cup sour cream
- Shredded cheddar cheese and minced fresh parsley, optional

In a large skillet, cook the beef, onion and garlic over medium heat until meat is no longer pink; drain. Stir in the beans, soup, salt, Worcestershire sauce, pepper and sour cream. Cover and simmer for 10 minutes or until heated through. Garnish with cheese and parsley if desired. **yield:** 4 servings.

lois joy ardery
murrieta, california

This stovetop supper gets you in and out of the kitchen in a jiffy. A friend served the tasty goulash to me many years ago, and I've been making it monthly for my family ever since.

beef skillet supper

This beef recipe is lighter in calories, fat and sodium.

tabitha allen
cypress, texas

Canned corn and tomato sauce put this cheesy pasta dinner on the fast track. Sometimes I make extra to ensure we have leftovers— they're great for lunch at work or school the next day.

prep/total time 30 minutes

- 1 package (8 ounces) medium egg noodles
- 1-1/2 pounds ground beef
- 1 medium onion, chopped
- 1 can (8 ounces) tomato sauce
- 1/2 cup water
- 1 can (11 ounces) Mexicorn, drained
- 1/2 teaspoon salt
- 1/4 teaspoon pepper
- 1 cup (4 ounces) shredded cheddar cheese

Cook noodles according to package directions. Meanwhile, in a skillet, cook beef and onion over medium heat until meat is no longer pink; drain. Add the tomato sauce and water. Cover and cook for 8 minutes.

Drain the noodles; add to beef mixture. Add the corn, salt and pepper. Sprinkle with the cheese; cover and cook until heated through and the cheese is melted. **yield:** 8-10 servings.

nutrition facts: 1 cup equals 268 calories, 10 g fat (5 g saturated fat), 67 mg cholesterol, 512 mg sodium, 25 g carbohydrate, 2 g fiber, 19 g protein.

country beef patties

prep 15 minutes | **cook** 1 hour

bernice morris
marshfield, missouri

For a home-style supper, try these flavor-packed patties. Bacon gives them a subtle smoky taste, and the well-seasoned tomato gravy adds a little zip.

1 pound ground beef
2 uncooked bacon strips, diced
1 teaspoon minced onion
1/2 teaspoon salt
1/8 teaspoon pepper

tomato gravy

2 tablespoons chopped green pepper
1 tablespoon chopped onion
1 can (14-1/2 ounces) diced tomatoes, undrained
1 to 2 bay leaves
1 teaspoon sugar
1/2 teaspoon celery salt
1/8 teaspoon salt
1/8 teaspoon pepper
1/2 cup water
2 tablespoons all-purpose flour

In a large bowl, combine the beef, bacon, onion, salt and pepper. Shape into four oval patties; brown in a skillet over medium heat. Remove patties and keep warm.

Drain all but 1 tablespoon drippings. In the same skillet, saute green pepper and onion in drippings until tender. Add the tomatoes, bay leaves, sugar, celery salt, salt and pepper.

Combine water and flour until smooth; add to tomato mixture, stirring constantly. Bring to a boil; cook and stir for 2 minutes or until thickened.

Return patties to gravy. Reduce heat; cover and simmer for 30 minutes. Uncover and simmer 10 minutes longer. Remove the bay leaves. **yield:** 4 servings.

bean and beef skillet

prep/total time 20 minutes

1 pound ground beef
1 medium onion, chopped
1 can (28 ounces) baked beans
1/4 cup barbecue sauce
1 cup (4 ounces) shredded cheddar cheese

rose purrington
windom, minnesota

In our house, this simple but delicious dish is a mainstay. I prefer to scoop it up with tortilla chips, but you could also crumble corn chips on top. Or, use taco sauce instead of barbecue sauce and roll up the mixture in your favorite tortillas.

In a large skillet, cook beef and onion over medium heat until meat is no longer pink; drain. Stir in beans and barbecue sauce; heat through. Sprinkle with cheese; cover and cook on low until cheese is melted. **yield:** 4 servings.

skillet bow tie lasagna

prep 5 minutes | **cook** 35 minutes

  1 pound ground beef
  1 small onion, chopped
  1 garlic clove, minced
  1 can (14-1/2 ounces) diced tomatoes, undrained
1-1/2 cups water
  1 can (6 ounces) tomato paste
  1 tablespoon dried parsley flakes
  2 teaspoons dried oregano
  1 teaspoon salt
2-1/2 cups uncooked bow tie pasta
  3/4 cup small-curd cottage cheese
  1/4 cup grated Parmesan cheese

In a large skillet, cook beef, onion and garlic until meat is no longer pink; drain. Add the tomatoes, water, tomato paste, parsley, oregano and salt; mix well. Stir in pasta; bring to a boil. Reduce heat; cover and simmer for 20-25 minutes or until pasta is tender, stirring once.

Combine cheeses; drop by rounded tablespoonfuls onto pasta mixture. Cover and cook for 5 minutes. **yield:** 4 servings.

arleta schurle

clay center, kansas

This Italian-style meal tastes just like lasagna but gives you the convenience of quick stovetop preparation. My family is always glad to hear this dish is on the menu.

skillet enchiladas

prep 10 minutes | **cook** 35 minutes

cathie beard
philomath, oregon

When our two grown children and grandchildren visit, I like to serve this Mexican-style dinner. Saucy and cheesy, it always disappears fast.

1 pound ground beef
1 medium onion, chopped
1 can (10-3/4 ounces) condensed cream of mushroom soup, undiluted
1 can (10 ounces) enchilada sauce
1/3 cup milk
1 to 2 tablespoons canned chopped green chilies
Vegetable oil
8 corn tortillas
2-1/2 cups (10 ounces) finely shredded cheddar cheese, *divided*
1/2 cup chopped ripe olives

In a large skillet, cook beef and onion over medium heat until meat is no longer pink; drain. Stir in the soup, enchilada sauce, milk and chilies. Bring to a boil. Reduce heat; cover and simmer for 20 minutes, stirring occasionally.

Meanwhile, in another skillet, heat 1/4 in. of oil. Dip each tortilla in hot oil for 3 seconds on each side or just until limp; drain on paper towels. Top each tortilla with 1/4 cup cheese and 1 tablespoon olives. Roll up and place over beef mixture, spooning some of mixture over the enchiladas.

Cover and cook until heated through, about 5 minutes. Sprinkle with remaining cheese; cover and cook until cheese is melted. **yield:** 8 enchiladas.

beef chow mein skillet

prep/total time 30 minutes

1 pound lean ground beef
1 large onion, chopped
3 cups chopped celery
1 package (8 ounces) fresh mushrooms, quartered
1-1/2 cups water
1 can (8 ounces) sliced water chestnuts, drained
3 tablespoons reduced-sodium soy sauce
1 tablespoon brown sugar
2 teaspoons reduced-sodium beef bouillon granules
1/4 teaspoon garlic powder
1/8 teaspoon pepper
2 tablespoons cornstarch
3 tablespoons cold water
Hot cooked rice
1 cup chow mein noodles

In a large nonstick skillet, cook beef and onion over medium heat until meat is no longer pink; drain. Stir in the celery, mushrooms, water, water chestnuts, soy sauce, brown sugar, bouillon granules, garlic powder and pepper. Bring to a boil. Reduce heat; cover and simmer for 15-20 minutes or until vegetables are tender.

Combine cornstarch and cold water until smooth; stir into beef mixture. Bring to a boil. Reduce heat; cook and stir for 2 minutes or until thickened. Serve over rice if desired. Top with chow mein noodles. **yield:** 4 servings.

lavonne hegland
st. michael, minnesota

Any time my family craves Chinese food, I pull out this easy, one-dish recipe. I use reduced-sodium ingredients to make it healthier.

oriental beef noodle toss

prep/total time 30 minutes

sue livangood
waukesha, wisconsin

If you're in the mood for "Far East" fare, try this recipe. It's a cinch to prepare and gives you a satisfying blend of Oriental flavors.

1 pound ground beef
2 packages (3 ounces *each*) Oriental-flavored ramen noodles
1 package (16 ounces) frozen Oriental vegetable blend
2 cups water
4 to 5 tablespoons soy sauce
1/4 teaspoon ground ginger
3 tablespoons thinly sliced green onions

In a large skillet, cook beef over medium heat until no longer pink; drain. Stir in contents of one noodle seasoning packet; set aside and keep warm.

Break the noodles; place in a large saucepan. Add the contents of second seasoning packet, vegetables, water, soy sauce and ginger. Bring to a boil. Reduce heat; cover and simmer for 6-10 minutes or until vegetables and noodles are tender. Stir in beef and onions. **yield:** 4-6 servings.

chili beef noodle skillet

prep/total time 30 minutes

deborah elliott
ridge spring, south carolina

My husband loves this hearty mix of beef, egg noodles, tomatoes and onion, all spiced up with chili powder. Add cheddar cheese for the perfect finishing touch.

1 package (8 ounces) egg noodles
2 pounds ground beef
1 medium onion, chopped
1/4 cup chopped celery
2 garlic cloves, minced
1 can (28 ounces) diced tomatoes, undrained
1 tablespoon chili powder
1/4 to 1/2 teaspoon salt
1/8 teaspoon pepper
1/2 to 1 cup shredded cheddar cheese

Cook noodles according to package directions. Meanwhile, in a large skillet, cook the beef, onion, celery and garlic over medium heat until meat is no longer pink and vegetables are tender; drain. Add the tomatoes, chili powder, salt and pepper. Cook and stir for 2 minutes or until heated through.

Drain noodles; stir into beef mixture and heat through. Remove from the heat. Sprinkle with cheese; cover and let stand for 5 minutes or until cheese is melted. **yield:** 8 servings.

chili mac skillet

prep/total time 15 minutes

This beef recipe is lighter in calories, fat and sodium.

tracy golder
bloomsburg, pennsylvania

Speedy stovetop preparation and zippy flavor make this dish a dinnertime winner. Both children and adults give it a thumbs-up.

1-1/4 cups uncooked elbow macaroni
    1 pound ground beef
    1 medium onion, chopped
    1 medium green pepper, chopped
    2 garlic cloves, minced
    2 cans (14-1/2 ounces *each*) diced tomatoes, undrained
    1 can (16 ounces) kidney beans, rinsed and drained
    1 package (10 ounces) frozen corn, thawed
    2 tablespoons chili powder
  1/2 to 1 teaspoon salt
  1/2 teaspoon ground cumin
  1/2 cup shredded pepper Jack cheese

Cook the macaroni according to package directions. Meanwhile, in a large skillet, cook the beef, onion, green pepper and garlic over medium heat or until meat is no longer pink and vegetables are tender; drain. Stir in the tomatoes, beans, corn, chili powder, salt and cumin. Bring to a boil. Reduce heat; cover and simmer for 15 minutes or until heated through.

Drain the macaroni and add to skillet; stir to coat. Sprinkle with cheese. **yield:** 8 servings.

nutrition facts: 1 cup equals 266 calories, 8 g fat (4 g saturated fat), 34 mg cholesterol, 402 mg sodium, 31 g carbohydrate, 6 g fiber, 19 g protein.

chili powder **CHOICE**

Along with ordinary table salt and cinnamon, chili powder is probably one of the most common seasonings found in American kitchens. It's used to spice up everything from chili, stews, soups and eggs to beefy dishes such as Chili Mac Skillet. In fact, you'll find chili powder used in many recipes in this book.

Chili powder isn't a single spice but a mixture of chili peppers, oregano, salt, cumin and sometimes cloves, coriander, pepper, garlic and/or allspice. Choose whatever blend appeals to you most.

Like other spices, chili powder is best purchased in small quantities because the flavor will diminish after opening. Store chili powder and other ground spices in tightly closed glass or heavy-duty plastic containers.

beefy beans 'n' rice

prep/total time 25 minutes

    1 pound ground beef
    1 medium onion, chopped
    2 cups cooked rice
    1 can (15 ounces) ranch-style *or* chili beans
    6 ounces process cheese (Velveeta), cubed
    3 tablespoons water

In a large skillet, cook beef and onion over medium heat until meat is no longer pink; drain. Stir in the rice, beans, cheese and water. Cook and stir over medium-low heat until cheese is melted. **yield:** 4 servings.

rebecca roberts
odessa, texas

This cheesy main course is satisfying all by itself and is so simple to prepare. After cooking the rice and beef, I just combine all of the ingredients in the skillet.

creamy beef and mushroom skillet

prep/total time 25 minutes

**taste of home
test kitchen**

greendale, wisconsin

*Enjoy the classic flavor of
Stroganoff with this recipe.
The saucy supper combines
lean ground beef, sliced fresh
mushrooms and onions in a
delicious brown gravy.*

- 1 pound lean ground beef
- 2 cups sliced fresh mushrooms
- 2 medium onions, sliced
- 1 jar (12 ounces) beef gravy
- 1/3 cup sour cream
- 1/3 cup plain yogurt
- 1 tablespoon Worcestershire sauce
- 1/4 teaspoon dried thyme
- 1/4 teaspoon pepper
- 1/4 teaspoon browning sauce
- Hot cooked noodles *or* rice
- 1/4 cup minced fresh parsley

In a large nonstick skillet, cook the beef,
mushrooms and onions over medium heat
until meat is no longer pink; drain. In a large
bowl, combine gravy, sour cream, yogurt,
Worcestershire sauce, thyme, pepper and
browning sauce. Stir into meat mixture;
heat through. Serve with noodles or rice.
Sprinkle with parsley. **yield:** 5 servings.

spicy rice skillet

prep/total time 30 minutes

- 2 pounds ground beef
- 1 large onion, chopped
- 1 large green pepper, chopped
- 1 can (10 ounces) diced tomatoes and green chilies, undrained
- 1 can (4 ounces) chopped green chilies
- 1 cup beef broth
- 2 tablespoons Worcestershire sauce
- 1 to 2 tablespoons chili powder
- 2 teaspoons salt
- 1 teaspoon pepper
- 1/4 teaspoon hot pepper sauce
- 4 cups cooked long grain rice
- 2 cups (16 ounces) sour cream
- 2 cups (8 ounces) shredded cheddar cheese
- Corn chips

katherine cruthis

roe, arkansas

*I've served this main dish to
countless guests. It has plenty
of zippy taste and is a snap to
prepare, even when I'm
getting ready for company.*

In a large skillet, cook the beef, onion and
green pepper over medium heat until the
meat is no longer pink; drain. Add the next
eight ingredients. Simmer, uncovered, for
10 minutes. Add rice, sour cream and
cheese; cook over low heat until cheese is
melted, about 6-8 minutes, stirring occasionally (do not boil). Serve over corn chips.
yield: 8-10 servings.

cleaning **CLUE**

To clean fresh mushrooms, gently remove dirt by rubbing with a mushroom brush or by wiping with a damp paper towel. Or, quickly rinse them under cold water, drain them and pat them dry with paper towels. Do not peel mushrooms.

stovetop mushroom beef patties

prep/total time 30 minutes

dale thelen
bedford, texas

I'm a "city boy," but my co-workers say I'm the most "country" one they know. Maybe that's because I like to share down-home recipes, including these easy patties.

2 tablespoons milk
1 tablespoon Worcestershire sauce
1/4 cup dry bread crumbs
1 teaspoon salt, *divided*
1/2 teaspoon pepper
1/2 teaspoon garlic powder
1 pound ground beef
1/2 pound sliced fresh mushrooms
1 teaspoon dried basil
5 tablespoons butter, *divided*
2 tablespoons all-purpose flour
1/2 cup half-and-half cream
1/2 to 3/4 cup water
1/4 teaspoon hot pepper sauce
1/4 cup shredded cheddar cheese
2 tablespoons chopped green onions

In a bowl, combine the milk, Worcestershire sauce, bread crumbs, 1/2 teaspoon salt, pepper and garlic powder. Crumble beef over mixture and mix well. Shape into three or four oval patties. In a large skillet, cook patties over medium heat until no longer pink.

In another skillet, saute mushrooms and basil in 2 tablespoons butter until tender; drain. Remove mushrooms with a slotted spoon and set aside.

In the same skillet, melt the remaining butter; stir in flour until smooth. Gradually whisk in the cream, 1/2 cup water, pepper sauce and remaining salt. Bring to a boil; cook and stir for 2 minutes or until thickened and bubbly. Add enough remaining water to make a medium-thin sauce. Add reserved mushrooms; heat though. Serve over beef patties; top with cheese and onions. **yield:** 3-4 servings.

chuck wagon tortilla stack

prep 15 minutes | **cook** 40 minutes

1 pound ground beef
2 to 3 garlic cloves, minced
1 can (16 ounces) baked beans
1 can (14-1/2 ounces) stewed tomatoes, undrained
1 can (11 ounces) whole kernel corn, drained
1 can (4 ounces) chopped green chilies
1/4 cup barbecue sauce
4-1/2 teaspoons chili powder
1-1/2 teaspoons ground cumin
4 flour tortillas (10 inches)
1-1/2 cups shredded pepper Jack cheese
Shredded lettuce, chopped red onion, sour cream *and/or* chopped tomatoes, optional

bernice janowski
stevens point, wisconsin

The first time I fixed this layered entree cooked in a deep skillet, every person at the table asked for seconds. Now I always plan on doubling the recipe!

In a large skillet, cook beef until meat is no longer pink; drain. Add the garlic, beans, tomatoes, corn, chilies, barbecue sauce, chili powder and cumin. Bring to a boil. Reduce heat; simmer, uncovered, for 10-12 minutes or until liquid is reduced.

Coat a large deep skillet with nonstick cooking spray. Place one tortilla in skillet; spread with 1-1/2 cups meat mixture. Sprinkle with 1/3 cup cheese. Repeat layers three times. Cover and cook on low for 15 minutes or until cheese is melted and tortillas are heated through. Cut into wedges. Serve with toppings of your choice. **yield:** 4-6 servings.

mexicana skillet stew

prep 5 minutes | **cook** 35 minutes

bobby walker
lake isabella, california

Bring a bit of the Southwest to dinnertime with this super supper. Sometimes I serve the hearty beef mixture in warm tortillas. You could even add some scrambled eggs to the leftovers the next morning for a great breakfast burrito.

1 pound ground beef
2 large potatoes, peeled and cut into 1/2-inch cubes
1 large onion, chopped
1 large green pepper, chopped
1 can (4 ounces) mushroom stems and pieces, undrained
3/4 cup picante sauce
Garlic salt and pepper to taste

In a large skillet, cook beef, potatoes, onion, green pepper and mushrooms over medium heat until meat is no longer pink; drain. Reduce heat; cover and simmer for 20 minutes or until potatoes are tender, stirring occasionally.

Add picante sauce, garlic salt and pepper. Cook 5 minutes longer or until heated through. **yield:** 4 servings.

country goulash skillet

prep 15 minutes | **cook** 20 minutes

- 1   pound ground beef
- 1   can (28 ounces) stewed tomatoes
- 1   can (10-3/4 ounces) condensed cream of mushroom soup, undiluted
- 2   cups fresh *or* frozen corn
- 1   medium green pepper, chopped
- 1   medium onion, chopped
- 1   tablespoon Worcestershire sauce
- 3   cups cooked elbow macaroni

In a large skillet, cook beef over medium heat until no longer pink; drain. Stir in the tomatoes, soup, corn, green pepper, onion and Worcestershire sauce. Bring to a boil. Reduce heat; cover and simmer for 20-25 minutes or until the vegetables are tender. Stir in macaroni and heat through. **yield:** 6-8 servings.

nutrition facts: 1 cup equals 277 calories, 10 g fat (3 g saturated fat), 39 mg cholesterol, 501 mg sodium, 33 g carbohydrate, 3 g fiber, 16 g protein.

This beef recipe is lighter in calories, fat and sodium.

lisa neubert

south ogden, utah

Simple but family-pleasing recipes like this one never go out of style. I like to prepare it using my homegrown onions, green peppers and corn.

stovetop hamburger casserole

prep 10 minutes | **bake** 25 minutes

edith landinger
longview, texas

Here is comfort food at its best! It's not only loaded with ground beef, pasta, veggies and cheddar cheese, but it also goes together in a jiffy.

1 package (7 ounces) small pasta shells
1-1/2 pounds ground beef
1 large onion, chopped
3 medium carrots, chopped
1 celery rib, chopped
3 garlic cloves, minced
3 cups cubed cooked red potatoes
1 can (15-1/4 ounces) whole kernel corn, drained
2 cans (8 ounces *each*) tomato sauce
1-1/2 teaspoons salt
1/2 teaspoon pepper
1 cup (4 ounces) shredded cheddar cheese

Cook pasta according to package directions. Meanwhile, in a large skillet, cook beef and onion over medium heat until meat is no longer pink; drain. Add the carrots, celery and garlic; cook and stir for 5 minutes or until vegetables are crisp-tender.

Stir in the potatoes, corn, tomato sauce, salt and pepper; heat through. Drain pasta and add to skillet; toss to coat. Sprinkle with cheese. Cover and cook until cheese is melted. **yield:** 6 servings.

carrot pepper skillet

prep 15 minutes | **cook** 30 minutes

6 medium green peppers
1-1/2 cups cooked rice
1 medium onion, chopped
1/3 cup tomato juice
1-1/4 cups water, *divided*
2 tablespoons Worcestershire sauce
2 teaspoons salt, *divided*
2 teaspoons sugar, *divided*
1 pound lean ground beef
4 cups sliced fresh carrots
1 tablespoon butter, melted
Dash ground ginger
Dash ground nutmeg
1 tablespoon corn syrup

Cut tops off peppers and remove seeds and membranes; set aside. In a large bowl, combine the rice, onion, tomato juice, 1/4 cup water, Worcestershire sauce, 1 teaspoon salt and 1 teaspoon sugar. Crumble beef over mixture and mix well. Spoon into peppers. Place around the edge of a 10-in. skillet.

In a large bowl, combine the carrots, butter, ginger, nutmeg and remaining salt and sugar. Place in the center of the skillet. Pour remaining water around peppers; cover and simmer for 30 minutes or until meat is no longer pink. Drizzle corn syrup over the carrots. **yield:** 6 servings.

esther shank
harrisonville, virginia

This creative recipe pairs stuffed peppers with nicely seasoned carrots…and everything is conveniently cooked in the same skillet for a meal-in-one.

hamburger rice skillet

prep/total time 25 minutes

1 pound ground beef
3 cups water
2 medium carrots, cut into 1/4-inch slices
1 celery rib, chopped
1 envelope onion soup mix
2 cups uncooked instant rice

In a large skillet, cook beef over medium heat until no longer pink; drain. stir in the water, carrots, celery and soup mix. Bring to a boil. Reduce heat; cover and simmer for 8 minutes or until vegetables are tender.

Return to a boil; add the rice. Remove from the heat; let stand for 5 minutes or until rice is tender. **yield:** 4 servings.

suzanne dolata
ripon, wisconsin

Onion soup mix mildy flavors this kid-pleasing blend of ground beef, instant rice and fresh vegetables. It can be served as either a main course or a hearty side dish.

keen on **CARROTS**

When choosing carrots, select smooth, crisp, firm, well-shaped ones with deep orange color. Smaller carrots are tender and sweet. Carrots sold in bunches with fern-like green tops are fresher than those sold in plastic bags but are not always available.

Store unwashed, unpeeled carrots in a sealed plastic bag in your refrigerator's crisper drawer for 1 to 2 weeks. Young carrots may be used unpeeled if they're well scrubbed. Larger ones should be thinly peeled with a vegetable peeler.

hamburger goulash

prep 5 minutes | **cook** 30 minutes

jennifer willingham
kansas city, missouri

When I was growing up, my birthday meal of choice was always goulash over mashed potatoes. Now I make my mother's tangy recipe for my own family to enjoy.

2-1/2 pounds ground beef
1 medium onion, chopped
2 cups water
3/4 cup ketchup
2 tablespoons Worcestershire sauce
2 teaspoons paprika
1 to 2 teaspoons sugar
1 teaspoon salt
1/2 teaspoon ground mustard
1/4 teaspoon garlic powder
2 tablespoons all-purpose flour
1/4 cup cold water
Hot cooked noodles *or* mashed potatoes

In a Dutch oven, cook beef and onion over medium heat until meat is no longer pink; drain. Add the water, ketchup, Worcestershire sauce, paprika, sugar, salt, mustard and garlic powder. Bring to a boil. Reduce heat; simmer, uncovered, for 20 minutes.

In a small bowl, combine flour and cold water until smooth; stir into the meat mixture. Bring to a boil; cook and stir for 2 minutes or until thickened. Serve over noodles or potatoes; or cool and freeze for up to 3 months.

TO USE FROZEN CASSEROLE: Thaw in the refrigerator overnight. Remove from the refrigerator 30 minutes before baking. Bake as directed. **yield:** 6 cups.

spaghetti skillet

prep/total time 25 minutes

1/2 pound ground beef
1/4 pound bulk Italian sausage
1 can (15 ounces) tomato sauce
1 can (14-1/2 ounces) stewed tomatoes
1 cup water
1 can (4 ounces) mushroom stems and pieces, drained
2 celery ribs, sliced
4 ounces uncooked spaghetti, broken in half
1/4 teaspoon dried oregano
Salt and pepper to taste

 This beef recipe is lighter in calories, fat and sodium.

margery bryan
moses lake, washington

No matter who is at your table, this beef-and-sausage supper can't miss. I like that the recipe saves a step—I don't have to precook the spaghetti before adding it to the skillet.

In a large skillet, cook beef and sausage over medium heat until no longer pink; drain. Add the remaining ingredients. Bring to a boil. Reduce heat; cover and simmer for 14-16 minutes or until spaghetti is tender. **yield:** 4-6 servings.

nutrition facts: 1 serving equals 204 calories, 6 g fat (2 g saturated fat), 26 mg cholesterol, 645 mg sodium, 24 g carbohydrate, 2 g fiber, 13 g protein.

hearty squash skillet

prep 15 minutes | **cook** 20 minutes

 This beef recipe is lighter in calories, fat and sodium.

vicki berry
galveston, indiana

This crowd-size recipe was a family favorite when I was growing up. We grew a lot of the vegetables for it in our backyard garden.

2 pounds lean ground beef
3 medium onions, chopped
2 medium green peppers, chopped
2 garlic cloves, minced
2 small butternut squash, peeled, seeded and thinly sliced
1 small acorn squash, peeled, seeded and cubed
3 small potatoes, diced
2 cans (8 ounces *each*) tomato sauce
1 tablespoon Worcestershire sauce
6 large tomatoes, peeled, seeded and chopped
1 small yellow squash, thinly sliced
1 medium zucchini, thinly sliced
1/2 teaspoon salt
1/4 teaspoon pepper
1 cup (4 ounces) shredded reduced-fat Swiss cheese
1 cup (4 ounces) shredded part-skim mozzarella cheese

In a large skillet, cook the beef, onions, green peppers and garlic until the meat is no longer pink; drain. Add the butternut squash, acorn squash, potatoes, tomato sauce and Worcestershire sauce. Bring to a boil. Reduce heat; cover and cook until the potatoes and squash are tender.

Add the tomatoes, yellow squash, zucchini, salt and pepper; heat through. Sprinkle with cheeses; cover and cook until cheese is melted. **yield:** 16 servings.

nutrition facts: 1 cup equals 231 calories, 6 g fat, (3 g saturated fat), 35 mg cholesterol, 317 mg sodium, 28 g carbohydrate, 6 g fiber, 18 g protein.

taco stovetop supper

prep 5 minutes | **cook** 30 minutes

barbara inglis
addy, washington

Green chilies, Mexicorn and taco seasoning give this dish south-of-the-border flair. The recipe makes a lot, so it's perfect for potluck guests—they can spoon the meaty mixture into tortillas and add their desired toppings.

2 pounds lean ground beef
2 cans (15-1/2 ounces *each*) hot chili beans
2 cans (10 ounces *each*) diced tomatoes and green chilies
1 can (11-1/2 ounces) picante V8 juice
1 can (11 ounces) Mexicorn, drained
2 envelopes taco seasoning

Optional garnishes: tortillas, shredded cheddar cheese, chopped onion, shredded lettuce *and/or* taco sauce

In a Dutch oven, cook beef over medium heat until no longer pink; drain. Stir in beans, tomatoes, V8 juice, corn and taco seasoning. Simmer, uncovered, for 15-20 minutes or until heated through. Garnish as desired. **yield:** 10-12 servings.

zippy ground beef skillet

prep/total time 25 minutes

This beef recipe is lighter in calories, fat and sodium.

vicki kerr

portland, maine

This zesty combination of ingredients creates a real fiesta of flavors. No one leaves the table hungry when I serve this filling supper dish hot from the stovetop.

8 ounces uncooked small tube pasta
1 pound lean ground beef
3/4 cup diced onion
3/4 cup diced green pepper
1 can (28 ounces) diced tomatoes, undrained
2 jalapeno peppers, seeded and chopped
1 tablespoon honey
2 to 3 teaspoons chili powder
3/4 teaspoon salt
1-1/2 cups reduced-fat sour cream

Cook pasta according to package directions. Meanwhile, in a large nonstick skillet, cook the beef, onion and green pepper over medium heat until meat is no longer pink; drain. Add the tomatoes, jalapenos, honey, chili powder and salt. Reduce heat to low; cook, uncovered, for 10 minutes, stirring occasionally.

Drain pasta; add to beef mixture. Add sour cream; cook and stir until heated through (do not boil). **yield:** 8 servings.

nutrition facts: 1 cup equals 307 calories, 10 g fat (5 g saturated fat), 36 mg cholesterol, 451 mg sodium, 33 g carbohydrate, 3 g fiber, 22 g protein.

editor's note: When cutting or seeding hot peppers, use rubber or plastic gloves to protect your hands. Avoid touching your face.

cuban ground beef hash

prep/total time 30 minutes

1-1/2 pounds ground beef
1 medium green pepper, chopped
1 medium onion, chopped
1 can (14-1/2 ounces) diced tomatoes, undrained
3 tablespoons tomato paste
1/3 cup raisins
1/3 cup sliced stuffed olives
1 tablespoon cider vinegar
3 garlic cloves, minced
2 teaspoons ground cumin
1/2 teaspoon salt
1/2 teaspoon pepper
1/2 cup frozen peas
Hot cooked rice

adrianna still cruz

weston, florida

Called "picadillo" in Spanish, this distinctive hash is terrific served over white rice...or even inside plain omelets for a hearty breakfast.

In a large skillet, cook the beef, green pepper and onion over medium heat until meat is no longer pink; drain. Stir in the tomatoes, tomato paste, raisins, olives, vinegar, garlic, cumin, salt and pepper. Bring to a boil. Reduce heat; cover and simmer for 5 minutes. Add peas; cover and cook 5 minutes longer or until heated through. Serve with rice. **yield:** 6 servings.

beefy spanish rice

prep/total time 30 minutes

- 1 pound ground beef
- 1 medium onion, chopped
- 1 green pepper, chopped
- 1 garlic clove, minced
- 1 can (14-1/2 ounces) stewed tomatoes
- 1-1/2 cups water
- 1 cup uncooked long grain rice
- 1 teaspoon salt
- 1/2 to 1 teaspoon chili powder
- 1/2 teaspoon dried thyme
- 1/4 teaspoon dried basil
- 1/4 teaspoon pepper
- 2 tablespoons tomato paste

French bread

In a large skillet, cook the ground beef, onion, green pepper and garlic until meat is no longer pink; drain. Stir in the next eight ingredients; bring to a boil. Reduce heat; cover and simmer for 20 minutes or until the rice is tender. Stir in tomato paste and cook until heated through. Serve with French bread. **yield:** 4-6 servings.

nutrition facts: 1 serving equals 273 calories, 7 g fat (3 g saturated fat), 37 mg cholesterol, 576 mg sodium, 35 g carbohydrate, 2 g fiber, 17 g protein.

 This beef recipe is lighter in calories, fat and sodium.

laurie smith murphy
foster, rhode island

I think this delicious rice dinner is best paired with French bread. Feel free to adjust the spice level to suit your taste. If I have leftover spaghetti sauce, I'll use that instead of the tomato paste.

hamburger macaroni skillet

prep 10 minutes | **cook** 30 minutes

teresa ray
lewisburg, tennessee

Who needs to buy hamburger dinner mixes when you have easy, tasty recipes like this one? While it simmers, you'll have time to toss together a salad or slice some bread.

1-1/2 pounds ground beef
2 cans (10-3/4 ounces *each*) condensed tomato soup, undiluted
2 cups uncooked elbow macaroni
2 cups frozen mixed vegetables
1-3/4 cups water
1-1/2 to 2 teaspoons garlic powder
1 teaspoon dried basil
1/2 teaspoon dried oregano

In a large skillet, cook beef over medium heat until no longer pink; drain. Stir in the soup, macaroni, vegetables, water, garlic powder, basil and oregano. Bring to a boil. Reduce heat; simmer, uncovered, for 20 minutes or until macaroni is tender. **yield:** 6-8 servings.

skillet ole

prep/total time 25 minutes

This beef recipe is lighter in calories, fat and sodium.

lillie glass

dripping springs, texas

I fix ranch-style beans and a green salad to go with this Southwestern dish, and the whole meal is ready in about

serve the beefy entree with your favorite salsa.

1/2 pound lean ground beef
1/2 pound lean ground turkey
1 small onion, chopped
1/4 cup chopped green pepper
1 can (8 ounces) no-salt-added tomato sauce
1 cup cooked rice
1 to 1-1/2 teaspoons chili powder
3/4 cup shredded reduced-fat cheddar cheese

In a large skillet, cook beef, turkey, onion and green pepper over medium heat until meat is no longer pink; drain. Stir in tomato sauce, rice and chili powder. Cook for 10 minutes; sprinkle with the cheese. Cover and cook for 2 minutes or until cheese is melted. **yield:** 4 servings.

nutrition facts: 1 serving equals 268 calories, 8 g fat (3 g saturated fat), 43 mg cholesterol, 236 mg sodium, 16 g carbohydrate, 2 g fiber, 32 g protein.

cabbage wedges with beef

prep 20 minutes | **cook** 15 minutes

1-1/2 pounds ground beef
1/2 cup *each* chopped onion, celery and green pepper
1 can (15 ounces) tomato sauce
3 tablespoons cider vinegar
3 tablespoons brown sugar
1-1/4 teaspoons salt
3 tablespoons quick-cooking oats
2 tablespoons minced fresh parsley
1/2 teaspoon garlic powder
1/8 teaspoon pepper
1 medium head cabbage

In a large skillet, cook the beef, onion, celery and green pepper over medium heat until meat is no longer pink; drain. In a small bowl, combine tomato sauce, vinegar, brown sugar and salt; add to skillet. Stir in the oats, parsley, garlic powder and pepper.

Core the cabbage and cut into six wedges; arrange over meat mixture. Cover and simmer for 15-20 minutes or until cabbage is tender. **yield:** 6 servings.

sue van dlac

everette, washington

This beef-and-veggie meal features onion, celery and green pepper in addition to the cabbage. I'm always happy to feed my family this wholesome dinner.

easy beef and rice

prep/total time 25 minutes

doris gill

sargent, nebraska

I rely on my microwave to cook this creamy main-dish casserole. Two canned soups and instant rice make it especially fast to fix.

1 pound ground beef
1 can (10-3/4 ounces) condensed cream of celery soup, undiluted
1 can (10-3/4 ounces) condensed cream of chicken soup, undiluted
1 cup water
1 cup uncooked instant rice
3 tablespoons chopped onion
1/2 teaspoon salt
1/4 teaspoon pepper

Crumble beef into an ungreased 2-qt. microwave-safe dish. Cover and microwave on high for 3 minutes or until no longer pink; drain. Stir in the remaining ingredients. Cover and heat on high for 9-10 minutes or until rice is tender. Let stand for 5 minutes before serving. **yield:** 4 servings.

editor's note: This recipe was tested in a 1,100-watt microwave.

lots of **LEAVES**

Plan on making Cabbage Bundles with Kraut? If you remove the head of cabbage from the boiling water and find that you didn't get enough leaves, simply place the head back in simmering water for a minute or two.

cabbage bundles with kraut

prep 30 minutes | **cook** 1 hour 15 minutes

jean kubley
glidden, wisconsin

In our area, cabbage rolls are a popular dish at potluck dinners. My family loves these bundles, which are cooked with plenty of sauerkraut.

1 large head cabbage
2 eggs
1 medium onion, chopped
1/2 cup uncooked long grain rice
2 teaspoons salt
1/4 teaspoon pepper
2 pounds ground beef
1 can (27 ounces) sauerkraut, rinsed and drained
2 cups water

In a large saucepan, cook cabbage in boiling water just until leaves fall off the head. Set aside 10 large leaves for bundles (refrigerate remaining cabbage for another use). Cut out the thick vein from each reserved leaf, making a V-shaped cut; set aside.

In a bowl, combine the eggs, onion, rice, salt and pepper. Crumble beef over mixture and mix well. Place about 1/2 cup meat mixture on each cabbage leaf; overlap the cut ends of leaf. Fold in the sides, beginning from the cut end. Roll up completely to enclose the filling.

Place five bundles in a Dutch oven. Top with sauerkraut and remaining bundles. Pour water over all. Bring to a boil over medium heat. reduce heat; cover and simmer for 1-1/4 to 1-1/2 hours or until meat is no longer pink and cabbage is tender. **yield:** 5 servings.

taco stir-fry

prep/total time 25 minutes

nila towler

baird, texas

To spice up dinnertime, try this meaty Mexican stir-fry. It's a fun variation on a taco salad…and is especially good on a warm summer day.

1 pound lean ground beef
1/4 cup chopped onion
1 can (14-1/2 ounces) stewed tomatoes
1 cup frozen corn
2 tablespoons chili powder
1 teaspoon sugar
1/2 teaspoon dried oregano
1/4 teaspoon salt
1/8 teaspoon pepper
1 cup (4 ounces) shredded reduced-fat cheddar cheese
1 medium head iceberg lettuce, shredded
Tortilla chips
1 cup salsa

In a nonstick skillet, cook beef and onion over medium heat until meat is no longer pink; drain. Stir in the tomatoes, corn, chili powder, sugar, oregano, salt and pepper. Bring to a boil. Reduce heat; cover and simmer for 10 minutes, stirring occasionally. Stir in cheese.

Place shredded lettuce and 10 tortilla chips on each plate; top with taco mixture and 2 tablespoons salsa. **yield:** 8 servings.

sauerbraten patties

prep 20 minutes | **cook** 1 hour

chris christoffers

lake worth, florida

I have fond memories of my mother serving this family favorite years ago. A roast was out of the question on our budget, but no one felt deprived when these tasty patties were on the table.

2 eggs
1 cup water, *divided*
1 cup seasoned bread crumbs
1/4 cup chopped onion
3/4 teaspoon poultry seasoning
3/4 teaspoon salt
1/4 teaspoon pepper
1-1/2 pounds ground beef
1 cup beef broth
1/4 cup red wine vinegar
1 to 2 tablespoons brown sugar
10 whole cloves
1 bay leaf
12 gingersnaps, crumbled

In a large bowl, combine the eggs, 3/4 cup water, bread crumbs, onion, poultry seasoning, salt and pepper. Crumble beef over mixture; mix well. Shape into eight patties.

In a large skillet, brown patties on both sides; drain. Add the broth, vinegar, brown sugar, cloves, bay leaf, gingersnaps and remaining water. Bring to a boil over medium heat. Reduce heat; cover and simmer for 1 hour or until meat is no longer pink. Discard cloves and bay leaf. **yield:** 6-8 servings.

swiss cheese lasagna

prep 1 hour | **bake** 40 minutes + standing

This beef recipe is lighter in calories, fat and sodium.

susan rourke

dartmouth, nova scotia

An old favorite from my mother-in-law's collection, this recipe is now a staple in our family. We like the

garlic bread and a Caesar salad or coleslaw.

1 pound ground beef
1 large onion, chopped
1 garlic clove, minced
3 cups water
1 can (12 ounces) tomato paste
2 teaspoons salt
1/2 to 1 teaspoon dried rosemary, crushed
1/4 teaspoon pepper
1 package (8 ounces) lasagna noodles
  ____ ____ sliced Swiss cheese
1-1/2 cups (12 ____ ____ cheese
1/2 cup shredded part-skim mozzarella cheese

In a large skillet, cook the beef, onion and garlic over medium heat until meat is no longer pink; drain. Stir in the water, tomato paste, salt, rosemary and pepper. Bring to a boil. Reduce heat; simmer, uncovered, for 30 minutes.

Meanwhile, cook the lasagna noodles according to the package directions; drain. In a greased 13-in. x 9-in. x 2-in. baking dish, layer a third of the meat sauce, lasagna noodles and Swiss cheese. Repeat layers. Top with the cottage cheese and remaining Swiss cheese, noodles and sauce. Sprinkle with the mozzarella cheese.

Cover and bake at 350° for 30 minutes. Uncover; bake 10-15 minutes longer or until bubbly. Let stand for 10 minutes before serving. **yield:** 12 servings.

nutrition facts: 1 serving equals 275 calories, 11 g fat (7 g saturated fat), 48 mg cholesterol, 596 mg sodium, 23 g carbohydrate, 3 g fiber, 20 g protein.

beef mushroom spaghetti

prep 15 minutes + freezing | **bake** 35 minutes

1 pound ground beef
1 medium onion, chopped
1 can (15 ounces) tomato sauce
1 can (10-3/4 ounces) condensed cream of mushroom soup, undiluted
1/4 cup water
1 package (7 ounces) thin spaghetti, cooked and drained

In a large skillet, cook beef and onion over medium heat until the meat is no longer pink; drain. Stir in tomato sauce, soup and water. Add spaghetti; mix well. Place in a greased 8-in. square baking dish. Cover and freeze for up to 3 months.

TO USE FROZEN CASSEROLE: Thaw in the refrigerator. Cover and bake at 350° for 35-40 minutes or until heated through. **yield:** 4 servings.

norene wright

manilla, indiana

You'll need just six simple ingredients to prepare this freezer-friendly spaghetti casserole. I often garnish it with a little Parmesan.

cheesy beef spirals

prep 25 minutes | **bake** 30 minutes

brenda marschall
poplar bluff, missouri

My mom shared the recipe for this easy-to-fix beef casserole, which is excellent with garlic toast. Large shell macaroni or ziti noodles could replace the spiral pasta.

2 cups uncooked spiral pasta
2 pounds ground beef
2 small onions, chopped
1 garlic clove, minced
1 jar (26 ounces) spaghetti sauce
1 jar (4-1/2 ounces) sliced mushrooms, drained
1/2 cup sour cream
1/2 pound process cheese (Velveeta), cubed
2 cups (8 ounces) shredded part-skim mozzarella cheese

Cook pasta according to package directions. Meanwhile, in a large saucepan, cook the beef, onions and garlic over medium heat until meat is no longer pink; drain. Stir in spaghetti sauce and mushrooms; bring to a boil. Reduce heat; cover and simmer for 20 minutes.

Place 1/2 cup of meat sauce in a greased shallow 2-1/2-qt. baking dish. Drain pasta; place half over sauce. Top with half of the remaining meat sauce; spread with sour cream. Top with cheese cubes and remaining pasta and meat sauce. Sprinkle with mozzarella cheese.

Cover and bake at 350° for 25-30 minutes. Uncover; bake 5-10 minutes longer or until bubbly. **yield:** 8-10 servings.

quick 'n' easy lasagna

prep 25 minutes | **bake** 35 minutes

- 16   lasagna noodles
- 2   pounds ground beef
- 1   jar (28 ounces) spaghetti sauce
- 1   pound process cheese (Velveeta), cubed

Cook noodles according to package directions. Meanwhile, in a large skillet, cook beef over medium heat until no longer pink; drain. Add spaghetti sauce; heat through. Rinse and drain the noodles.

In a greased 13-in. x 9-in. x 2-in. baking dish, layer a third of the meat sauce and half of the noodles and cheese. Repeat layers. Top with remaining meat sauce. Cover and bake at 350° for 35 minutes or until bubbly. **yield:** 6-8 servings.

brenda richardson
rison, arizona

If you think lasagna has to be complicated, give this four-ingredient version a try. I like to make it when my husband and I have friends over to play cards.

sloppy joe pasta

prep 10 minutes | **bake** 30 minutes

lynne leih
idyllvild, california

Since ___ d this recipe a few years a___ become a regular part ___ nu plans. Everyone ___ combination of sloppy ___ ingredients, shell pasta and cheddar cheese.

- 1   pound ground beef
- 1   envelope sloppy joe mix
- 1   cup water
- 1   can (8 ounces) tomato sauce
- 1   can (6 ounces) tomato paste
- 1   package (7 ounces) small shell pasta, cooked and drained
- 1   cup small-curd cottage cheese
- 1/2   cup shredded cheddar cheese

In a ___ rge saucepan, cook beef over medium heat ___ ntil no longer pink; drain. Stir in the slopp___ oe mix, water, tomato sauce and tomato ___ aste. Bring to a boil. Reduce heat; simmer___ ncovered, for 5-8 minutes or until hea___ d through. Remove from the heat; stir in ___ asta.

Spoon ha___ nto a greased 2-1/2-qt. baking dish. Top ___ ith cottage cheese and remaining pasta ___ ixture. Sprinkle with cheddar cheese. Ba___ uncovered, at 350° for 30-35 minutes o___ ntil bubbly and cheese is melted. **yield:** 4-6 ___ rvings.

mexican-style spaghetti

prep 15 minutes | **cook** 2 hours

2 pounds lean ground beef
2 medium onions, chopped
1 medium green pepper, chopped
3 garlic cloves, minced
1 can (29 ounces) tomato puree
1 can (15-1/2 ounces) kidney beans,
    rinsed and drained
1 cup water
1/4 cup chopped fresh parsley
2 tablespoons chili powder
1 teaspoon ground cumin
1 teaspoon dried marjoram
1 teaspoon dried oregano
1 teaspoon salt, optional
1/4 to 1/2 teaspoon cayenne pepper
1 package (12 ounces) spaghetti,
    cooked and drained

In a Dutch oven, cook the beef, onions, green pepper and garlic over medium heat until the meat is no longer pink; drain. Add the next 10 ingredients. Cover and simmer for 2 hours, stirring occasionally. Serve with spaghetti. **yield:** 8 servings.

nutrition facts: 1/8 recipe (calculated without added salt) equals 379 calories, 11 g fat (0 saturated fat), 61 mg cholesterol, 495 mg sodium, 39 g carbohydrate, 0 fiber, 32 g protein.

 This beef recipe is lighter in calories, fat and sodium.

mary detweiler
west farmington, ohio

When my family gets tired of the "same old" spaghetti, I spice things up with this south-of-the-border version. Cumin, chili powder and cayenne give it a twist.

---

beef and bean macaroni

prep 20 minutes | **bake** 30 minutes

 This beef recipe is lighter in calories, fat and sodium.

sally norcutt
chatham, virginia

This hearty casserole with ground beef, kidney beans, macaroni and more is a full meal in itself. Using reduced-fat ingredients makes it lighter, too.

1 pound lean ground beef
1 package (7 ounces) elbow macaroni,
    cooked and drained
2 cups (8 ounces) shredded
    reduced-fat cheddar cheese, *divided*
1 can (16 ounces) kidney beans, rinsed
    and drained
1 can (14-1/2 ounces) stewed
    tomatoes
1 medium green pepper, diced
1 medium onion, finely chopped
1/4 teaspoon garlic powder
Crushed red pepper flakes and pepper to
    taste
2 tablespoons grated Parmesan
    cheese

In a large skillet, cook beef over medium heat until no longer pink; drain. In a large bowl, combine the macaroni, 1-1/2 cups cheddar cheese, beans, tomatoes, green pepper and onion. Stir in beef, garlic powder, pepper flakes and pepper.

Spoon into a 13-in. x 9-in. x 2-in. baking dish coated with nonstick cooking spray. Sprinkle with Parmesan and remaining cheddar cheese. Cover and bake at 375° for 30 minutes or until heated through. **yield:** 10 servings.

nutrition facts: 1 cup equals 289 calories, 6 g fat (3 g saturated fat), 22 mg cholesterol, 289 mg sodium, 33 g carbohydrate, 6 g fiber, 24 g protein.

ravioli lasagna

prep 25 minutes | **bake** 40 minutes

1 pound ground beef
1 jar (28 ounces) spaghetti sauce
1 package (25 ounces) frozen sausage *or* cheese ravioli
1-1/2 cups (6 ounces) shredded part-skim mozzarella cheese

In a large skillet, cook beef over medium heat until no longer pink; drain. In a greased 2-1/2-qt. baking dish, layer a third of the spaghetti sauce, half of the ravioli and beef and 1/2 cup cheese; repeat layers. Top with remaining sauce and cheese.

Cover and bake at 400° for 40-45 minutes or until heated through. **yield:** 6-8 servings.

patricia smith
asheboro, north carolina

When people sample this, they think it came from a complicated, from-scratch recipe. But the lasagna actually starts with frozen ravioli and requires just three other ingredients.

cut and **DRIED**

To keep lasagna from becoming watery when baking, it's important to drain the noodles well. Try this method:

Drain and rinse the cooked noodles in a colander. Take each noodle, shake off the excess water and lay the noodle flat

most of the water has evaporated.

meaty chili lasagna

prep 20 minutes | **bake** 45 minutes + standing

melba nesmith

corsicana, texas

This luscious lasagna from my mother-in-law is in great demand at family gatherings and potluck suppers. Chili powder and jalapenos give it fantastic flavor.

 12 uncooked lasagna noodles
1-1/2 pounds ground beef
  1 medium onion, chopped
  1 medium green pepper, chopped
  2 to 3 jalapeno peppers, seeded and chopped
  1 to 2 tablespoons chili powder
  1 garlic clove, minced
  1 can (10-3/4 ounces) condensed cream of mushroom soup, undiluted
  1 cup frozen corn
  1 can (8 ounces) tomato sauce
  3 tablespoons tomato paste
  1 can (2-1/4 ounces) sliced ripe olives, drained
  4 cups (16 ounces) shredded cheddar cheese

Cook noodles according to package directions. Meanwhile, in a large skillet, cook beef, onion, peppers, chili powder and garlic over medium heat until meat is no longer pink; drain. Add the soup, corn, tomato sauce, tomato paste and olives; simmer until heated through.

Drain noodles. Spread 1/2 cup meat sauce in a greased 13-in. x 9-in. x 2-in. baking dish. Layer with four noodles, half of the remaining sauce and a third of the cheese. Repeat layers once. Top with remaining noodles and cheese.

Cover and bake at 350° for 30 minutes. Uncover; bake 15 minutes longer or until cheese is melted. Let stand for 15 minutes before cutting. **yield:** 12 servings.

editor's note: When cutting or seeding hot peppers, use rubber or plastic gloves to protect your hands. Avoid touching your face.

classic lasagna

prep 45 minutes | **bake** 55 minutes

- 1/2 pound bulk Italian sausage
- 1/2 pound ground beef
- 1-1/2 cups chopped onion
- 1 cup chopped carrot
- 3 garlic cloves, minced
- 1/4 teaspoon crushed red pepper flakes
- 2 cans (28 ounces *each*) whole tomatoes, undrained
- 2 tablespoons tomato paste
- 1 teaspoon *each* sugar, dried oregano and basil
- 1 teaspoon salt
- 1 teaspoon pepper, *divided*
- 2 cartons (15 ounces *each*) ricotta cheese
- 3/4 cup grated Parmesan cheese, *divided*
- 1 egg
- 1/3 cup minced fresh parsley
- 1 package (12 ounces) lasagna noodles, cooked, rinsed and drained
- 2 cups (8 ounces) shredded part-skim mozzarella cheese

In a large saucepan, cook the sausage, beef, onion, carrot, garlic and red pepper flakes over medium heat until meat is no longer pink; drain.

Add the tomatoes, tomato paste, sugar, oregano, basil, salt and 1/2 teaspoon pepper; bring to a boil. Reduce heat; simmer, uncovered, for 45 minutes or until thick, stirring occasionally.

In a small bowl, combine ricotta, 1/2 cup Parmesan cheese, egg, parsley and remaining pepper.

In a greased 13-in. x 9-in. x 2-in. baking dish, layer a fourth of the noodles, a third of the ricotta mixture, a fourth of the meat sauce and 1/2 cup mozzarella cheese. Repeat layers twice. Top with the remaining noodles, sauce and Parmesan.

Cover and bake at 400° for 45 minutes. Sprinkle with remaining mozzarella; bake, uncovered, 10 minutes longer. Let stand 15 minutes before serving. **yield:** 12 servings.

suzanne barker
bellingham, washington

My parents were Hungarian, but I've always had a weakness for Italian food. This traditional lasagna is thick, meaty and cheesy—just the way I like it.

beefy pasta and rice

prep 5 minutes | **bake** 30 minutes

heidi butts

streetsboro, ohio

Here's a recipe that's doubly appealing—it tastes great and is inexpensive as well. I usually round out the meal with homemade applesauce and oven-fresh biscuits.

1 pound ground beef
1 medium onion, chopped
1 cup uncooked long grain rice
8 ounces uncooked spaghetti, broken into 1-inch pieces
1/4 cup butter, cubed
4 cups chicken broth
1 package (10 ounces) frozen peas
Salt and pepper to taste

In a large skillet, cook beef and onion over medium heat until meat is no longer pink; drain. In another skillet, brown rice and spaghetti in butter. Stir in the beef mixture, broth, peas, salt and pepper. Cover and simmer for 20 minutes or until the rice and spaghetti are tender. **yield:** 8 servings.

cheesy shell lasagna

prep 25 minutes | **bake** 45 minutes + standing

1-1/2 pounds lean ground beef
2 medium onions, chopped
1 garlic clove, minced
1 can (14-1/2 ounces) diced tomatoes
1 jar (14 ounces) meatless spaghetti sauce
1 can (4 ounces) mushroom stems and pieces, undrained
8 ounces uncooked small shell pasta
2 cups (16 ounces) sour cream
11 slices (8 ounces) provolone cheese
1 cup (4 ounces) shredded part-skim mozzarella cheese

mrs. leo merchant

jackson, mississippi

This layered casserole went over big with our children when they were young, and now they fix it for their own children. It has zesty flavor and is easier to make than traditional lasagna.

In a nonstick skillet, cook the beef, onions and garlic over medium heat until meat is no longer pink; drain. Stir in the tomatoes, spaghetti sauce and mushrooms. Bring to a boil. Reduce heat; simmer, uncovered, for 20 minutes.

Meanwhile, cook the pasta according to package directions; drain. Place half of the pasta in an ungreased 13-in. x 9-in. x 2-in. baking dish. Top with half of the meat sauce, sour cream and provolone cheese. Repeat the layers. Sprinkle with the mozzarella cheese.

Cover and bake at 350° for 35-40 minutes. Uncover; bake 10 minutes longer or until cheese begins to brown. Let stand for 10 minutes before cutting. **yield:** 12 servings.

microwave mexican manicotti

prep 15 minutes | **cook** 30 minutes

1/2 pound lean ground beef
1 cup refried beans
1 teaspoon dried oregano
1/2 teaspoon ground cumin
8 uncooked manicotti shells
1-1/4 cups water
1 cup taco *or* picante sauce
1 cup (8 ounces) sour cream
1/4 cup finely chopped green onions
1/4 cup sliced ripe olives
1/2 cup shredded Monterey Jack cheese

In a large bowl, combine the beef, beans, oregano and cumin. Stuff into manicotti shells; place in an ungreased 11-in. x 7-in. x 2-in. microwave-safe dish.

In a small bowl, combine water and taco sauce; pour over shells. Loosely cover dish; microwave on high for 3-4 minutes. Turn shells with tongs. Microwave 3-4 minutes longer; turn shells again.

Cover and cook at 50% power for 12-15 minutes or until the pasta is tender and the meat juices run clear, turning the dish a half turn once.

Spoon the sour cream lengthwise down the center; sprinkle with the onions, olives and cheese. Microwave, uncovered, on high for 1-2 minutes or until the cheese is melted. **yield:** 4 servings.

editor's note: This recipe was tested in a 1,100-watt microwave.

nancy ensor
oviedo, florida

With this time-saving recipe, you don't need to precook the pasta or beef. Everything goes in the microwave… and the result is a delicious, change-of-pace dish.

To easily separate the eggs for Meatball Stroganoff with Noodles, use an egg separator. Simply place it over a custard cup and crack the eggs into the separator. Keep in mind that it's easier to separate eggs when they are cold.

meatball stroganoff with noodles

prep 40 minutes + standing | **cook** 15 minutes

carol schurvinske

geneseo, illinois

My great-nephews and great-niece ask me to fix this dish as their special birthday meal. With homemade noodles and meatballs, this saucy Stroganoff is hard to beat.

2 cups all-purpose flour
1 teaspoon salt
3 egg yolks
1 egg
6 tablespoons water

meatballs

1 egg, lightly beaten
2 tablespoons ketchup
1/4 cup quick-cooking oats
1 tablespoon finely chopped onion
1/2 teaspoon salt
1 pound ground beef

sauce

2 cans (10-3/4 ounces *each*) condensed cream of mushroom soup, undiluted
1 cup (8 ounces) sour cream
1 cup milk
1 tablespoon paprika
2 quarts water
1 teaspoon salt
1 tablespoon butter
1 tablespoon minced parsley

In a large bowl, combine flour and salt. Make a well in the center. Beat egg yolks, egg and water; pour into well. Stir together, forming a dough. Turn dough onto a floured surface; knead 8-10 times. Divide into thirds; roll out each as thin as possible. Let stand for 20 minutes or until partially dried. Cut into 1/4-in. strips, then into 2-in. pieces; set aside.

In another large bowl, combine the egg, ketchup, oats, onion and salt. Crumble beef over mixture; mix well. Shape into 1-1/2-in. balls. Place meatballs on a greased rack in a shallow baking pan. Bake, uncovered, at 400° for 10-15 minutes or until no longer pink; drain.

In a large saucepan, combine the soup, sour cream, milk and paprika; heat through. Add meatballs; cover and cook until heated through, stirring frequently.

In another saucepan, bring water and salt to a boil; add noodles. Cook for 12-15 minutes or until noodles are tender; drain. Toss with butter and parsley. Serve with meatballs. **yield:** 6 servings.

hearty mac 'n' cheese

prep/total time 25 minutes

- 1 pound ground beef
- 1 small onion, chopped
- 2 packages (7-1/4 ounces *each*) macaroni and cheese dinner mix
- 1 cup (4 ounces) shredded part-skim mozzarella cheese
- 6 bacon strips, cooked and crumbled

In a large skillet, cook beef and onion over medium heat until the meat is no longer pink. Meanwhile, prepare macaroni and cheese according to package directions.

Drain the beef mixture; stir into the macaroni and cheese. Transfer to a greased shallow 2-1/2-qt. baking dish. Sprinkle with the mozzarella cheese and bacon. Broil for 2-3 minutes or until the cheese is melted. **yield:** 6-8 servings.

tiffanie froese
athena, oregon

I do most of the cooking for our family of eight, and this bacon-topped main dish pleases everyone at the table. Preparation is a cinch with a boxed macaroni mix.

beefy barbecue macaroni

prep/total time 15 minutes

mary petrara
lancaster, pennsylvania

While I was visiting a friend, she had to work late one night, so I threw together this all in one skillet supper using pantry staples. Her family was so impressed that she now makes it once a week!

- 3/4 pound ground beef
- 1/2 cup chopped onion
- 3 garlic cloves, minced
- 3-1/2 cups cooked elbow macaroni
- 3/4 cup barbecue sauce
- 1/4 teaspoon pepper
- Dash cayenne pepper
- 1/4 cup milk
- 1 tablespoon butter
- 1 cup (4 ounces) shredded sharp cheddar cheese
- Additional cheddar cheese, optional

In a large skillet, cook the beef, onion and garlic over medium heat until meat is no longer pink; drain. Add the macaroni, barbecue sauce, pepper and cayenne.

In a small saucepan, heat milk and butter over medium heat until butter is melted. Stir in cheese until melted. Pour over the macaroni mixture; gently toss to coat. Sprinkle with additional cheese if desired. **yield:** 4 servings.

mexican lasagna

prep 15 minutes | **bake** 60 minutes

- 1 pound lean ground beef
- 1 can (16 ounces) refried beans
- 2 teaspoons dried oregano
- 1 teaspoon ground cumin
- 3/4 teaspoon garlic powder
- 9 uncooked lasagna noodles
- 1 jar (16 ounces) salsa
- 2 cups water
- 2 cups (16 ounces) sour cream
- 1 can (2-1/4 ounces) sliced ripe olives, drained
- 1 cup (4 ounces) shredded Mexican cheese blend
- 1/2 cup thinly sliced green onions

sheree swistun
winnipeg, manitoba

When I was in the mood for something a little different, I gave my traditional Italian lasagna a Mexican accent. The shredded cheese, green onions and ripe olives make an attractive topping.

In a nonstick skillet, cook beef over medium heat until no longer pink; drain. Add the refried beans, oregano, cumin and garlic powder; heat through.

Place three noodles in a 13-in. x 9-in. x 2-in. baking dish coated with nonstick cooking spray; cover with half of the meat mixture. Repeat layers. Top with remaining noodles. Combine the salsa and water; pour over noodles.

Cover and bake at 350° for 60-70 minutes or until noodles are tender. Spread with sour cream. Sprinkle with olives, cheese and onions. **yield:** 9 servings.

swift spaghetti

prep/total time 30 minutes

louise miller
westminster, maryland

I add dry onion soup mix to the water when cooking my spaghetti, then stir in nicely seasoned beef. It results in so much flavor, I'm always asked for the recipe.

- 5-1/2 cups water
- 1 package (7 ounces) spaghetti
- 1 envelope onion soup mix
- 1 pound ground beef
- 1 can (8 ounces) tomato sauce
- 1 can (6 ounces) tomato paste
- 1 tablespoon dried parsley flakes
- 1 teaspoon dried oregano
- 1/2 teaspoon dried basil
- 1/4 to 1/2 teaspoon garlic powder

In a large saucepan, bring water to a boil. Add spaghetti and dry soup mix. Cook for 12-15 minutes or until spaghetti is tender (do not drain).

Meanwhile, in a large skillet, cook beef over medium heat until no longer pink; drain. Stir in the tomato sauce, tomato paste, parsley, oregano, basil and garlic powder. Add to the spaghetti mixture; heat through. **yield:** 4-6 servings.

golden burger spirals

prep 15 minutes | **bake** 30 minutes

- 1 pound ground beef
- 1 medium onion, chopped
- 1 medium green pepper, chopped
- 1 can (10-3/4 ounces) condensed golden mushroom soup, undiluted
- 1 can (8 ounces) tomato sauce
- 1-1/2 cups (6 ounces) shredded cheddar cheese, *divided*
- 1/2 teaspoon salt
- 1 package (8 ounces) spiral pasta, cooked and drained

In a large skillet, cook the beef, onion and green pepper over medium heat until the meat is no longer pink; drain. Add the soup, tomato sauce, 1 cup cheese and salt. Stir in pasta.

Transfer to a greased 2-1/2-qt. baking dish. Sprinkle with remaining cheese. Bake, uncovered, at 350° for 30 minutes or until bubbly. **yield:** 4-6 servings.

lisa sinyard
lexington, alabama

After a busy day, I use popular cheeseburger ingredients and a few other items to fix this quick casserole for my family. It's also an excellent dish for potlucks and church socials.

mom's lasagna

prep 40 minutes | **bake** 45 minutes + standing

kim orr
louisville, kentucky

One of my mom's special recipes, this Italian classic is requested time and again. The made-from-scratch sauce gives each cheesy slice home-style flavor and a softer texture than many other versions of lasagna.

- 1 pound ground beef
- 2 garlic cloves, minced
- 1-1/2 cups water
- 1 can (15 ounces) tomato sauce
- 1 can (6 ounces) tomato paste
- 1/2 to 1 envelope onion soup mix
- 1 teaspoon dried oregano
- 1/2 teaspoon sugar
- 1/4 teaspoon pepper
- 9 lasagna noodles, cooked and drained
- 2 cups (16 ounces) 4% cottage cheese
- 4 cups (16 ounces) shredded part-skim mozzarella cheese
- 2 cups grated Parmesan cheese

In a large saucepan, cook beef and garlic over medium heat until meat is no longer pink; drain. Stir in the water, tomato sauce and paste, soup mix, oregano, sugar and pepper. Bring to a boil. Reduce heat; cover and simmer for 30 minutes.

Spoon 1/2 cup meat sauce into a greased 13-in. x 9-in. x 2-in. baking dish. Layer with three noodles and a third of the cottage cheese, mozzarella, meat sauce and Parmesan cheese. Repeat layers twice.

Cover and bake at 350° for 40 minutes or until bubbly and heated through. Uncover; bake 5-10 minutes longer. Let stand for 10 minutes before cutting. **yield:** 12 servings.

pizza lasagna

prep 10 minutes | **bake** 80 minutes

 This beef recipe is lighter in calories, fat and sodium.

vicki melies

glenwood, iowa

My husband and I love pizza and lasagna, and we have the best of both worlds in this luscious dish. Because we're watching our weight, I lightened up the recipe.

1/2 pound lean ground beef
2 cans (14-1/2 ounces *each*) diced tomatoes, undrained
1 can (15 ounces) ready-to-serve creamy tomato soup
1 can (6 ounces) tomato paste
1/2 cup water
1 medium onion, chopped
1 teaspoon garlic powder
1 teaspoon dried oregano
1/2 teaspoon salt
9 uncooked lasagna noodles
4 ounces sliced turkey pepperoni
1-1/2 cups (6 ounces) shredded part-skim mozzarella cheese, *divided*
1/2 pound fresh mushrooms, sliced
1 medium sweet red pepper, diced
6 green onions, chopped
1 can (2-1/4 ounces) sliced ripe olives, drained

In a nonstick skillet, cook the beef over medium heat until no longer pink; drain. For the sauce, in a large bowl, combine the tomatoes, soup, tomato paste, water, onion and seasonings.

Spread 1/2 cup sauce in a 13-in. x 9-in. x 2-in. baking dish coated with nonstick cooking spray. Top with three noodles and a third of the sauce, then pepperoni. Sprinkle with 1 cup cheese. Top with three noodles and a third of the sauce. Top with mushrooms, red pepper, green onions and beef. Top with remaining noodles, sauce and cheese. Sprinkle with olives.

Cover and bake at 350° for 70-80 minutes or until noodles are tender. Uncover; bake 10 minutes longer or until the cheese is melted. Let stand for 10 minutes. **yield:** 12 servings.

nutrition facts: 1 piece equals 191 calories, 6 g fat (3 g saturated fat), 29 mg cholesterol, 568 mg sodium, 22 g carbohydrate, 4 g fiber, 14 g protein.

editor's note: This recipe was tested with Healthy Choice Creamy Tomato Soup.

italian noodles

prep/total time 25 minutes

4 cups uncooked egg noodles
1/2 pound ground beef
1/4 pound miniature smoked sausage links
2 cups frozen corn, thawed
1 jar (26 ounces) spaghetti sauce
1 cup (8 ounces) 4% cottage cheese
1/4 teaspoon garlic powder
1/2 cup shredded part-skim mozzarella cheese

Cook noodles according to package directions. Meanwhile, in a large skillet, cook beef and sausage over medium heat until beef is no longer pink; drain. Add the corn, spaghetti sauce, cottage cheese and garlic powder; heat through.

Drain noodles and stir into beef mixture. Sprinkle with mozzarella cheese. Cover and cook for 5 minutes or until cheese is melted. **yield:** 4-6 servings.

barbara thomas

mankato, kansas

I seldom know if I'm going to have one, two or 15 people at the dinner table, so I rely on recipes that are fast and simple. This skillet supper is both, and people of all ages find it delicious.

savory beef and noodles

prep/total time 20 minutes

1 pound ground beef
1 can (10-1/2 ounces) condensed French onion soup, undiluted
1/2 cup beef gravy
1 can (4 ounces) mushroom stems and pieces, drained
1 tablespoon all-purpose flour
1 tablespoon water
Hot cooked noodles
Minced fresh parsley, optional

In a large skillet, cook beef over medium heat until no longer pink; drain. Stir in the soup, gravy and mushrooms. Bring to a boil. Reduce heat; cover and simmer for 5 minutes.

In a small bowl, combine flour and water until smooth; stir into beef mixture. Bring to a boil; cook and stir for 2 minutes or until thickened. Serve over hot cooked noodles. Garnish with fresh parsley if desired. **yield:** 4 servings.

taste of home test kitchen
greendale, wisconsin

This hearty, home-style dish is true comfort food. The saucy, beefy pasta is sure to leave everyone at the table feeling full and satisfied.

southwestern spaghetti

prep/total time 30 minutes

This beef recipe is lighter in calories, fat and sodium.

beth coffee
hartford city, indiana

Chili powder and cumin give mild Mexican flavor to this colorful, one-skillet supper. With chunks of fresh zucchini, it's a nice alternative to the usual spaghetti dishes.

3/4	pound lean ground beef
2-1/4	cups water
1	can (15 ounces) tomato sauce
2	teaspoons chili powder
1/2	teaspoon garlic powder
1/2	teaspoon salt, optional
1/2	teaspoon ground cumin
1	package (7 ounces) thin spaghetti, broken into thirds
6	small zucchini (about 1 pound), cut into chunks
1/2	cup shredded reduced-fat cheddar cheese

In a large skillet, cook beef over medium heat until no longer pink; drain. Remove beef and keep warm. In the same skillet, combine the water, tomato sauce, chili powder, garlic powder, salt if desired and cumin; bring to a boil. Stir in spaghetti; return to a boil. Boil for 6 minutes.

Add the zucchini. Cook 4-5 minutes longer or until spaghetti and zucchini are tender, stirring several times. Stir in the beef; sprinkle with cheese. **yield:** 5 servings.

nutrition facts: 1 serving (prepared without salt) equals 340 calories, 10 g fat (4 g saturated fat), 0 cholesterol, 676 mg sodium, 39 g carbohydrate, 3 g fiber, 24 g protein.

plantation supper

prep 10 minutes | **cook** 20 minutes

1-1/2 pounds ground beef
1 medium onion, chopped
1 can (15-1/4 ounces) whole kernel corn, drained
1 can (10-3/4 ounces) condensed cream of mushroom soup, undiluted
1 package (8 ounces) cream cheese, cubed
1 cup milk
1 teaspoon beef bouillon granules
1/4 teaspoon pepper
4-1/2 cups uncooked wide egg noodles

In a large skillet, cook beef and onion over medium heat until meat is no longer pink; drain. Add the corn, soup, cream cheese, milk, bouillon and pepper. Cook and stir until cheese is melted.

Meanwhile, cook noodles according to package directions; rinse and drain. Add to skillet; heat through. **yield:** 8 servings.

linda heller
allison, iowa

This rich and creamy skillet meal always goes over big, especially with my husband. We think it tastes even better the next day…although we rarely have leftovers!

mexican stuffed shells

prep 15 minutes | **bake** 25 minutes

This beef recipe is lighter in calories, fat and sodium.

norma jean shaw
stephens city, virginia

My husband and I are fans of Mexican food—and the hotter, the better! But our children and friends prefer milder dishes, so I created this versatile recipe. The heat level depends on the type of salsa you choose.

24 uncooked jumbo pasta shells
1 pound lean ground beef
2 cups salsa
1 can (8 ounces) tomato sauce
1 cup frozen corn
1/2 cup canned black beans, rinsed and drained
1 cup (4 ounces) shredded reduced-fat Mexican cheese blend

toppings
8 tablespoons reduced-fat sour cream
8 tablespoons salsa
1/4 cup sliced ripe olives
1/4 cup sliced green onions

Cook pasta shells according to package directions; drain. In a large nonstick skillet, cook beef over medium heat until no longer pink; drain. Stir in the salsa, tomato sauce, corn and beans. Spoon into pasta shells.

Place in a 13-in. x 9-in. x 2-in. baking dish coated with nonstick cooking spray. Sprinkle with cheese. Cover and bake at 350° for 25-30 minutes or until heated through. Top with sour cream, salsa, olives and onions. **yield:** 8 servings.

nutrition facts: 3 stuffed shells (calculated with 1 tablespoon each sour cream and salsa and 1-1/2 teaspoons each olives and onions) equals 315 calories, 9 g fat (4 g saturated fat), 43 mg cholesterol, 696 mg sodium, 33 g carbohydrate, 2 g fiber, 22 g protein.

one-pot dinner

prep/total time 30 minutes

 This beef recipe is lighter in calories, fat and sodium.

bonnie morrow
spencerport, new york

Everyone comes back for seconds when I serve this well-seasoned skillet supper. I like the fact that it's on the table in just 30 minutes.

1/2 pound lean ground beef
1 medium onion, chopped
1 cup chopped celery
3/4 cup chopped green pepper
2 teaspoons Worcestershire sauce
1 teaspoon salt, optional
1/2 teaspoon dried basil
1/4 teaspoon pepper
2 cups uncooked medium no-yolk egg noodles
1 can (16 ounces) kidney beans, rinsed and drained
1 can (14-1/2 ounces) no-salt-added stewed tomatoes
3/4 cup water
1 reduced-sodium beef bouillon cube

In a large saucepan or skillet, cook beef, onion, celery and green pepper over medium heat until meat is no longer pink; drain. Add Worcestershire sauce, salt if desired, basil and pepper. Stir in noodles, beans, tomatoes, water and bouillon.

Bring to a boil. Reduce the heat; cover and simmer for 20 minutes or until the noodles are tender, stirring occasionally. **yield:** 5 servings.

nutrition facts: 1 cup (prepared without salt) equals 282 calories, 5 g fat (0 saturated fat), 29 mg cholesterol, 91 mg sodium, 39 g carbohydrate, 0 fiber, 19 g protein.

chili spaghetti

prep 15 minutes | **bake** 65 minutes + standing

1 pound ground beef
1/2 cup chopped onion
2 garlic cloves, minced
3 cups tomato juice
1 can (16 ounces) kidney beans, rinsed and drained
6 ounces spaghetti, broken into 3-inch pieces
1 tablespoon Worcestershire sauce
2 to 3 teaspoons chili powder
1 teaspoon salt
1/2 teaspoon pepper

pam thompson
girard, illinois

My husband often asked his grandmother to make this hearty pasta casserole. With a combination of chili ingredients and spaghetti, it's always a winner.

In a large skillet, cook the beef, onion and garlic over medium heat until the meat is no longer pink; drain. Transfer to a greased 2-1/2-qt. baking dish; stir in the remaining ingredients.

Cover and bake at 350° for 65-70 minutes or until spaghetti is just tender. Let stand, covered, for 10 minutes. **yield:** 6 servings.

double-cheese beef pasta

prep 30 minutes | **bake** 40 minutes

2-1/2 cups uncooked medium shell pasta
2 pounds ground beef
2 medium onions, chopped
1 jar (14 ounces) spaghetti sauce
1 can (14-1/2 ounces) stewed tomatoes, undrained and finely chopped
1 jar (4-1/2 ounces) sliced mushrooms, drained
1 garlic clove, minced
1 teaspoon salt
1/2 teaspoon pepper
2 cups (16 ounces) sour cream
1 package (6 ounces) sliced provolone cheese
1 cup (4 ounces) shredded part-skim mozzarella cheese

Cook pasta according to package directions. Meanwhile, in a large skillet, cook beef and onions over medium heat until meat is no longer pink; drain. Add the spaghetti sauce, tomatoes, mushrooms, garlic, salt and pepper. Bring to a boil. Reduce heat; simmer, uncovered, for 20 minutes, stirring occasionally.

Drain pasta; place half in a greased 3-qt. baking dish. Top with half of the beef mixture. Layer with sour cream and provolone cheese. Top with remaining pasta and beef mixture. Sprinkle with mozzarella cheese. Cover and bake at 350° for 40 minutes. Uncover; bake 5-10 minutes longer or until cheese is melted. **yield:** 6-8 servings.

marilyn pearson
billings, montana

Provolone and mozzarella cheeses star in this rich, comforting pasta casserole. My mother shared the recipe with me years ago when I was a newlywed.

taco noodle dinner

prep 15 minutes | **cook** 35 minutes

marcy cella
l'anse, michigan

Taco seasoning provides the family-pleasing Southwestern flavor in this skillet supper. The topping of sour cream and fresh parsley is the perfect finishing touch.

1 pound ground beef
1/4 cup chopped onion
3/4 cup water
1 envelope taco seasoning
1/2 teaspoon salt
1 can (4 ounces) mushroom stems and pieces, drained
3 cups uncooked fine egg noodles
2-1/2 to 3 cups tomato juice
1 cup (8 ounces) sour cream
1 tablespoon minced fresh parsley

In a large skillet, cook the ground beef and onion over medium heat until the meat is no longer pink; drain. Stir in the water, taco seasoning and salt. Reduce the heat; simmer for 2-3 minutes.

Add the mushrooms. Sprinkle the egg noodles over the top. Pour the tomato juice over the noodles and stir gently. Cover and simmer for 20-25 minutes or until the noodles are tender.

Remove from the heat. Combine sour cream and parsley; spread over the top. Cover and let stand for 5 minutes. **yield:** 6 servings.

market SMARTS

To help keep ground beef cold when returning from the supermarket, make the meat department your last stop in the store. Refrigerate the package as soon as you get home. In warm weather, have your grocer pack all refrigerated items together. If your ride home is long, consider keeping a cooler in your trunk.

MEAT PIES
& pizzas

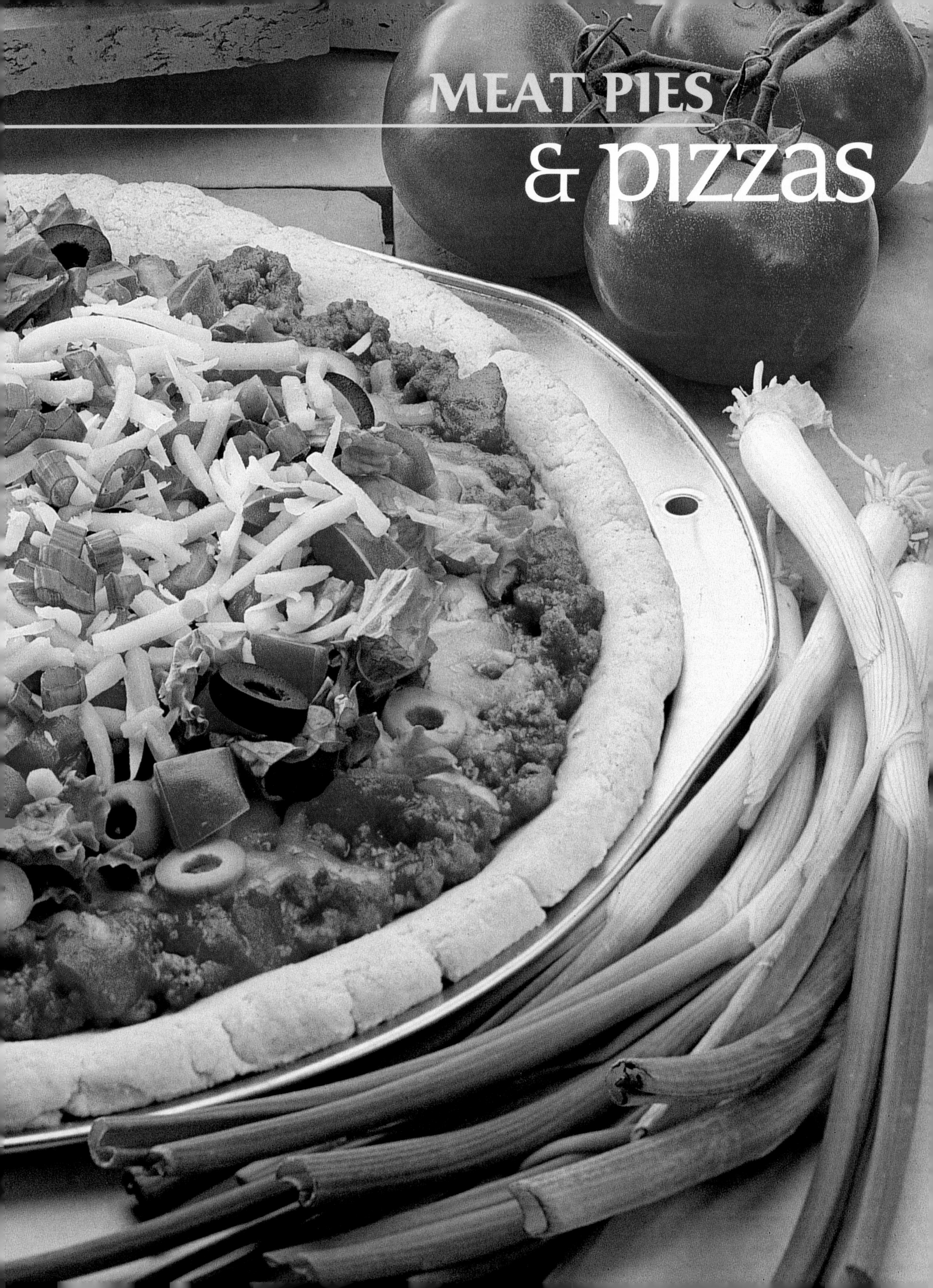

spinach beef pie

prep 25 minutes | **bake** 30 minutes

meg stankiewicz
garfield heights, ohio

This attractive dish blends nutritious spinach and tomatoes with plenty of beef, cheddar and seasonings. A simple, homemade oat crust adds to the great combination of flavors.

1 cup all-purpose flour
1/3 cup old-fashioned oats
7 tablespoons cold butter
2 to 3 tablespoons cold water
1 pound ground beef
1 medium onion, chopped
1 medium green pepper, chopped
1 garlic clove, minced
1/4 cup ketchup
1 teaspoon salt
1 teaspoon dried oregano
1/2 teaspoon dried basil
1/2 teaspoon dried marjoram
1/4 teaspoon pepper
1 package (10 ounces) frozen chopped spinach, thawed and squeezed dry
3 eggs, lightly beaten
2 cups (8 ounces) shredded cheddar cheese, *divided*
1 large tomato, seeded and diced

In a large bowl, combine flour and oats; cut in the butter until crumbly. Gradually add water, tossing with a fork until dough forms a ball. Roll out dough to fit a 9-in. pie plate. Transfer dough to plate; trim and flute edges.

In a large skillet, cook beef, onion, green pepper and garlic over medium heat until meat is no longer pink; drain. Stir in ketchup and seasonings. Fold in spinach; cool slightly. Stir in eggs and 1 cup cheese until combined; spoon into crust.

Bake at 400° for 25-30 minutes or until the center is set. Sprinkle with tomato and remaining cheese around edge of pie. Bake 5-10 minutes longer or until cheese is melted. Let stand for 5-10 minutes before cutting. **yield:** 6-8 servings.

upside-down meat pie

prep/total time 30 minutes

- 1   pound ground beef
- 1/2 cup chopped celery
- 1/2 cup chopped onion
- 1/4 cup chopped green pepper
- 1   can (10-3/4 ounces) condensed tomato soup, undiluted
- 1   teaspoon prepared mustard
- 1-1/2 cups biscuit/baking mix
- 1/3 cup water
- 3   slices process American cheese, halved diagonally

Green pepper rings, optional

In a large skillet, cook the beef, celery, onion and green pepper over medium heat until the meat is no longer pink; drain. Stir in soup and mustard. Transfer to a greased 9-in. pie plate.

Meanwhile, in a large bowl, combine dry baking mix and water until a soft dough forms. Turn onto a lightly floured surface; roll into a 9-in. circle.

Place over meat mixture. Bake at 425° for 20 minutes or until golden brown. Cool for 5 minutes.

Run a knife around edge to loosen biscuit; invert onto a serving platter. Arrange cheese slices in a pinwheel pattern on top. Garnish with green pepper rings if desired. **yield:** 6 servings.

jennifer eilts
central city, nebraska

Thanks to the sloppy joe flavor of this dinner, kids will dig right in…and adults will, too. Plus, I can get it on the table in just half an hour.

shepherd's pie

prep 10 minutes | **bake** 30 minutes

2 pounds ground beef
2 cans (10-1/4 ounces *each*) beef gravy
2 cups frozen corn
2 cups frozen peas and carrots
2 teaspoons dried minced onion

additional ingredients (for each casserole):

2 to 3 cups mashed potatoes
2 tablespoons butter, melted
Paprika

In a Dutch oven, cook beef over medium heat until no longer pink; drain. Add the gravy, vegetables and onion. Spoon half into a greased 2-qt. baking dish. Top with mashed potatoes. Drizzle with butter and sprinkle with paprika.

Bake, uncovered, at 350° for 30-35 minutes or until heated through. Place the remaining beef mixture in a freezer container and freeze for up to 3 months.

TO USE FROZEN BEEF: Thaw in the refrigerator; transfer to a greased 2-qt. baking dish. Top with the potatoes, butter and paprika; bake as directed. **yield:** 2 casseroles (4 servings each).

paula zsiray
logan, utah

This classic recipe makes one pie to eat right away and one batch of meat mixture to freeze for another day. Just pull out the frozen beef any time you have some leftover mashed potatoes.

sloppy joe pizza

prep/total time 25 minutes

This beef recipe is lighter in calories, fat and sodium.

brenda rohlman
kingman, kansas

If your children like sloppy joes, they're sure to like this change-of-pace pizza. The six-ingredient recipe has kid-pleasing flavor and goes together in a flash.

2 tubes (10 ounces *each*) refrigerated pizza crust
1 pound ground beef
1 can (15-1/2 ounces) sloppy joe sauce
2 cups (8 ounces) shredded part-skim mozzarella cheese
1 cup (4 ounces) shredded cheddar cheese
1/2 cup grated Parmesan cheese

Unroll pizza dough; place on two greased 12-in. pizza pans. Bake at 425° for 6-7 minutes or until golden brown.

In a large skillet, cook beef over medium heat until no longer pink; drain. Add sloppy joe sauce. Spread over crusts. Sprinkle with cheeses. Bake at 425° for 6-8 minutes or until the cheese is melted. **yield:** 2 pizzas (8 slices each).

nutrition facts: 1 slice equals 218 calories, 12 g fat (7 g saturated fat), 47 mg cholesterol, 482 mg sodium, 12 g carbohydrate, 1 g fiber, 14 g protein.

two-tater shepherd's pie

prep 20 minutes | **bake** 40 minutes

1-1/2 pounds ground beef
1 can (10-3/4 ounces) condensed cream of mushroom soup, undiluted
1/2 teaspoon garlic salt
1/4 teaspoon pepper
6 cups frozen Tater Tots
2 cups frozen French-style green beans, thawed
3 cups hot mashed potatoes
1 cup (4 ounces) shredded Colby cheese

In a large skillet, cook beef over medium heat until no longer pink; drain. Stir in the soup, garlic salt and pepper.

Place Tater Tots in a greased 13-in. x 9-in. x 2-in. baking dish. Top with beef mixture and green beans. Spread mashed potatoes over the top; sprinkle with cheese. Bake, uncovered, at 350° for 40-45 minutes or until heated through. **yield:** 8 servings.

cindy rebain
robertsdale, alabama

Shepherd's pie is one of my favorite dinners, but our oldest son doesn't care for some of the ingredients. So I adjusted my recipe to come up with this Tater Tot version everyone enjoys.

beef 'n' green bean pie

prep 25 minutes | **bake** 20 minutes

jane hotaling
longmeadow, massachusetts

In our house, this is a mainstay for supper on Sunday night. The crust couldn't be much easier to make—I just press refrigerated crescent roll dough into the pie plate.

1 pound ground beef
1/2 cup chopped onion
1/4 cup chopped green pepper, optional
1 can (8 ounces) tomato sauce
1 can (14-1/2 ounces) cut green beans, drained
1/2 teaspoon salt
1/4 teaspoon garlic salt
1 tube (8 ounces) refrigerated crescent rolls
1 egg
2 cups (8 ounces) shredded cheddar cheese, *divided*

Paprika

In a large skillet, cook the beef, onion and green pepper if desired over medium heat until the meat is no longer pink; drain. Stir in the tomato sauce, green beans, salt and garlic salt. Simmer for 8 minutes or until heated through.

Meanwhile, separate crescent dough into eight triangles; place in an ungreased 9-in. pie plate with points toward the center. Press onto the bottom and up the sides to form a crust; seal perforations.

In a large bowl, beat egg and 1 cup cheese; spread over crust. Stir 1/2 cup cheese into meat mixture; spoon into crust.

Sprinkle with paprika and remaining cheese. Bake, uncovered, at 375° for 20-25 minutes or until golden brown. Let stand for 5 minutes before cutting. **yield:** 4-6 servings.

facts on **FREEZING**

Uncooked ground beef may be frozen for 2 weeks in its original packaging. For the highest quality, don't refreeze beef that's been frozen and defrosted.

To freeze it for up to 3 months, it's a good idea to remove the meat from its packaging and wrap it in freezer paper, plastic freezer bags or heavy-duty aluminum foil. This will help prevent the meat from becoming dried out and getting freezer burn. For quicker thawing and easier stacking, keep each package flat and uniform in size.

hearty meat pie

prep 30 minutes | **bake** 1 hour 15 minutes

twila burkholder

middleburg, pennsylvania

A savory mushroom gravy is served alongside this homey meat-and-vegetable pie. I spend a little extra time making two of them, but the reward comes later when I pull the second pie out of the freezer and pop it in the oven.

Pastry for two double-crust pies
- 2 cups grated peeled potatoes
- 1-1/4 cups diced celery
- 1 cup grated carrots
- 1/4 cup chopped onion
- 2 tablespoons Worcestershire sauce
- 1 teaspoon salt
- 1/4 teaspoon pepper
- 3/4 pound lean ground beef

mushroom gravy (for each pie):
- 1 can (4 ounces) mushroom stems and pieces
- 2 tablespoons all-purpose flour
- 2 tablespoons vegetable oil
- 1 teaspoon beef bouillon granules
- 4 drops browning sauce, optional

Divide the pastry into fourths. On a lightly floured surface, roll out one portion to fit a 9-in. pie plate. In a large bowl, combine the next seven ingredients; crumble the beef over the mixture and mix well. Spoon half into crust.

Roll out another portion of pastry to fit top of pie; place over filling and seal edges. Cut vents in top pastry. Repeat with remaining pastry and filling. Cover and freeze one pie for up to 3 months.

Bake the second pie at 375° for 15 minutes. Reduce the heat; bake at 350° for 1 hour. Meanwhile, drain the mushrooms, reserving the liquid. Add water to the liquid to measure 1 cup; set aside.

In a small saucepan, cook mushrooms and flour in oil until bubbly. Remove from the heat; stir in bouillon and reserved mushroom liquid. Bring to a boil; cook and stir for 1 minute or until thickened. Stir in browning sauce if desired. Serve with pie.

TO USE FROZEN PIE: Bake at 375° for 70 minutes. Prepare gravy as directed. Serve with pie. **yield:** 2 pies (6-8 servings each).

loaded pizza

prep 30 minutes | **bake** 20 minutes

- 1 can (8 ounces) mushroom stems and pieces, drained
- 1/4 cup *each* chopped green pepper, sweet red pepper, ripe olives, white onion and red onion
- 2 garlic cloves, minced
- 3 tablespoons olive oil, *divided*
- 1/2 pound ground beef
- 1/4 pound bulk pork sausage
- 2 teaspoons cornmeal
- 1 loaf (1 pound) frozen bread dough, thawed
- 1/2 teaspoon garlic powder
- 1 can (8 ounces) tomato sauce
- 2 tablespoons minced fresh parsley
- 4 teaspoons Italian seasoning
- 1/4 teaspoon pepper
- 27 pepperoni slices (1-3/4 ounces)
- 2 cups (8 ounces) shredded Italian cheese blend
- 1/4 cup shredded cheddar cheese

In a large skillet, saute the mushrooms, peppers, olives, onions and garlic in 1 tablespoon oil until tender; remove and set aside. In the same skillet, cook beef and sausage over medium heat until no longer pink; drain.

Grease a 14-in. pizza pan and sprinkle with cornmeal. On a floured surface, roll dough into a 15-in. circle. Transfer to prepared pan. Build up edges slightly; prick dough thoroughly with a fork. Brush with remaining oil; sprinkle with garlic powder. Bake at 400° for 8-10 minutes or until edges are lightly browned.

In a small bowl, combine the tomato sauce, parsley, Italian seasoning and pepper; spread over crust.

Top with the vegetables, meat mixture and pepperoni. Sprinkle with cheeses. Bake for 17-20 minutes or until crust is golden and cheese is melted. **yield:** 8 servings.

louie rossignolo
athens, alabama

This big pizza smothered with toppings is one of my specialties. I like to prepare a bunch at Christmastime, dress up as Santa Claus and deliver them to friends.

---

beef and cheddar quiche

prep 15 minutes | **bake** 45 minutes

jeanne lee
terrace park, ohio

Do you think quiche is too complicated and time-consuming to make? Try this simplified version. The beefy, cheesy dish starts with a convenient purchased pastry shell.

- 3/4 pound ground beef
- 1 unbaked pastry shell (9 inches)
- 3 eggs, lightly beaten
- 1/2 cup mayonnaise
- 1/2 cup milk
- 1/2 cup chopped onion
- 4 teaspoons cornstarch
- 1 teaspoon salt
- 1/2 teaspoon pepper
- 2 cups (8 ounces) shredded cheddar cheese, *divided*

In a large skillet, cook the beef over medium heat until no longer pink. Meanwhile, line unpricked pastry shell with a double thickness of heavy-duty foil. Bake at 450° for 5 minutes. Remove foil; bake for 5 minutes more. Set aside.

Drain beef; place in a large bowl. Add the eggs, mayonnaise, milk, onion, cornstarch, salt, pepper and 1 cup cheese. Pour into crust. Bake at 350° for 35-40 minutes or until a knife inserted near the center comes out clean.

If necessary, cover the edges of crust with foil to prevent overbrowning. Sprinkle with remaining cheese. Let stand 5-10 minutes before cutting. **yield:** 6-8 servings.

editor's note: Reduced-fat or fat-free mayonnaise is not recommended for this recipe.

french canadian meat pie

prep 15 minutes | **bake** 30 minutes

1 pound ground beef
3/4 pound ground pork
3/4 cup chopped onion
2 celery ribs, chopped
2 garlic cloves, minced
6 cups hot mashed potatoes (prepared without milk and butter)
1/4 cup chicken broth
1/2 teaspoon dried rosemary, crushed
1/2 teaspoon rubbed sage
1/2 teaspoon dried thyme
1/4 teaspoon dried marjoram
Salt and pepper to taste
Pastry for two double-crust pies (9 inches)
Milk, optional

diane davies
indian trail, north carolina

It was tradition for my mom's family in Quebec to have this beef-and-pork pie on Christmas Eve. The recipe was passed down through at least four generations and was translated from my grandmother's copy written in French.

In a large skillet, cook the beef, pork, onion, celery and garlic over medium heat until meat is no longer pink; drain. Remove from the heat. Stir in the potatoes, broth and seasonings.

Line two 9-in. pie plates with pastry. Divide meat mixture between crusts. Top with remaining pastry; trim, seal and flute edges.

Cut slits in top. Brush with milk if desired. Bake at 375° for 30-35 minutes or until golden brown. **yield:** 2 pies (6-8 servings each).

pizza english muffins

prep 35 minutes | **bake** 15 minutes

This beef recipe is lighter in calories, fat and sodium.

lea deluca
st. paul, minnesota

My mother fixed these fun mini pizzas for me from the time I started elementary school until I went to college. The meaty muffins please people of all ages and freeze well, too.

2 pounds ground beef
1-1/2 pounds bulk pork sausage
1 medium onion, chopped
1 can (6 ounces) tomato paste
1 teaspoon garlic salt
1 teaspoon dried oregano
1/2 teaspoon cayenne pepper
3 packages (12 ounces *each*) English muffins, split
3 cups (12 ounces) shredded part-skim mozzarella cheese
2 cups (8 ounces) shredded cheddar cheese
2 cups (8 ounces) shredded Swiss cheese

In a Dutch oven, cook the beef, sausage and onion over medium heat until meat is no longer pink; drain. Stir in the tomato paste, garlic salt, oregano and cayenne. Spread over the cut side of each English muffin. Place on baking sheets. Combine the cheeses; sprinkle over meat mixture.

Freeze for up to 3 months or bake at 350° for 15-20 minutes or until heated through. **yield:** 6 dozen.

TO USE FROZEN PIZZA ENGLISH MUFFINS: Bake at 350° for 30 minutes.

nutrition facts: 1 English muffin pizza equals 92 calories, 6 g fat (3 g saturated fat), 21 mg cholesterol, 142 mg sodium, 3 g carbohydrate, trace fiber, 6 g protein.

crescent cheeseburger pie

prep/total time 30 minutes

- 1 pound ground beef
- 1 small onion, chopped
- 1 can (8 ounces) tomato sauce
- 1/3 cup ketchup
- 1/2 teaspoon salt
- 1/4 teaspoon pepper
- 5 to 6 slices process cheese (Velveeta)
- 1 tube (8 ounces) refrigerated crescent rolls

In a skillet, cook the beef and onion over medium heat until the meat is no longer pink; drain. Stir in tomato sauce, ketchup, salt and pepper; heat through. Spoon into an ungreased 9-in. pie plate. Arrange the cheese on top.

Bake at 400° for 2-3 minutes or until cheese begins to warm. Unroll crescent roll dough and separate into triangles. Place over cheese, pressing down on edges of pie plate to seal. Bake 10-12 minutes longer or until golden brown. Let stand for 5 minutes before cutting. **yield:** 8 servings.

carolyn hayes
marion, illinois

For a main course that's quick but will still get smiles from everyone at the table, I grab this recipe. Just add a side salad, and presto— your dinner is done!

nacho pie

prep 25 minutes | **bake** 20 minutes

doris gill
sargent, nebraska

I like to spend time in the garden, so I look for recipes that don't require hours in the kitchen. This Southwestern pie has a short list of ingredients and is a snap to prepare.

- 1 pound ground beef
- 1/2 cup chopped onion
- 1 can (8 ounces) tomato sauce
- 2 tablespoons taco seasoning
- 1 tube (8 ounces) refrigerated crescent rolls
- 1-1/2 cups crushed nacho tortilla chips, *divided*
- 1 cup (8 ounces) sour cream
- 1 cup (4 ounces) shredded Mexican cheese blend

In a large skillet, cook beef and onion over medium heat until meat is no longer pink; drain. Stir in tomato sauce and taco seasoning. Bring to a boil. Reduce heat; simmer, uncovered, for 5 minutes.

Meanwhile, separate crescent dough into eight triangles; place in a greased 9-in. pie plate with points toward the center. Press onto the bottom and up the sides to form a crust; seal perforations.

Sprinkle 1 cup chips over crust. Top with meat mixture. Carefully spread sour cream over meat mixture. Sprinkle with cheese and remaining chips. Bake at 350° for 20-25 minutes or until cheese is melted and crust is golden brown. Let stand for 5 minutes before cutting. **yield:** 6-8 servings.

french bread pizza

prep/total time 25 minutes

- 1/2 pound ground beef
- 1 can (15 ounces) pizza sauce
- 1 jar (8 ounces) sliced mushrooms, drained
- 1 loaf (1 pound) French bread
- 2 cups (8 ounces) shredded part-skim mozzarella cheese

In a large skillet, cook beef over medium heat until no longer pink; drain. Stir in pizza sauce and mushrooms; set aside.

Cut bread in half lengthwise, then into eight pieces. Spread meat sauce on bread; place on a greased baking sheet. Sprinkle with mozzarella. Bake, uncovered, at 400° for 10 minutes or until cheese is melted and bubbly. **yield:** 6-8 servings.

nutrition facts: 2 pieces equals 296 calories, 9 g fat (4 g saturated fat), 30 mg cholesterol, 764 mg sodium, 35 g carbohydrate, 3 g fiber, 18 g protein.

 This beef recipe is lighter in calories, fat and sodium.

sue mclaughlin
onawa, iowa

Slices of this hearty French bread are guaranteed to please. I sometimes substitute spaghetti sauce for the pizza sauce…or add our favorite veggies to the toppings.

tortilla pie

prep/total time 30 minutes

This beef recipe is lighter in calories, fat and sodium.

lisa king
caledonia, michigan

My husband and I can't get enough of this delicious layered entree, which uses lightened-up ingredients. Even our two daughters enjoy the pleasantly mild flavor.

- 1/2 pound lean ground beef
- 1/4 cup chopped onion
- 1 garlic clove, minced
- 1 can (14-1/2 ounces) Italian *or* Mexican diced tomatoes, drained
- 1/2 teaspoon chili powder
- 1/4 teaspoon ground cumin
- 3/4 cup part-skim ricotta cheese
- 1/4 cup shredded part-skim mozzarella cheese
- 3 tablespoons minced fresh cilantro, *divided*
- 4 flour tortillas (8 inches)
- 1/2 cup shredded reduced-fat cheddar cheese

In a large nonstick skillet, cook the beef, onion and garlic over medium heat until meat is no longer pink; drain. Stir in the tomatoes, chili powder and cumin. Bring to a boil; remove from the heat. In a small bowl, combine the ricotta cheese, mozzarella cheese and 2 tablespoons cilantro.

Place one tortilla in a 9-in. round baking pan coated with nonstick cooking spray. Layer with half of the meat sauce, one tortilla, all of the ricotta mixture, another tortilla and the remaining meat sauce. Top with remaining tortilla; sprinkle with cheddar cheese and remaining cilantro.

Cover and bake at 400° for 15 minutes or until heated through and cheese is melted. **yield:** 6 servings.

nutrition facts: 1 piece equals 250 calories, 9 g fat (4 g saturated fat), 28 mg cholesterol, 439 mg sodium, 22 g carbohydrate, 1 g fiber, 19 g protein.

taco pizza

prep 30 minutes | **bake** 25 minutes + cooling

1-1/4 cups cornmeal
1-1/4 cups all-purpose flour
2 teaspoons baking powder
1-1/2 teaspoons salt
2/3 cup milk
1/3 cup butter, melted
1/2 pound ground beef
1/2 pound bulk pork sausage
1 can (6 ounces) tomato paste
1 can (14-1/2 ounces) diced tomatoes, undrained
1 envelope taco seasoning
3/4 cup water
1-1/2 cups (6 ounces) shredded cheddar cheese
1 cup (4 ounces) shredded Monterey Jack cheese
2 cups chopped lettuce
1 cup diced fresh tomato
1/2 cup sliced ripe olives
1/2 cup sliced green onions

In a large bowl, combine the cornmeal, flour, baking powder and salt. Add milk and butter; mix well. Press onto the bottom and sides of a 12- to 14-in. pizza pan. Bake at 400° for 10 minutes or until edges are lightly browned. Cool.

In a large skillet, cook beef and sausage over medium heat until no longer pink; drain. Stir in the tomato paste, canned tomatoes, taco seasoning and water; bring to a boil. Simmer, uncovered, for 5 minutes. Spread over crust.

Combine cheeses; sprinkle 2 cups over the meat layer. Bake at 400° for 15 minutes or until cheese melts. Top with lettuce, fresh tomato, olives, onions and remaining cheese. **yield:** 4-6 servings.

gladys shaffer
elma, washington

This colorful, summery pizza puts fresh vegetables, cheese and a savory meat sauce on top of a crispy cornmeal crust. You may have a hard time eating just one slice!

meatball pie

prep 30 minutes | **bake** 45 minutes + standing

susan keith
fort plain, new york

Growing up on a farm, I took part in 4-H cooking club activities. I still love to prepare and serve classic, wholesome recipes such as this meal-in-one pie.

1 pound ground beef
3/4 cup soft bread crumbs
1/4 cup chopped onion
2 tablespoons minced fresh parsley
1 teaspoon salt
1/2 teaspoon dried marjoram
1/8 teaspoon pepper
1/4 cup milk
1 egg, lightly beaten
1 can (14-1/2 ounces) stewed tomatoes
1 tablespoon cornstarch
2 teaspoons beef bouillon granules
1 cup frozen peas
1 cup sliced carrots, cooked

crust

2-2/3 cups all-purpose flour
1/2 teaspoon salt
1 cup shortening
7 to 8 tablespoons ice water
Half-and-half cream

In a large bowl, combine the first nine ingredients (mixture will be soft). Divide into fourths; shape each portion into 12 small meatballs. Brown meatballs, a few at a time, in a large skillet; drain and set aside.

Drain tomatoes, reserving liquid. Combine the liquid with cornstarch; pour into the skillet. Add tomatoes and bouillon; bring to a boil over medium heat, stirring constantly. Stir in peas and carrots. Remove from the heat and set aside.

For crust, in a large bowl, combine flour and salt. Cut in shortening until the mixture resembles coarse crumbs. Add water, 1 tablespoon at a time, tossing lightly with a fork until dough forms a ball. On a lightly floured surface, roll half of dough to fit a 10-in. pie plate.

Place in ungreased plate; add meatballs. Spoon tomato mixture over top. Roll remaining pastry to fit top of pie. Place over filling; seal and flute edges. Cut vents in top crust. Brush with cream.

Bake at 400° for 45-50 minutes or until golden brown. If needed, cover edges with foil for the last 10 minutes to prevent over-browning. Let stand for 10 minutes before cutting. **yield:** 6 servings.

mexican chili pie

prep 40 minutes | **bake** 15 minutes

- 1 pound ground beef
- 1 medium onion, chopped
- 3 garlic cloves, minced
- 2 teaspoons chili powder
- 1 teaspoon ground mustard
- 1/4 teaspoon ground cumin
- 1/4 teaspoon crushed red pepper flakes
- 1/4 teaspoon dried oregano
- 1 can (14-1/2 ounces) diced tomatoes, undrained
- 1/2 cup chopped green pepper
- 1 can (16 ounces) kidney beans, rinsed and drained

topping

- 3/4 cup cornmeal
- 1/2 cup all-purpose flour
- 1/2 teaspoon *each* baking soda, salt and sugar
- 1 cup (4 ounces) shredded cheddar cheese
- 3/4 cup buttermilk
- 1 egg, lightly beaten
- 2 tablespoons vegetable oil

In a large skillet, cook beef, onion and garlic over medium heat until the meat is no longer pink; drain. Add seasonings and tomatoes. Simmer, uncovered, for 20 minutes. Add green pepper. Spoon 2 cups into an ungreased 2-1/2-qt. shallow baking dish; top with half of the beans. Repeat layers.

For topping, combine dry ingredients in a large bowl. Stir in cheese. Combine buttermilk, egg and oil; stir into dry ingredients just until moistened. Spread over filling. Bake at 450° for 15 minutes or until topping is lightly browned and filling is bubbly. **yield:** 4-6 servings.

heather thurmeier
pense, saskatchewan

On wintry days, I turn up the heat with this spicy main dish. The topping is crunchy, and the chili has just enough of a kick to warm you up in even the coldest weather.

taco potato pie

prep 15 minutes | **bake** 30 minutes

betty jorsvick
olds, alberta

I made several of these Southwestern-style pies for visitors at our cattle ranch, and everyone requested the recipe. With mashed potatoes, ground beef and vegetables, it's truly a meal in itself.

- 2 cups cold mashed potatoes (prepared with milk and butter)
- 1 envelope taco seasoning, *divided*
- 1 pound ground beef
- 1/2 cup chopped onion
- 1 can (16 ounces) refried beans
- 1/2 cup barbecue sauce
- 1/4 cup water
- 1 cup shredded lettuce
- 1 medium tomato, seeded and chopped
- 1 cup (4 ounces) shredded cheddar cheese
- Sour cream

Combine the potatoes and 2 tablespoons taco seasoning. Press into a greased 9-in. deep-dish pie plate; set aside.

In a skillet, cook the beef and onion over medium heat until the meat is no longer pink; drain. Stir in the refried beans, barbecue sauce, water and remaining seasoning. Cook and stir until hot and bubbly. Spoon into the potato crust.

Bake at 350° for 30-35 minutes or until heated through. Top with lettuce, tomato, cheese and sour cream. **yield:** 4-6 servings.

grilled cheeseburger pizza

prep 25 minutes | **grill** 15 minutes

tanya gutierro
beacon falls, connecticut

I combined our daughter's two favorite foods—pizza and grilled cheeseburgers— to create this main dish. It's a fun change of pace for a backyard cookout.

3/4 pound ground beef
  1 cup ketchup
  2 tablespoons prepared mustard
  1 prebaked Italian bread shell crust (14 ounces)
  1 cup shredded lettuce
  1 medium tomato, thinly sliced
1/8 teaspoon salt
1/8 teaspoon pepper
  1 small sweet onion, thinly sliced
1/2 cup dill pickle slices
  1 cup (4 ounces) shredded cheddar cheese
  1 cup (4 ounces) shredded part-skim mozzarella cheese

Shape beef into three 1/2-in.-thick patties. Grill, covered, over medium-hot heat for 5 minutes on each side or until meat is no longer pink.

Meanwhile, combine ketchup and mustard; spread over the crust to within 1 in. of edge. Sprinkle with lettuce; top with tomato. Sprinkle with salt and pepper. When beef patties are cooked, cut into 1/2-in. pieces; arrange over tomato slices. Top with onion, pickles and cheeses.

Place pizza on a 16-in. square piece of heavy-duty foil. Prepare grill for indirect heat. Grill, covered, over medium indirect heat for 12-15 minutes or until cheese is melted and crust is lightly browned. Let stand for 5-10 minutes before slicing. **yield:** 4-6 servings.

pizza crescent bake

prep 20 minutes | **bake** 30 minutes

- 2 tubes (8 ounces *each*) refrigerated crescent rolls
- 1-1/2 pounds ground beef
- 1 can (15 ounces) pizza sauce
- 1 cup (4 ounces) shredded cheddar cheese
- 1 cup (4 ounces) shredded part-skim mozzarella cheese

Unroll one tube of crescent dough; place in a lightly greased 13-in. x 9-in. x 2-in. baking dish. Press to seal perforations.

In a large skillet, cook beef over medium heat until no longer pink; drain. Sprinkle over dough. Top with pizza sauce and sprinkle with cheeses.

Unroll remaining crescent dough and place over cheese; seal perforations. Bake, uncovered, at 350° for 30 minutes or until golden brown. **yield:** 6-8 servings.

laurie malyuk
river falls, wisconsin

As a new bride, I didn't have a large collection of recipes. When my cousin found out, she wrote out nearly 50 of them—including this easy, pizza-like supper dish.

sloppy joe pie

prep 30 minutes | **bake** 20 minutes

kathy mccreary
goddard, kansas

People are usually pretty quiet when I serve this pie—they're not talking because they're too busy eating! I created the recipe when I needed something fast.

- 1 pound ground beef
- 1/2 cup chopped onion
- 1 can (8 ounces) tomato sauce
- 1 can (8-3/4 ounces) whole kernel corn, drained
- 1/4 cup water
- 1 envelope sloppy joe mix
- 1 tube (10 ounces) refrigerated biscuits
- 2 tablespoons milk
- 1/3 cup cornmeal
- 1 cup (8 ounces) shredded cheddar cheese, *divided*

In a large skillet, cook beef and onion over medium heat until meat is no longer pink; drain. Stir in the tomato sauce, corn, water and sloppy joe seasoning; cook over medium heat until bubbly. Reduce heat and simmer for 5 minutes; remove from heat and set aside.

Separate the biscuits; flatten each to a 3-1/2-in. circle. Place the milk and cornmeal in separate shallow bowls; dip both sides of each biscuit into the milk and then into the cornmeal. Place seven biscuits around the sides and three on the bottom of an ungreased 9-in. pie plate.

Press biscuits together to form a crust, leaving a scalloped edge around rim. Sprinkle with 1/2 cup cheese. Spoon meat mixture over cheese. Bake at 375° for 20-25 minutes or until crust is deep golden brown. Sprinkle with remaining cheese. Let stand for 5 minutes before serving. **yield:** 7 servings.

southwestern meat loaf pie

prep 10 minutes | **bake** 35 minutes

1 egg
2 cups salsa, *divided*
1/2 cup finely crushed saltines (about 15 crackers)
1/2 teaspoon ground cumin
1/2 teaspoon salt
1/4 teaspoon pepper
1 pound ground beef
3 cups cooked rice
1 cup (4 ounces) shredded cheddar cheese, *divided*
Additional salsa, optional

In a large bowl, combine the egg, 3/4 cup salsa, cracker crumbs, cumin, salt and pepper. Crumble beef over mixture and mix well. Press onto the bottom and up the sides of a greased 9-in. pie plate. Bake, uncovered, at 350° for 25 minutes; drain.

Combine the rice, 1/2 cup cheese and remaining salsa. Spread over meat shell. Sprinkle with remaining cheese.

Bake 10-15 minutes longer or until heated through. Let stand for 5-10 minutes before cutting. Serve with additional salsa if desired. **yield:** 6 servings.

karen ann bland
gove, kansas

My family loves spicy food, so my file is full of recipes that use salsa and cumin. This south-of-the-border spin on meat loaf is a supper I rely on time and time again.

south-of-the-border pizza

prep/total time 30 minutes

This beef recipe is lighter in calories, fat and sodium.

eileen becker
homer, alaska

When we moved from Santa Barbara, California to Alaska over 30 years ago, my friends gave me copies of their best Mexican recipes. This easy entree remains a favorite.

1 tablespoon cornmeal
1 loaf (1 pound) frozen bread dough, thawed
1/2 pound lean ground beef
1 medium onion, chopped
1 sweet yellow pepper, chopped
1 garlic clove, minced
1 can (16 ounces) fat-free refried beans
1 cup salsa
1 can (4 ounces) chopped green chilies
1 to 2 teaspoons chili powder
2 cups (8 ounces) shredded reduced-fat Mexican-blend cheese
2 medium tomatoes, chopped
2 cups shredded lettuce

Coat two 12-in. pizza pans with nonstick cooking spray; sprinkle with cornmeal. Divide the bread dough in half; roll each portion into a 12-in. circle.

Transfer to prepared pans. Build up edges slightly; prick dough thoroughly with a fork. Bake at 425° for 12 minutes or until lightly browned.

Meanwhile, in a large skillet, cook the beef, onion, yellow pepper and garlic over medium heat until meat is no longer pink; drain. Stir in refried beans, salsa, chilies and chili powder; heat through.

Spread over the crusts; sprinkle with cheese. Bake 6-7 minutes longer or until cheese is melted. Top with tomatoes and lettuce; serve immediately. **yield:** 2 pizzas (6 slices each).

nutrition facts: 1 slice equals 250 calories, 7 g fat (3 g saturated fat), 20 mg cholesterol, 706 mg sodium, 31 g carbohydrate, 5 g fiber, 17 g protein.

vegetable beef potpie

prep 40 minutes | **bake** 25 minutes

1	pound ground beef
1/2	teaspoon pepper
1/4	teaspoon salt
2	cups frozen pearl onions, thawed
1-1/2	cups baby carrots, halved
1	medium parsnip, peeled, halved lengthwise and sliced
2	tablespoons butter
3	garlic cloves, minced
1/4	cup all-purpose flour
1-1/3	cups beef broth
4-1/2	teaspoons red wine vinegar
4-1/2	teaspoons Dijon mustard
3	teaspoons minced fresh rosemary, *divided*
1	sheet frozen puff pastry, thawed
1	egg, lightly beaten

In a large skillet, cook beef over medium heat until no longer pink; drain. Stir in pepper and salt; remove and set aside. In the same skillet, saute the onions, carrots and parsnip in butter for 7 minutes. Add garlic; cook 2 minutes longer or until vegetables are crisp-tender. Stir in flour.

Combine the broth, vinegar and mustard; gradually stir into vegetable mixture. Bring to a boil; cook and stir for 2-3 minutes or until thickened. Stir in beef mixture and 2 teaspoons rosemary; heat through. Transfer to a greased 8-in. square baking dish.

On a lightly floured surface, roll pastry into a 10-in. square. Sprinkle with remaining rosemary; press into pastry. Place over filling; flute edges and cut slits in top. Brush with egg. Bake, uncovered, at 400° for 25-30 minutes or until crust is golden brown. **yield:** 6 servings.

trudy williams
shannonville, ontario

This good, old-fashioned potpie is tried-and-true comfort food. Its golden crust and savory filling look wonderful on the table... and don't disappoint when you dig in.

SOUTHWESTERN favorites

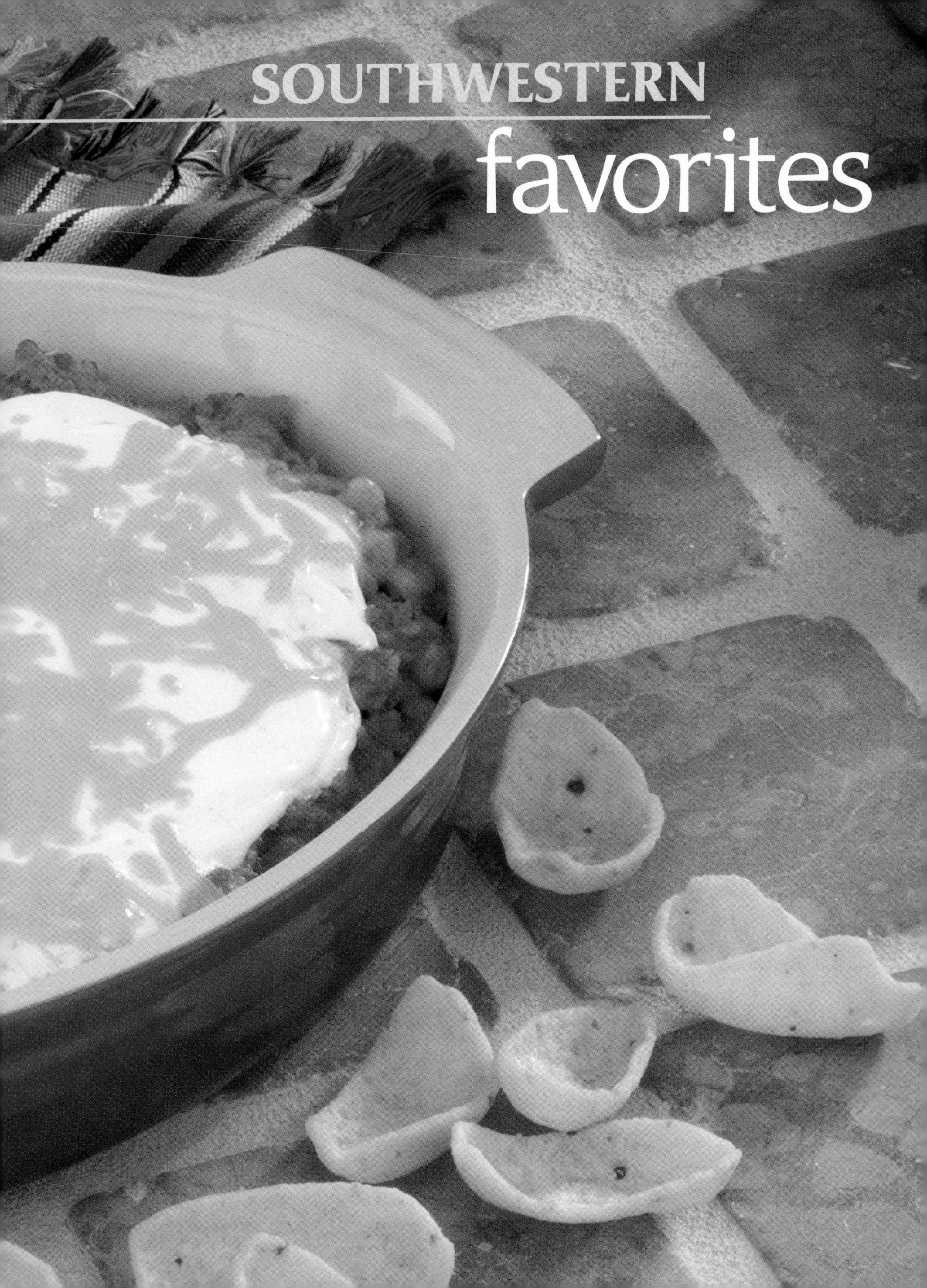

rice **REDO**

Have cooked rice left over from a home-made stir-fry dinner…or from Chinese food takeout? The extras are perfect to use in Mexican-Style Stuffed Peppers. Plus, they'll save you the extra step of cooking a new batch of rice.

mexican-style stuffed peppers

prep 15 minutes | **bake** 50 minutes

This beef recipe is lighter in calories, fat and sodium.

ladonna reed
ponca city, oklahoma

Fans of traditional stuffed peppers are pleasantly surprised by these mildly spicy versions. For convenience, I sometimes assemble them ahead of time and then pop them in the oven later.

6 medium green *or* sweet red peppers
1 pound lean ground beef
1/3 cup chopped onion
1/3 cup chopped celery
3 cups cooked rice
1-1/4 cups salsa, *divided*
1 tablespoon chopped green chilies
2 teaspoons chili powder
1/4 teaspoon salt
1 cup (4 ounces) shredded reduced-fat Mexican blend cheese

Cut tops off peppers and discard; remove seeds. In a Dutch oven or large kettle, cook peppers in boiling water for 3-5 minutes. Drain and rinse in cold water; set aside.

In a nonstick skillet, cook the beef, onion and celery over medium heat until meat is no longer pink; drain. Stir in the rice, 1 cup salsa, chilies, chili powder and salt. Spoon into peppers.

Place in a 13-in. x 9-in. x 2-in. baking dish coated with nonstick cooking spray. Add 1/4 cup water to dish. Cover and bake at 350° for 45-50 minutes or until heated through. Uncover; sprinkle with cheese and top with remaining salsa. Bake 2-3 minutes longer or until cheese is melted. **yield:** 6 servings.

nutrition facts: 1 stuffed pepper equals 334 calories, 9 g fat (4 g saturated fat), 44 mg cholesterol, 665 mg sodium, 41 g carbohydrate, 3 g fiber, 23 g protein.

green chili burritos

prep/total time 30 minutes

1 can (16 ounces) refried beans
8 flour tortillas (6 inches), warmed
1/2 pound ground beef, cooked and drained
1 cup (4 ounces) shredded sharp cheddar cheese, *divided*
1 can (4-1/2 ounces) chopped green chilies

Spread refried beans over tortillas. Top each with beef and 2 tablespoons of cheese. Fold ends and sides over filling and roll up; place seam side down in a greased 13-in. x 9-in. x 2-in. baking dish. Sprinkle with chilies and remaining cheese.

Bake, uncovered, at 350° for 20 minutes or until heated through. **yield:** 4 servings.

kathy ybarra
rock springs, wyoming

Both my husband and I love home-cooked Mexican food, so I usually have all of the ingredients for these tasty burritos on hand. A woman from our church shared the simple recipe.

firecracker casserole

prep 15 minutes | **bake** 25 minutes

teressa eastman
el dorado, kansas

Growing up, I couldn't get enough of this Southwestern casserole my mother often made. Now I fix it for my husband and me. The flavor reminds us of enchiladas.

2 pounds ground beef
1 medium onion, chopped
1 can (15 ounces) black beans, rinsed and drained
1 to 2 tablespoons chili powder
2 to 3 teaspoons ground cumin
1/2 teaspoon salt
4 flour tortillas (6 inches)
1 can (10-3/4 ounces) condensed cream of mushroom soup, undiluted
1 can (10 ounces) diced tomatoes and green chilies, undrained
1 cup (4 ounces) shredded cheddar cheese

In a skillet, cook the beef and onion over medium heat until the meat is no longer pink; drain. Add beans, chili powder, cumin and salt.

Transfer to a greased 13-in. x 9-in. x 2-in. baking dish. Arrange tortillas over the top. Combine soup and tomatoes; pour over the tortillas. Sprinkle with cheese.

Bake, uncovered, at 350° for 25-30 minutes or until heated through. **yield:** 8 servings.

beef quesadillas

prep/total time 30 minutes

3/4   pound ground beef
1/2   cup refried beans
1   can (4 ounces) chopped green chilies, drained
1/2   teaspoon dried oregano
1/2   teaspoon ground cumin
1/4   teaspoon salt
4   flour tortillas (8 inches)
2   tablespoons butter, melted
1-1/3   cups shredded taco cheese
Paprika

In a large skillet, cook the beef over medium heat until no longer pink; drain. Stir in the beans, chilies, oregano, cumin and salt. Cook over medium-low heat for 3-4 minutes or until heated through.

Brush one side of each tortilla with butter. Spoon 1/2 cup of the meat mixture over half of unbuttered side. Sprinkle with 1/3 cup cheese; fold in half.

Place on a lightly greased baking sheet. Sprinkle with paprika. Bake at 475° for 10 minutes or until crisp and golden brown. Cut into wedges. **yield:** 4 servings.

taste of home test kitchen
greendale, wisconsin

For a 30-minute Mexican meal, try these quesadillas. They're especially good with toppings such as sour cream, salsa, guacamole, chopped tomatoes and lettuce.

western chili casserole

prep/total time 25 minutes

terri mock
american falls, idaho

In our busy household, easy yet scrumptious meals are a must. This crunchy bake that uses convenient canned chili really fills the bill.

1   pound ground beef
1   large onion, chopped
1   celery rib, chopped
1   can (15 ounces) chili with beans
1-1/2   cups corn chips, coarsely crushed, *divided*
3/4   cup shredded cheddar cheese

In a large skillet, cook the beef, onion and celery over medium heat until meat is no longer pink and vegetables are tender; drain. Stir in the chili and 1/2 cup of chips.

Transfer to a greased 1-1/2-qt. baking dish. Sprinkle remaining chips around edge of dish; fill center with cheese. Bake, uncovered, at 350° for 10 minutes or until heated through. **yield:** 4 servings.

beef chimichangas

prep 25 minutes | **cook** 15 minutes

1 pound ground beef
1/2 cup finely chopped onion
1 can (16 ounces) refried beans
3 cans (8 ounces *each*) tomato sauce, *divided*
2 teaspoons chili powder
1 teaspoon minced garlic
1/2 teaspoon ground cumin
12 flour tortillas (10 inches)
1 can (4 ounces) chopped green chilies
1 can (4 ounces) chopped jalapeno peppers
Oil for deep-fat frying
1-1/2 cups (6 ounces) shredded cheddar cheese

In a large skillet, cook beef over medium heat until no longer pink; drain. Stir in the onion, beans, 1/2 cup tomato sauce, chili powder, garlic and cumin.

Spoon about 1/3 cup of the beef mixture off-center on each tortilla. Fold the edge nearest the filling up and over to cover. Fold in both sides and roll up. Fasten with toothpicks. In a large saucepan, combine the chilies, peppers and remaining tomato sauce; heat through.

In an electric skillet or deep-fat fryer, heat 1 in. of oil to 375°. Fry the chimichangas for 1-1/2 to 2 minutes on each side or until browned. Drain on paper towels. Sprinkle with cheese. Serve with sauce. **yield:** 1 dozen.

editor's note: Chimichangas may be baked instead of fried. Brush with melted butter and bake at 350° for 25-30 minutes or until golden brown (if frozen, thaw before baking).

schelby thompson
camden wyoming, delaware

A spicy sauce adds spark to these tasty beef-and-bean tortillas. I just fry them for a few minutes, sprinkle on some cheese and serve.

quick taco platter

prep/total time 30 minutes

2 pounds ground beef
2 cans (15 ounces *each*) tomato sauce
2 envelopes taco seasoning
Tortilla *or* corn chips
Shredded lettuce, chopped tomato, chopped onion and shredded cheddar cheese

In a skillet, cook the beef over medium heat until no longer pink; drain. Stir in tomato sauce and taco seasoning; simmer for 15 minutes, stirring occasionally. Cover a serving platter with chips; top with lettuce. Layer with beef mixture, tomato, onion and cheese. **yield:** 6-8 servings.

celia rixman

sylmar, california

This speedy main dish is like a huge, layered taco salad. It's great to have a recipe that's so simple to fix yet pleases the whole gang.

popular potluck casserole

prep 25 minutes | **bake** 25 minutes

debbi smith

crossett, arkansas

For a crowd-size amount, count on this macaroni casserole. It has plenty of Tex-Mex taste and never lasts long on a potluck table.

1 package (7 ounces) ring macaroni
2 pounds ground beef
1 medium onion, chopped
1/4 cup chopped green pepper
1/4 cup thinly sliced celery
1 can (10-3/4 ounces) condensed cream of mushroom soup, undiluted
1 can (10 ounces) diced tomatoes with green chilies
1 can (8 ounces) tomato sauce
1 to 2 tablespoons chili powder
1 can (15-1/4 ounces) whole kernel corn, drained
2 cups (8 ounces) shredded cheddar cheese, *divided*

Cook macaroni according to package directions. Meanwhile, in a large skillet, cook the beef, onion, green pepper and celery over medium heat until meat is no longer pink and vegetables are tender; drain. Stir in the soup, tomatoes, tomato sauce and chili powder until combined.

Drain the macaroni; stir into beef mixture. Add corn and 1-1/2 cups of cheddar cheese. Transfer to a greased 13-in. x 9-in. x 2-in. baking dish. Sprinkle with the remaining cheese. Bake, uncovered, at 350° for 25-30 minutes or until heated through. **yield:** 10-12 servings.

au gratin taco bake

prep 15 minutes | **bake** 70 minutes

1 pound ground beef
1 package (4.9 ounces) au gratin potatoes
1 can (15-1/4 ounces) whole kernel corn, undrained
1 can (14-1/2 ounces) no-salt-added stewed tomatoes, undrained
3/4 cup milk
1/2 cup water
2 tablespoons taco seasoning
1 cup (4 ounces) shredded cheddar cheese

In a large skillet, cook beef over medium heat until no longer pink; drain. Stir in the potatoes and contents of sauce mix, corn, tomatoes, milk, water and taco seasoning. Transfer to a greased 2-qt. baking dish.

Cover and bake at 350° for 65-70 minutes or until potatoes are tender. Sprinkle with cheddar cheese. Bake, uncovered, 5 minutes longer or until cheese is melted. **yield:** 4-6 servings.

linda muir

big lake, minnesota

This hearty hot dish takes advantage of packaged au gratin potatoes. Chock-full of beef, corn, tomatoes and cheddar, the Southwestern casserole is a winner with everyone who tastes it.

beef 'n' bean enchiladas

prep/total time 30 minutes

linda lundmark

martinton, illinois

After cooking ground beef in the microwave, I combine it with canned bean dip and chilies to fill flour tortillas. Cheese and olives jazz up the prepared enchilada sauce.

3 tablespoons all-purpose flour
1 teaspoon salt, *divided*
1/4 teaspoon paprika
1-1/2 cups milk
1 can (10 ounces) enchilada sauce
1 cup (4 ounces) shredded cheddar cheese
1 can (2-1/4 ounces) sliced ripe olives, drained
3/4 pound ground beef
1 medium onion, chopped
1 can (9 ounces) bean dip
1 can (4 ounces) chopped green chilies
1/8 teaspoon pepper
1 large tomato, seeded and diced
9 white *or* yellow corn tortillas (6 inches), warmed

In a 1-qt. microwave-safe bowl, combine the flour, 1/2 teaspoon salt, paprika, milk and enchilada sauce until smooth. Microwave, uncovered, on high for 1-1/2 minutes; stir. Cook 3-4 minutes longer or until thickened, stirring every minute. Stir in cheese and olives; set aside.

Place beef and onion in a microwave-safe dish. Cover and microwave on high for 3-4 minutes or until meat is no longer pink; drain. Stir in the bean dip, chilies, pepper and remaining salt.

Spoon about 1/3 cup meat mixture and 1 tablespoon of diced tomato down the center of each tortilla; roll up tightly.

Place enchiladas seam side down in an ungreased 11-in. x 7-in. x 2-in. microwave-safe dish. Top with sauce. Microwave, uncovered, on high for 7-8 minutes or until bubbly around the edges, rotating dish twice. **yield:** 4 servings.

editor's note: This recipe was tested in a 1,100-watt microwave.

chuck wagon wraps

prep/total time 25 minutes

  1 pound lean ground beef
  1 can (28 ounces) barbecue-flavored baked beans
  2 cups frozen corn, thawed
4-1/2 teaspoons Worcestershire sauce
  1 cup (4 ounces) shredded cheddar cheese
  12 flour tortillas (8 inches), warmed
  3 cups shredded lettuce
1-1/2 cups chopped fresh tomatoes
  3/4 cup sour cream

wendy conger
winfield, illinois

If you're a fan of baked beans, you'll love this robust wrap. I mix the beans with beef, corn and cheese, then roll it all up in tortillas.

In a large nonstick skillet, cook beef over medium heat until no longer pink; drain. Stir in beans, corn and Worcestershire sauce; mix well. Bring to a boil.

Reduce heat; simmer, uncovered, for 4-5 minutes or until heated through. Sprinkle with cheese; cook 1-2 minutes longer. Spoon about 1/2 cup off center on each tortilla; top with lettuce, tomatoes and sour cream. Roll up. **yield:** 12 servings.

southwestern rice bake

prep 15 minutes | **bake** 20 minutes

sheila johnson
red feather lakes, colorado

Whenever I'm wondering what to make for dinner, my husband requests his favorite casserole. It's so satisfying, no side dishes are ever necessary!

  3 cups cooked brown *or* white rice
1/2 pound ground beef, cooked and drained
1-1/4 cups sour cream
  1 cup (4 ounces) shredded Monterey Jack cheese, *divided*
  1 cup (4 ounces) shredded cheddar cheese, *divided*
  1 can (4 ounces) chopped green chilies
1/2 teaspoon salt
1/4 teaspoon pepper
Sliced ripe olives, chopped tomatoes and green onions, optional

In a large bowl, combine the rice, beef, sour cream, 3/4 cup of Monterey Jack cheese, 3/4 cup of cheddar cheese, chilies, salt and pepper.

Spoon into a greased 1-1/2-qt. baking dish. Sprinkle with remaining cheeses. Bake, uncovered, at 350° for 20-25 minutes or until heated through. Serve with olives, tomatoes and onions if desired. **yield:** 4 servings.

cheddar beef enchiladas

prep 30 minutes | **bake** 20 minutes

- 1 pound ground beef
- 1 envelope taco seasoning
- 1 cup water
- 2 cups cooked rice
- 1 can (16 ounces) refried beans
- 2 cups (8 ounces) shredded cheddar cheese, *divided*
- 10 to 12 flour tortillas (8 inches), warmed
- 1 jar (16 ounces) salsa
- 1 can (10-3/4 ounces) condensed cream of chicken soup, undiluted

In a large skillet, cook the beef over medium heat until no longer pink; drain. Stir in the taco seasoning and water. Bring to a boil. Reduce the heat; simmer, uncovered, for 5 minutes. Stir in the rice. Cook and stir until the liquid is evaporated.

Spread about 2 tablespoons of refried beans, 1/4 cup beef mixture and 1 tablespoon cheese down the center of each tortilla; roll up. Place seam side down in two greased 13-in. x 9-in. x 2-in. baking dishes.

Combine salsa and soup; pour down the center of enchiladas. Sprinkle with remaining cheese. Bake one casserole, uncovered, at 350° for 20-25 minutes or until heated through and cheese is melted. Cover and freeze remaining casserole for up to 3 months.

TO USE FROZEN CASSEROLE: Thaw in the refrigerator overnight. Cover and bake at 350° for 30 minutes. Uncover; bake 5-10 minutes longer or until heated through and cheese is melted. **yield:** 2 casseroles (5-6 enchiladas each).

stacy cizek
conrad, iowa

When these cheesy roll-ups pleased the picky eaters in our family, I knew I had a winning main dish. The recipe makes two pans— one to keep in the freezer for another time.

crispy beef tostadas

prep 35 minutes + resting | **cook** 20 minutes

joy rackham
chimacum, washington

I experimented with the ingredients in this one-dish meal many times, and now it's a favorite. I even made several batches of tostadas and served them at a party.

3 cups all-purpose flour
5 teaspoons baking powder
1-1/4 cups milk
1 pound ground beef
2 garlic cloves, minced
1 can (4 ounces) chopped green chilies
1 envelope taco seasoning
3/4 cup water
1 can (16 ounces) refried beans
Oil for deep-fat frying
Picante sauce
Shredded lettuce
Finely chopped green onions
Diced tomatoes
Shredded cheddar cheese

In a large bowl, combine flour and baking powder; add the milk to form a soft dough. Cover and let rest for 1 hour.

About 30 minutes before serving, in a large skillet, cook beef over medium heat until no longer pink; drain. Stir in garlic, chilies, taco seasoning and water; simmer for 10 minutes. Stir in beans; heat through and keep warm.

Divide dough into sixths. On a lightly floured surface, roll each portion into a 7-in. circle. In a deep-fat fryer, preheat oil to 375°. Fry tostadas in hot oil until golden, turning once; drain on paper towels. Top each with meat mixture, picante sauce, lettuce, onions, tomatoes and cheese. **yield:** 6 servings.

taco casserole

prep 20 minutes | **bake** 20 minutes

- 2-1/2 pounds ground beef
- 2 packages taco seasoning
- 2/3 cup water
- 1 can (16 ounces) kidney beans, rinsed and drained
- 1 cup (4 ounces) shredded Monterey Jack *or* pepper Jack cheese
- 2 eggs, lightly beaten
- 1 cup milk
- 1-1/2 cups biscuit/baking mix
- 1 cup (8 ounces) sour cream
- 1 cup (4 ounces) shredded cheddar cheese
- 2 cups shredded lettuce
- 1 medium tomato, diced
- 1 can (2-1/4 ounces) sliced ripe olives, drained

In a large skillet, cook the beef over medium heat until no longer pink; drain. Stir in the taco seasoning and water. Bring to a boil. Reduce the heat and simmer for 5 minutes. Stir in the beans.

Spoon meat mixture into a greased 8-in. square baking dish. Sprinkle with Monterey Jack cheese. In a large bowl, combine the eggs, milk and biscuit mix until moistened. Pour over cheese.

Bake, uncovered, at 400° for 20-25 minutes or until lightly browned and a knife inserted near the center comes out clean. Spread with sour cream. Top with cheddar cheese, lettuce, tomato and olives. **yield:** 6-8 servings.

bonnie king
lansing, michigan

When you're bored with traditional tacos, give this filling main dish a try. It puts the same Southwestern taste into a comforting casserole.

southwest pasta bake

prep 15 minutes | **bake** 30 minutes + standing

carol lepak
sheboygan, wisconsin

Cream cheese and cheddar make this pasta casserole wonderfully rich and creamy. It's a great way to get family members to eat spinach!

- 8 ounces uncooked penne pasta
- 1 package (8 ounces) cream cheese, cubed
- 1/2 cup milk
- 1 package (10 ounces) frozen chopped spinach, thawed and squeezed dry
- 1 teaspoon dried oregano
- 1 pound lean ground beef
- 2 garlic cloves, minced
- 1 jar (16 ounces) picante sauce
- 1 can (8 ounces) tomato sauce
- 1 can (6 ounces) tomato paste
- 2 teaspoons chili powder
- 1 teaspoon ground cumin
- 1 cup (4 ounces) shredded cheddar cheese
- 1 can (2-1/4 ounces) sliced ripe olives, drained
- 1/4 cup sliced green onions

Cook pasta according to package directions. Meanwhile, in a small mixing bowl, beat cream cheese until smooth. Beat in milk. Stir in spinach and oregano; set aside.

In a nonstick skillet, cook beef and garlic over medium heat until meat is no longer pink; drain. Stir in the picante sauce, tomato sauce, tomato paste, chili powder and cumin; bring to a boil. Reduce heat; simmer, uncovered, for 5 minutes. Drain pasta; stir into meat mixture.

In a 13-in. x 9-in. x 2-in. baking dish coated with nonstick cooking spray, layer half of the meat mixture and all of the spinach mixture. Top with remaining meat mixture.

Cover and bake at 350° for 30 minutes. Uncover; sprinkle with cheese. Bake 5 minutes longer or until cheese is melted. Sprinkle with olives and onions. Let stand for 10 minutes before serving. **yield:** 8 servings.

sensational SAGE

In recipes such as Garlic Beef Enchiladas that use "rubbed" sage, take the whole dried leaf and crush or rub it to make a finely textured powder. Most dried sage sold in the spice section of the grocery store is rubbed this way.

garlic beef enchiladas

prep 30 minutes | **bake** 40 minutes

jennifer standridge
dallas, georgia

Enchiladas are typically prepared with corn tortillas, but my husband and I prefer the flour variety. That's what I use in this saucy casserole.

1 pound ground beef
1 medium onion, chopped
2 tablespoons all-purpose flour
1 tablespoon chili powder
1 teaspoon salt
1 teaspoon garlic powder
1/2 teaspoon ground cumin
1/4 teaspoon rubbed sage
1 can (14-1/2 ounces) stewed tomatoes

sauce
4 to 6 garlic cloves, minced
1/3 cup butter
1/2 cup all-purpose flour
1 can (14-1/2 ounces) beef broth
1 can (15 ounces) tomato sauce
1 to 2 tablespoons chili powder
1 to 2 teaspoons ground cumin
1 to 2 teaspoons rubbed sage
1/2 teaspoon salt
10 flour tortillas (7 inches)
2 cups (8 ounces) shredded Colby-Monterey Jack cheese

In a saucepan, cook beef and onion over medium heat until meat is no longer pink; drain. Stir in the flour and seasonings until blended. Stir in tomatoes; bring to a boil. Reduce heat; cover and simmer for 15 minutes.

Meanwhile, in another saucepan, saute garlic in butter until tender. Stir in flour until blended. Gradually stir in broth; bring to a boil. Cook and stir for 2 minutes or until thickened. Stir in tomato sauce and seasonings; heat through.

Pour about 1-1/2 cups sauce into an ungreased 13-in. x 9-in. x 2-in. baking dish. Spread about 1/4 cup beef mixture down the center of each tortilla; top with 1-2 tablespoons cheese. Roll up tightly; place seam side down over sauce. Top with the remaining sauce.

Cover and bake at 350° for 30-35 minutes. Sprinkle with remaining cheese. Bake, uncovered, 10-15 minutes longer or until the cheese is melted. **yield:** 4-6 servings.

chilies rellenos casserole

prep 15 minutes | **bake** 45 minutes

nadine estes
alto, new mexico

I love green chilies and like to cook with them when I entertain. This beefy main dish gives you big pepper taste in every bite.

1 can (7 ounces) whole green chilies
1-1/2 cups (6 ounces) shredded Colby-Monterey Jack cheese
3/4 pound ground beef
1/4 cup chopped onion
1 cup milk
4 eggs
1/4 cup all-purpose flour
1/4 teaspoon salt
1/8 teaspoon pepper

Split chilies and remove seeds; dry on paper towels. Arrange chilies on the bottom of a greased 2-qt. baking dish. Top with cheese. In a skillet, cook beef and onion over medium heat until meat is no longer pink; drain. Spoon over the cheese.

In a mixing bowl, beat milk, eggs, flour, salt and pepper until smooth; pour over beef mixture. Bake, uncovered, at 350° for 45-50 minutes or until a knife inserted near the center comes out clean. Let stand 5 minutes before serving. **yield:** 6 servings.

editor's note: When cutting or seeding hot peppers, use rubber or plastic gloves to protect your hands. Avoid touching your face.

---

taco plate for two

prep/total time 15 minutes

1/2 pound ground beef
1/2 cup chopped onion
1/3 cup taco sauce
1/4 cup chopped green chilies
1/4 teaspoon salt
1 cup broken tortilla chips
1/2 cup shredded cheddar cheese

sue ross
casa grande, arizona

My husband and I enjoy splitting this two-serving taco plate and don't have to worry about leftovers. But the recipe is easy to double if needed.

In a skillet, cook beef and onion over medium heat until meat is no longer pink; drain. Stir in the taco sauce, chilies and salt. Cover and cook over medium-low heat for 6-8 minutes or until heated though. Spoon over chips; sprinkle with cheese. **yield:** 2 servings.

mexican chip casserole

prep/total time 20 minutes

1 pound ground beef
1 medium onion, chopped
1 garlic clove, minced
1 can (10-3/4 ounces) condensed cream of mushroom soup, undiluted
1 can (11 ounces) Mexicorn
1 can (4 ounces) chopped green chilies
1 package (10-1/2 ounces) corn chips
1 can (10 ounces) enchilada sauce
1 to 2 cups (4 to 8 ounces) shredded Colby-Monterey Jack cheese

doris heath
franklin, north carolina

From start to finish, this crunchy casserole takes a mere 20 minutes to make. I have time to set the table while it's in the oven.

In a skillet, cook beef, onion and garlic over medium heat until meat is no longer pink and onion is tender; drain. Add soup, corn and chilies; mix well.

In an ungreased shallow 3-qt. baking dish, layer meat mixture, chips and sauce; top with cheese. Bake, uncovered, at 350° for 8-10 minutes or until heated through. **yield:** 6 servings.

tamale casserole

prep 10 minutes | bake 45 minutes + standing

kathleen reid
petaluma, california

Want to "heat up" your dinner routine? With diced jalapeno pepper, this easy main dish is guaranteed to put a little kick in your menu.

1 pound lean ground beef
1 jalapeno pepper, seeded and diced
2 cups frozen corn, thawed
1 can (28 ounces) diced tomatoes, undrained
1-1/2 cups milk
1 cup cornmeal
1 can (4 ounces) chopped green chilies, drained
1 can (2-1/2 ounces) sliced ripe olives, drained
2 egg whites, lightly beaten
1 envelope taco seasoning
1 cup (4 ounces) shredded cheddar cheese
1 cup salsa

In a large nonstick skillet, cook beef and jalapeno over medium heat until meat is no longer pink; drain. Stir in the corn, tomatoes, milk, cornmeal, chilies, olives, egg whites and taco seasoning until blended.

Transfer to a 13-in. x 9-in. x 2-in. baking dish coated with nonstick cooking spray. Bake, uncovered, at 350° for 40 minutes. Sprinkle with cheese. Bake 5 minutes longer or until cheese is melted. Let stand for 10 minutes before cutting. Serve with salsa. **yield:** 8 servings.

editor's note: When cutting or seeding hot peppers, use rubber or plastic gloves to protect your hands. Avoid touching your face.

sour cream beef 'n' beans

prep/total time 15 minutes

1   pound ground beef
1   can (15 ounces) pinto beans, rinsed and drained
1   can (15 ounces) enchilada sauce
1-1/2   cups (6 ounces) shredded cheddar cheese, *divided*
1   can (4 ounces) chopped green chilies, undrained
1-1/2   cups crushed corn chips
1   tablespoon dried minced onion
1   cup (8 ounces) sour cream
Additional corn chips

Crumble beef into an ungreased 2-qt. microwave-safe dish; cover with waxed paper. Cook on high for 3-4 minutes or until meat is no longer pink, stirring twice; drain. Stir in the beans, enchilada sauce, 1 cup of cheese, chilies, crushed corn chips and onion. Cover and microwave on high for 2 to 2-1/2 minutes or until heated through, stirring once.

Top with the sour cream and remaining cheese. Heat, uncovered, at 70% power for 1-2 minutes or until cheese is melted. Serve with corn chips. **yield:** 4-6 servings.

editor's note: This recipe was tested in a 1,100-watt microwave.

joyce marten
cottonwood, arizona

This was originally an oven recipe that I adapted for the microwave. When I serve the creamy beef and beans to friends, I always hear raves.

tortilla **TREAT**

Have an opened package of tortillas left over from the Taco Burritos? Make a fast dessert. Simply brush the tortillas with butter and sprinkle on some cinnamon-sugar. Then cut them into wedges and bake them on a cookie sheet until crisp.

taco burritos

prep/total time 25 minutes

katie koziolek

hartland, minnesota

Full of beef, peppers and south-of-the-border flair, these burritos are a great way to spice up dinnertime. The flour tortillas bake to a wonderful crispness.

1-1/2   pounds ground beef
1   green pepper, chopped
1   medium onion, chopped
2   garlic cloves, minced
1   envelope taco seasoning
1/4   cup water
8   flour tortillas
1   tablespoon vegetable oil
Taco toppings of your choice

In a large skillet, cook the beef, green pepper and onion over medium heat until meat is no longer pink; drain. Add the garlic, taco seasoning and water. Simmer, uncovered, for 2 minutes.

Place four tortillas on a microwave-safe plate; microwave on high for 20 seconds. Place 1/2 cup of meat mixture on each; fold over sides and ends. Place seam side down in a greased 13-in. x 9-in. x 2-in. baking dish. Repeat with remaining tortillas and filling.

Brush burritos with oil. Bake, uncovered, at 450° for 9-10 minutes or until lightly browned and slightly crisp. Serve with toppings of your choice. **yield:** 8 servings.

taco pie

prep 20 minutes | **bake** 25 minutes

1   pound ground beef
1   large onion, chopped
1/2   cup salsa
2   tablespoons taco seasoning
1/4   teaspoon pepper
1   cup (4 ounces) shredded cheddar cheese
2   eggs
1   cup milk
1/2   cup biscuit/baking mix

In a large skillet, cook beef and onion over medium heat until meat is no longer pink; drain. Stir in salsa, taco seasoning and pepper. Transfer to a greased 9-in. pie plate; sprinkle with cheese.

In a large bowl, combine the eggs, milk and biscuit mix just until blended; pour over cheese. Bake at 400° for 25-30 minutes or until a knife inserted near the center comes out clean. **yield:** 6 servings.

shelly winkleblack

interlaken, new york

Biscuit ingredients and taco fixings are all you'll need to create this zippy pie. Use your favorite salsa to make it as mild or as hot as you wish.

meaty mexican sandwiches

prep 20 minutes | **cook** 30 minutes

1/2 pound ground pork
1/2 pound ground beef
1 small onion, chopped
1 garlic clove, minced
3/4 cup ketchup
1/2 cup raisins
1 teaspoon red wine vinegar
1/2 teaspoon ground cinnamon
1/2 teaspoon chili powder
1/2 teaspoon salt
1/4 teaspoon pepper
1/8 teaspoon ground cumin
Pinch ground cloves
1/2 cup slivered almonds, toasted
6 hard rolls, split
1-1/2 cups (6 ounces) shredded cheddar cheese
2 cups shredded lettuce

In a large skillet, cook pork, beef, onion and garlic over medium heat until meat is no longer pink; drain. Stir in the ketchup, raisins, vinegar and seasonings. Cover and simmer for 20-25 minutes, stirring occasionally. Stir in almonds.

Hollow out the top and bottom of each roll, leaving a 1/2-in. shell. (Discard removed bread or save for another use.) Fill each roll with about 1/2 cup meat mixture. Top with cheese and lettuce; replace top of roll. **yield:** 6 servings.

teri spaulding
durham, california

I like to serve these hearty sandwiches on Super Bowl Sunday along with a salad and beans. Everyone raves about the great combination of flavors and textures.

texas taco platter

prep 20 minutes | **cook** 1-1/2 hours

kathy young
weatherford, texas

This fun dish is one of my top menu choices when I'm entertaining. No one can resist the beefy entree topped with cheese, lettuce, tomatoes and olives.

2 pounds ground beef
1 large onion, chopped
1 can (14-1/2 ounces) diced tomatoes, undrained
1 can (12 ounces) tomato paste
1 can (15 ounces) tomato puree
2 tablespoons chili powder
1 teaspoon ground cumin
1/2 teaspoon garlic powder
2 teaspoons salt
2 cans (15 ounces *each*) ranch-style beans, undrained
1 package (10-1/2 ounces) corn chips
2 cups hot cooked rice

toppings
2 cups (8 ounces *each*) shredded cheddar cheese
1 medium onion, chopped
1 medium head iceberg lettuce, shredded
3 medium tomatoes, chopped
1 can (2-1/4 ounces) sliced ripe olives, drained
1 cup picante sauce, optional

In a large skillet or Dutch oven, cook beef and onion over medium heat until meat is no longer pink; drain. Add next seven ingredients; simmer for 1-1/2 hours.

Add beans and heat though. On a platter, layer the corn chips, rice, meat mixture, cheese, onion, lettuce, tomatoes and olives. Serve with picante sauce if desired. **yield:** 10-12 servings.

enchilada stack

prep/total time 30 minutes

doreen adams

sacramento, california

I tried this fast and flavorful casserole when I bought my first microwave many years ago. The easy enchilada dish is still a family favorite.

1 pound ground beef
1/4 cup chopped onion
1 garlic clove, minced
1 can (8 ounces) tomato sauce
1/4 cup water
1 to 2 teaspoons chili powder
1/2 teaspoon salt
1/4 teaspoon pepper
4 corn tortillas (6 inches)
2 cups (8 ounces) shredded cheddar cheese

In an ungreased 2-qt. microwave-safe dish, combine the beef, onion and garlic. Cover and cook on high for 3-4 minutes or until meat is no longer pink, stirring once; drain. Stir in tomato sauce, water, chili powder, salt and pepper. Cover and cook on high for 6 minutes, stirring once.

In an ungreased 1-1/2-qt. round dish, layer one tortilla, 1/2 cup meat sauce and 1/2 cup cheese. Repeat layers three times. Heat, uncovered, on high for 45 seconds or until the cheese is melted. **yield:** 4 servings.

editor's note: This recipe was tested in a 1,100-watt microwave.

corn bread taco bake

prep 20 minutes | **bake** 25 minutes

1-1/2 pounds ground beef
1 can (15-1/4 ounces) whole kernel corn, drained
1 can (8 ounces) tomato sauce
1/2 cup water
1/2 cup chopped green pepper
1 envelope taco seasoning
1 package (8-1/2 ounces) corn bread/muffin mix
1 can (2.8 ounces) french-fried onions, *divided*
1/3 cup shredded cheddar cheese

vicki good

oscoda, michigan

A packaged corn bread mix speeds up the preparation of this can't-miss casserole. The cheddar cheese and french-fried onions make an irresistible topping.

In a large skillet, cook beef over medium heat until no longer pink; drain. Stir in the corn, tomato sauce, water, green pepper and taco seasoning. Spoon into a greased 2-qt. baking dish.

Prepare the corn bread mix according to the package directions for corn bread. Stir in half of the onions. Spread over the beef mixture. Bake, uncovered, at 400° for 20 minutes.

Sprinkle with cheese and remaining onions. Bake 3-5 minutes longer or until cheese is melted and a toothpick inserted into corn bread layer comes out clean. **yield:** 6 servings.

mom's tamale pie

prep 25 minutes | **bake** 20 minutes

- 2 pounds ground beef
- 1 large onion, chopped
- 1 large green pepper, chopped
- 1 can (15-1/4 ounces) whole kernel corn, undrained
- 1-1/2 cups chopped fresh tomatoes
- 5 tablespoons tomato paste
- 1 envelope chili seasoning
- 1-1/2 teaspoons sugar
- 1 teaspoon garlic powder
- 1 teaspoon dried basil
- 1 teaspoon dried oregano
- 6 cups cooked grits (prepared with butter and salt)
- 1-1/2 teaspoons chili powder, *divided*
- 1-1/2 cups (6 ounces) shredded cheddar cheese

In a large skillet, cook the beef, onion and green pepper over medium heat until meat is no longer pink; drain. Add the corn, tomatoes, tomato paste, chili seasoning, sugar, garlic powder, basil and oregano. Cook and stir until heated through; keep warm.

Spread half of the grits in a greased 3-qt. baking dish. Sprinkle with 1 teaspoon chili powder. Top with beef mixture and cheese. Pipe remaining grits around edge of dish; sprinkle with remaining chili powder.

Bake, uncovered, at 325° for 20-25 minutes or until cheese is melted. Let stand for 5 minutes before serving. **yield:** 12 servings.

nutrition facts: 1 serving equals 296 calories, 12 g fat (6 g saturated fat), 52 mg cholesterol, 725 mg sodium, 27 g carbohydrate, 2 g fiber, 20 g protein.

  This beef recipe is lighter in calories, fat and sodium.

waldine guillott
dequincy, louisiana

I don't recall my mom ever using a recipe for her tamale pie, but I came up with this version that tastes very much like hers did. The grits add a Southern accent.

beef tortilla casserole

prep/total time 30 minutes

- 2 pounds ground beef
- 1 medium onion, chopped
- 1 bottle (8 ounces) taco sauce
- 6 corn tortillas (6 inches), halved and cut into 1-inch strips
- 2 cups (16 ounces) sour cream
- 1 cup (4 ounces) shredded cheddar cheese
- 1 cup (4 ounces) shredded part-skim mozzarella cheese

Crumble beef into a large microwave-safe dish. Stir in onion. Microwave, uncovered, on high for 6-7 minutes or until meat is no longer pink, stirring and draining every 2 minutes. Stir in taco sauce and tortillas.

In a greased 2-1/2-qt. microwave-safe dish, layer half of the beef mixture, sour cream and cheeses. Repeat layers. Cover and cook at 70% power for 7-9 minutes or until heated through. Let stand for 2-4 minutes before serving. **yield:** 6-8 servings.

editor's note: This recipe was tested in a 1,100-watt microwave.

patty burchett
louisville, kentucky

Your favorite taco sauce will add the spark to this beefy bake. Mozzarella, cheddar and sour cream make every helping rich and satisfying.

enchilada casserole

prep 20 minutes | **bake** 40 minutes

julie huffman
new lebanon, ohio

I get two family-pleasing casseroles when I prepare this convenient recipe. I pop one in the freezer and serve the other one with some rice and black beans.

- 1-1/2 pounds ground beef
- 1 large onion, chopped
- 1 cup water
- 2 to 3 tablespoons chili powder
- 1-1/2 teaspoons salt
- 1/2 teaspoon pepper
- 1/4 teaspoon garlic powder
- 2 cups salsa, *divided*
- 10 flour tortillas (8 inches), cut into 3/4-inch strips, *divided*
- 1 cup (8 ounces) sour cream
- 2 cans (15-1/4 ounces *each*) whole kernel corn, drained
- 4 cups (16 ounces) shredded part-skim mozzarella cheese

In a large skillet, cook beef and onion over medium heat until meat is no longer pink; drain. Stir in water, chili powder, salt, pepper and garlic powder. Bring to a boil. Reduce heat; simmer, uncovered, for 10 minutes.

Place 1/4 cup salsa each in two greased 8-in. square baking dishes. Layer each dish with a fourth of the tortillas and 1/4 cup salsa.

Divide meat mixture, sour cream and corn between the two casseroles. Top with remaining tortillas, salsa and cheese.

Cover and freeze one casserole for up to 1 month. Cover and bake second casserole at 350° for 35 minutes. Uncover; bake 5-10 minutes longer or until heated through.

TO USE FROZEN CASSEROLE: Thaw the casserole in the refrigerator for 24 hours. Remove from the refrigerator 30 minutes before baking. Bake as directed above. **yield:** 2 casseroles (4-6 servings each).

seasoned taco meat

prep 25 minutes | **cook** 10 minutes

This beef recipe is lighter in calories, fat and sodium.

margaret peterson
forest city, iowa

This party-size recipe blends plenty of ground beef and zippy seasonings. Turn the big batch of meat into a taco supper for hungry guests.

4 pounds ground beef
3 tablespoons chopped onion
1 can (14-1/2 ounces) beef broth
1 can (8 ounces) tomato sauce
1/4 cup chili powder
2 tablespoons paprika
1 tablespoon beef bouillon granules
1 tablespoon ground cumin
1 teaspoon chicken bouillon granules
1 teaspoon garlic powder
1 teaspoon cayenne pepper
1/2 teaspoon pepper
1/2 teaspoon lime juice
1/4 teaspoon onion powder
1/4 teaspoon sugar
1/4 teaspoon salt
1/4 teaspoon garlic salt
Taco shells *or* flour tortillas
Shredded cheese and salsa

In a Dutch oven, cook the beef and onion over medium heat until meat is no longer pink; drain. Stir in the next 15 ingredients. Bring to a boil. Reduce heat; cover and simmer for 10 minutes.

Serve in taco shells or tortillas with shredded cheese and salsa. **yield:** 8 cups.

nutrition facts: 1/4 cup equals 98 calories, 5 g fat (2 g saturated fat), 28 mg cholesterol, 260 mg sodium, 2 g carbohydrate, 1 g fiber, 10 g protein.

defrosting DO'S

For best results, defrost ground beef in the refrigerator and use it within 1 to 2 days. Allow 24 hours for a 1- to 1-1/2-inch-thick package to defrost. To catch the juices as the meat thaws, place the frozen package in a shallow dish.

Short on time? You can quickly thaw frozen ground beef in the microwave. Follow the manufacturer's directions for suggested defrosting times. Completely defrost the beef before cooking and cook it immediately after thawing.

deep-dish taco squares

prep 10 minutes | **bake** 20 minutes

1 pound lean ground beef
1 cup (4 ounces) shredded cheddar cheese
1/3 cup mayonnaise
1/3 cup sour cream
1 tablespoon finely chopped onion
1 cup biscuit/baking mix
1/4 cup cold water
1 small tomato, sliced

In a nonstick skillet, cook beef over medium heat until no longer pink; drain. Remove from the heat; stir in the cheese, mayonnaise, sour cream and onion.

In a large bowl, combine biscuit mix and water. Spread into an 8-in. square baking dish coated with nonstick cooking spray. Top with beef mixture and tomato. Bake, uncovered, at 375° for 20 minutes or until bottom crust is golden brown. **yield:** 6 servings.

barb tropansky
bella vista, arkansas

Hearty and comforting, this dish has a biscuit crust topped with a thick layer of beef and cheese. It's a terrific menu choice any night of the week.

hearty burritos

prep 20 minutes | **bake** 25 minutes

- 1/2 pound ground beef
- 1 large green pepper, chopped
- 1 medium onion, chopped
- 1 package (16 ounces) frozen cubed hash brown potatoes, thawed
- 1 can (15 ounces) black beans, rinsed and drained
- 1 can (14-1/2 ounces) Mexican diced tomatoes, undrained
- 1 cup frozen corn, thawed
- 1/2 cup salsa
- 1/2 cup cooked rice
- 2 teaspoons chili powder
- 1/2 teaspoon salt
- 2 cups (8 ounces) shredded cheddar cheese
- 8 flour tortillas (10 inches)

Sour cream, chopped tomatoes, guacamole, additional shredded cheddar cheese and salsa, optional

In a large skillet, cook beef, green pepper and onion over medium heat until meat is no longer pink; drain. Add potatoes, beans, tomatoes, corn, salsa, rice, chili powder and salt. Sprinkle 1/4 cup cheese off-center on each tortilla; top with about 1 cup beef mixture. Fold sides and ends over filling.

Wrap the burritos individually in foil and freeze for up to 3 months. Or place the burritos seam side down on a baking sheet. Bake at 350° for 25 minutes or until heated through. Serve burritos with sour cream, tomatoes, guacamole, additional cheese and salsa if desired.

TO USE FROZEN BURRITOS: Thaw in the refrigerator overnight. Bake and serve as directed. **yield:** 8 burritos.

janelle mceachern
riverside, california

These beyond-compare burritos are chock-full of tasty ingredients and frozen individually, so you can bake only as many as needed.

beefy jalapeno corn bake

prep 20 minutes | **bake** 55 minutes

james coleman
charlotte, north carolina

You'll love digging into these squares of beefed-up corn bread. Loaded with cheese, corn and jalapenos, it's a filling main dish.

- 1 pound ground beef
- 2 eggs
- 1 can (14-3/4 ounces) cream-style corn
- 1 cup milk
- 1/2 cup vegetable oil
- 1 cup cornmeal
- 3 tablespoons all-purpose flour
- 1-1/2 teaspoons baking powder
- 3/4 teaspoon salt
- 4 cups (16 ounces) shredded cheddar cheese, *divided*
- 1 medium onion, chopped
- 4 jalapeno peppers, seeded and chopped

In a large skillet, cook beef over medium heat until no longer pink; drain and set aside. In a large bowl, beat eggs, corn, milk and oil. Combine the cornmeal, flour, baking powder and salt; add to egg mixture and mix well.

Pour half of the batter into a greased 13-in. x 9-in. x 2-in. baking dish. Sprinkle with 2 cups cheese; top with the beef, onion and jalapenos. Sprinkle with remaining cheese; top with remaining batter.

Bake, uncovered, at 350° for 55-60 minutes or until a toothpick inserted into the corn bread topping comes out clean. Serve casserole warm. Refrigerate any leftovers. **yield:** 12 servings.

editor's note: When cutting or seeding hot peppers, use rubber or plastic gloves to protect your hands. Avoid touching your face.

kinds of **CORNMEAL**

Cornmeal can be either white, yellow or blue depending on which strain of corn is used. Traditionally, white cornmeal is more popular in the South and yellow is preferred in the North. The blue variety can be found in specialty stores.

All three types of cornmeal may be used interchangeably in recipes, including Southwestern Pizza.

southwestern pizza

prep 40 minutes | **bake** 5 minutes

1-1/4 cups all-purpose flour
3/4 cup cornmeal
1/4 cup sugar
2 teaspoons baking powder
1 teaspoon cayenne pepper
1 teaspoon chili powder
1/2 teaspoon salt
1 cup milk
1/4 cup vegetable oil
1 egg
3/4 cup shredded cheddar cheese
3/4 cup shredded Monterey Jack cheese

topping
1-1/2 pounds ground beef
2/3 cup water
2 envelopes taco seasoning, *divided*
2 cups (16 ounces) sour cream
1-3/4 cups shredded cheddar cheese
1-3/4 cups shredded Monterey Jack cheese
1 can (15-1/4 ounces) whole kernel corn, drained
1 can (15 ounces) black beans, rinsed and drained
1 cup salsa

In a large bowl, combine the flour, cornmeal, sugar, baking powder, cayenne, chili powder and salt. Combine the milk, oil and egg; stir into dry ingredients just until moistened. Stir in the cheeses.

Spread into a greased 15-in. x 10-in. x 1-in. baking pan. Bake at 400° for 10-12 minutes or until a toothpick inserted into the crust comes out clean.

In a large skillet, cook beef over medium heat until no longer pink; drain. Stir in water and one envelope of taco seasoning. Bring to a boil. Reduce heat; simmer, uncovered, for 5 minutes. Set aside.

In a small bowl, combine the sour cream and remaining taco seasoning; mix well. Spread over crust. Sprinkle with the beef mixture and half of the cheeses.

Combine the corn, beans and salsa; spoon over cheese. Sprinkle with remaining cheese. Broil 5-10 minutes or until cheese is melted. **yield:** 12-15 servings.

caroline grooms
dickinson, north dakota

Seasoned ground beef, corn and black beans deliciously top off a cornmeal crust in this hearty appetizer pizza. Larger helpings could even make a main course.

FUN FARE for kids

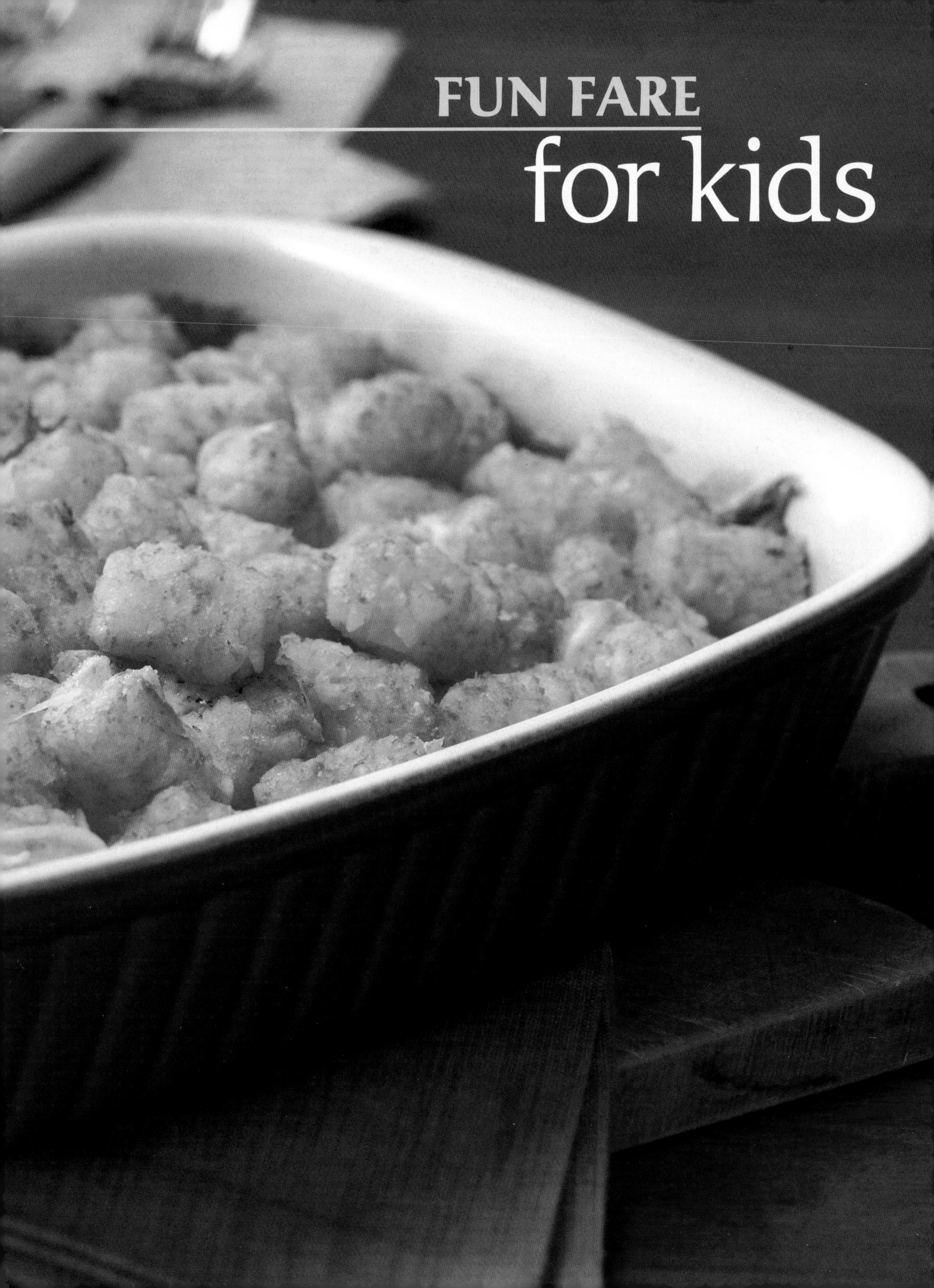

no-noodle lasagna

prep 20 minutes | **bake** 25 minutes

mary moore
omaha, nebraska

This convenient recipe gives you classic lasagna flavor without all the work. I seal the beef, cheese and other ingredients between two layers of refrigerated crescent roll dough.

1-1/2 pounds ground beef
1/2 cup chopped onion
1 can (6 ounces) tomato paste
1 tablespoon dried parsley flakes
1/2 teaspoon dried basil
1/2 teaspoon dried oregano
1/2 teaspoon salt
1/2 teaspoon pepper
Dash garlic salt
1 egg
1-1/2 cups (12 ounces) 4% cottage cheese
1/4 cup grated Parmesan cheese
2 tubes (8 ounces *each*) refrigerated crescent rolls
8 slices part-skim mozzarella cheese
1 tablespoon milk
1 tablespoon sesame seeds

In a large skillet, cook beef and onion over medium heat until meat is no longer pink; drain. Stir in tomato paste and seasonings. In a small bowl, combine the egg, cottage cheese and Parmesan cheese.

Roll out each tube of crescent dough between waxed paper into a 15-in. x 10-in. rectangle. Transfer one rectangle to a greased 15-in. x 10-in. x 1-in. baking pan. Spread with half of the meat mixture to within 1 in. of the edges; top with half of the cheese mixture. Repeat the meat and cheese layers.

Top with mozzarella. Carefully place second dough rectangle on top; press edges to seal. Brush with milk; sprinkle with sesame seeds. Bake, uncovered, at 350° for 25-30 minutes or until golden brown. **yield:** 6 servings.

cheesy pizza macaroni

prep 20 minutes | **bake** 30 minutes

kathryn mccafferty

camdenton, missouri

Here's an easy way to jazz up a boxed macaroni mix. My family likes to have this at least once a month—preferably more often!

1-1/2 pounds ground beef
2 packages (7-1/4 ounces *each*) macaroni and cheese
2 cans (15 ounces *each*) pizza sauce
2 cups (8 ounces) shredded cheddar cheese
2 cups (8 ounces) shredded part-skim mozzarella cheese

In a large skillet, cook the beef until no longer pink; drain. Prepare macaroni and cheese according to package directions.

Spread one can of pizza sauce into a greased 13-in. x 9-in. x 2-in. baking dish; layer with half the beef, macaroni and cheese, and cheddar and mozzarella cheeses. Repeat layers (dish will be full). Bake, uncovered, at 350° for 30-35 minutes or until bubbly. **yield:** 10-12 servings.

chili-ghetti

prep/total time 30 minutes

1 package (7 ounces) spaghetti
1 pound ground beef
1 small onion, chopped
1 can (16 ounces) kidney beans, rinsed and drained
1 can (14-1/2 ounces) diced tomatoes, undrained
1 can (4 ounces) mushroom stems and pieces, drained
1/3 cup water
1 envelope chili seasoning
2 tablespoons grated Parmesan cheese
1/4 cup shredded part-skim mozzarella cheese

Cook spaghetti according to package directions. Meanwhile, in a large skillet, cook beef and onion over medium heat until meat is no longer pink; drain.

Drain spaghetti; add to beef mixture. Stir in the beans, tomatoes, mushrooms, water, chili seasoning and Parmesan cheese. Cover and simmer for 10 minutes. Sprinkle with mozzarella cheese. **yield:** 8 servings.

nutrition facts: 1 cup equals 293 calories, 9 g fat (3 g saturated fat), 41 mg cholesterol, 590 mg sodium, 33 g carbohydrate, 5 g fiber, 21 g protein.

 This beef recipe is lighter in calories, fat and sodium.

cindy cuykendall

skaneateles, new york

I came up with this recipe when unexpected guests stopped by and I didn't have enough chili. The spur-of-the-moment main dish is now a favorite.

sloppy joe wagon wheels

prep/total time 20 minutes

lou ellen mcclinton

jacksonville, north carolina

Sloppy joe sauce gives some sweetness to the spaghetti sauce in this meaty mixture. Serve it over wagon wheel pasta, and kids will dig in.

1 package (16 ounces) wagon wheel pasta
2 pounds ground beef
1 medium green pepper, chopped
1 medium onion, chopped
1 jar (28 ounces) meatless spaghetti sauce
1 jar (15-1/2 ounces) sloppy joe sauce

Cook pasta according to package directions. Meanwhile, in a large skillet, cook the beef, green pepper and onion until meat is no longer pink; drain. Stir in the sauces; cook until heated through.

Drain pasta; transfer to a large serving bowl; top with beef mixture. **yield:** 8 servings.

pizzawiches

prep 20 minutes | **bake** 10 minutes + freezing

jennifer short
omaha, nebraska

People of all ages like these pizza-flavored sandwiches, which can be made ahead of time and stored in the freezer. Frozen ones don't need to thaw before baking, so you'll have a meal in a flash.

 2 pounds ground beef
 1 medium onion, chopped
 2 cans (10-3/4 ounces *each*) condensed tomato soup, undiluted
 1 teaspoon dried oregano
 1 teaspoon chili powder
 1/2 teaspoon garlic salt
 1 cup (4 ounces) shredded cheddar cheese
 1 cup (4 ounces) shredded part-skim mozzarella cheese
 12 hamburger buns, split
 3 to 4 tablespoons butter, melted

In a large skillet, cook beef and onion over medium heat until meat is no longer pink; drain. Stir in the soup, oregano, chili powder and garlic salt. Bring to a boil. Remove from the heat; stir in cheeses. Place about 1/3 cup meat mixture on each bun. Brush tops of buns with butter.

Place on an ungreased baking sheet. Bake at 375° for 7-9 minutes or until cheese is melted. Or wrap sandwiches in foil and freeze for up to 3 months.

TO BAKE FROZEN SANDWICHES: Place foil-wrapped buns on an ungreased baking sheet. Bake at 375° for 35-40 minutes or until heated through. **yield:** 12 sandwiches.

walk-along chili

prep 15 minutes | **cook** 1 hour

 2 pounds ground beef
 1 small onion, chopped
 2 garlic cloves, minced
 1 can (28 ounces) diced tomatoes, undrained
 1 can (8 ounces) tomato sauce
 1 can (6 ounces) tomato paste
 2 to 3 tablespoons chili powder
 1 tablespoon paprika
 1 tablespoon dried oregano
 1-1/2 teaspoons salt
 1 teaspoon ground cumin
 16 bags (1-1/4 ounces *each*) corn chips
Shredded cheddar cheese

 This beef recipe is lighter in calories, fat and sodium.

joyce vonstempa
jeffersontown, kentucky

Getting children to eat this playful beef chili is a cinch. Each helping is served over crunchy corn chips right inside a small chip bag!

In a large saucepan or Dutch oven, cook the beef over medium heat until no longer pink; drain. Add the onion and garlic; cook and stir for 5 minutes. Stir in the next eight ingredients. Bring to a boil. Cover and simmer for 1 hour.

To serve, split open bags of chips at the back seam or cut an "x" in the bag; add 1/2 cup of chili to each. Sprinkle with cheese. **yield:** 16 servings.

nutrition facts: 1 cup equals 132 calories, 6 g fat (2 g saturated fat), 28 mg cholesterol, 414 mg sodium, 8 g carbohydrate, 2 g fiber, 11 g protein.

chili macaroni soup

prep/total time 30 minutes

- 1 pound ground beef
- 1 medium onion, chopped
- 1/4 cup chopped green pepper
- 5 cups water
- 1 can (14-1/2 ounces) diced tomatoes, undrained
- 1 package (7-1/2 ounces) chili macaroni dinner mix
- 1 teaspoon chili powder
- 1/2 teaspoon garlic salt
- 1/4 teaspoon salt
- 1 can (8-3/4 ounces) whole kernel corn, drained
- 2 tablespoons sliced ripe olives

In a large saucepan or soup kettle, cook the beef, onion and green pepper over medium heat until the meat is no longer pink; drain. Add the water, tomatoes, contents of sauce mix from the dinner mix, chili powder, garlic salt and salt. Simmer, uncovered, for 10 minutes.

Add macaroni from dinner mix, corn and olives. Cover and simmer for 10 minutes or until macaroni is tender, stirring occasionally. **yield:** 9 servings (about 2 quarts).

nutrition facts: 1 cup equals 145 calories, 6 g fat (2 g saturated fat), 33 mg cholesterol, 416 mg sodium, 10 g carbohydrate, 2 g fiber, 13 g protein.

This beef recipe is lighter in calories, fat and sodium.

flo burtnett

gage, oklahoma

Turn a macaroni dinner into a thick, zesty soup with this recipe. Each helping is chock-full of ground beef, tomatoes, corn and more.

cheeseburger biscuit bake

prep 15 minutes | **bake** 20 minutes

joy frasure

longmont, colorado

Popular cheeseburger ingredients create the tasty layers in this family-pleasing casserole. For the "bun," I use refrigerated biscuits to make a golden topping.

- 1 pound ground beef
- 1/4 cup chopped onion
- 1 can (8 ounces) tomato sauce
- 1/4 cup ketchup

Dash pepper

- 2 cups (8 ounces) shredded cheddar cheese, *divided*
- 1 tube (12 ounces) refrigerated buttermilk biscuits, separated into 10 biscuits

In a large skillet, cook beef and onion over medium heat until meat is no longer pink; drain. Stir in tomato sauce, ketchup and pepper. Spoon half into a greased 8-in. square baking dish; sprinkle with half of the cheese. Repeat layers.

Place biscuits around edges of dish. Bake, uncovered, at 400° for 18-22 minutes or until the meat mixture is bubbly and biscuits are golden brown. **yield:** 5 servings.

deluxe macaroni dinner

prep/total time 30 minutes

- 1/2 pound ground beef
- 1 small onion, chopped
- 2 garlic cloves, minced
- 10 cups water
- 1 package (14 ounces) deluxe four-cheese macaroni and cheese dinner
- 2 cups chopped fresh broccoli

In a large skillet, cook the beef, onion and garlic until meat is no longer pink; drain. In a large saucepan, bring the water to a boil. Add macaroni; cook for 5 minutes. Add broccoli; cook 4-5 minutes longer or until macaroni and broccoli are tender. Drain, reserving 1/4 cup cooking liquid. Place contents of cheese sauce mix in saucepan. Stir in macaroni mixture, beef mixture and reserved liquid; heat through. **yield:** 4-6 servings.

nutrition facts: 3/4 cup equals 300 calories, 11 g fat (6 g saturated fat), 42 mg cholesterol, 512 mg sodium, 32 g carbohydrate, 2 g fiber, 18 g protein.

This beef recipe is lighter in calories, fat and sodium.

michele odstrcilek

lemont, illinois

When this cheesy supper is on the table, I never have leftovers. The recipe starts with a convenient boxed mix and includes plenty of good-for-you broccoli.

life preserver meat loaves

prep 20 minutes | **bake** 25 minutes

1	egg
1	can (5-1/2 ounces) spicy-hot *or* picante V8
1/4	cup milk
1	cup seasoned bread crumbs
1-1/2	teaspoons seasoned salt
1	teaspoon chili powder
1-1/2	pounds lean ground beef

Ketchup and mustard

In a large bowl, combine the first six ingredients. Crumble beef over mixture and mix well. Shape into six balls; flatten slightly. Make a hole in the center of each ball with the end of a wooden spoon handle.

Place in a greased 15-in. x 10-in. x 1-in. baking pan. Bake, uncovered, at 350° for 25-30 minutes or until meat is no longer pink and a meat thermometer reads 160°. Decorate the loaves with ketchup and mustard. **yield:** 6 servings.

taste of home test kitchen
greendale, wisconsin

For a summer party or anytime, these miniature ring-shaped loaves are a "shore" hit with children. Piping on ketchup and mustard adds colorful markings to the little life preservers.

fly burgers

prep 20 minutes + rising | **bake** 10 minutes

This beef recipe is lighter in calories, fat and sodium.

lenore walters
oklahoma city, oklahoma

If your kids think bugs are "cool," they'll be buzzing over these playful burgers. I cut the top bun to make it look like a fly's wings, and green onion "eyes" peer out from the beef patties.

8	frozen bread dough dinner rolls, thawed
1	pound ground beef
1	egg
1/4	cup ketchup
32	thin green onions slices

Cut each roll in half; shape each into a ball. Place on an ungreased baking sheet; flatten slightly. Cover and let rise until doubled, about 30 minutes.

Bake at 350° for 10-12 minutes or until lightly browned. Cool on a wire rack.

In a small bowl, combine beef and egg. Shape into 16 patties, 2 in. each. In a large skillet, cook patties on both sides over medium heat until no longer pink. Drain on paper towels.

Split the rolls; place a beef patty on each bottom half. For the wings, cut a narrow V shape from each roll top; position on each

patty (discard removed sections). Secure with toothpicks. For the eyes, pipe two dots of ketchup near the edge of each patty opposite the V; top with onion slices. **yield:** 16 sandwiches.

nutrition facts: 1 burger equals 113 calories, 5 g fat (1 g saturated fat), 32 mg cholesterol, 160 mg sodium, 10 g carbohydrate, 1 g fiber, 8 g protein.

meat-za pie

prep/total time 25 minutes

1	can (5 ounces) evaporated milk
1/2	cup plain *or* seasoned dry bread crumbs
3/4	teaspoon garlic salt
1	pound lean ground beef
1/4	cup ketchup
1	teaspoon sugar
1/2	cup canned sliced mushrooms
3	slices process American cheese, cut into thin strips
1/4	teaspoon dried oregano
2	tablespoons grated Parmesan cheese

In a large bowl, combine the milk, bread crumbs and garlic salt; add beef. Stir with a fork just until mixed. Press onto the bottom and 1/2 in. up the sides of an ungreased 9-in. pie plate.

Combine the ketchup and sugar; spread over beef mixture. Sprinkle with the mushrooms. Arrange the cheese strips in a lattice pattern on top. Sprinkle with the oregano and Parmesan cheese.

Bake at 400° for 20 minutes or until the meat is no longer pink and a meat thermometer reads 160°; drain. Cut pie into wedges. **yield:** 4 servings.

denise albers
freeburg, illinois

This pizza-shaped meat loaf is so easy to make that children can help with the preparation. My daughter liked to do several of the steps all by herself.

fast **FUN**

If you don't have the kitchen tools or the time needed to pipe the design on the Layer Cake Meat Loaf, dress up the top mashed potato layer in an easier way. Just sprinkle on some shredded cheddar cheese or a little paprika.

layer cake meat loaf

prep 30 minutes | **bake** 15 minutes + standing

**taste of home
test kitchen**

greendale, wisconsin

For a birthday party or anytime, this topsy-turvy main course is guaranteed to get giggles! With mashed potatoes that resemble frosting, the layered loaf looks like dessert. But one bite proves that it's really a delicious beef dinner.

    2 eggs, lightly beaten
    1 can (5-1/2 ounces) spicy hot V8 juice
  1/2 cup seasoned bread crumbs
  1/2 cup quick-cooking oats
  2/3 cup chopped onion
    1 cup chopped green pepper
    1 teaspoon chili powder
  1/2 teaspoon salt
  1/2 teaspoon pepper
    2 pounds ground beef

mashed potatoes

  4-2/3 cups water
      1 cup milk plus 2 tablespoons milk
      7 tablespoons butter, *divided*
  1-3/4 teaspoons salt
  4-2/3 cups mashed potato flakes
Ketchup and mustard

In a large bowl, combine the first nine ingredients. Crumble beef over mixture and mix well. Pat into two ungreased 9-in. square baking pans. Bake at 350° for 15-20 minutes or until meat is no longer pink and a meat thermometer reads 160°; drain. Let stand for 10 minutes.

Meanwhile, in a large saucepan, bring the water, milk, butter and salt to a boil. Stir in potato flakes. Remove from the heat. Invert one meat loaf onto a serving platter; invert the second loaf onto a cutting board. Spread 1-1/2 cups mashed potatoes over loaf on the platter. Carefully slide second loaf onto the potatoes.

Spread 3-1/2 cups mashed potatoes over the top and sides. Spoon remaining mashed potatoes into a pastry bag with open star tip #195. Pipe a shell border around the bottom and top edges. Place ketchup and mustard in resealable plastic bags; cut a small hole in a corner of each bag. Pipe ketchup and mustard on cake. **yield:** 8-10 servings.

spaghetti mac

prep/total time 30 minutes

2 cups uncooked elbow macaroni
1/2 pound ground beef
1 can (10-3/4 ounces) condensed tomato soup, undiluted
1 can (8 ounces) tomato sauce
1 teaspoon dried minced onion
1 teaspoon dried parsley flakes
1/2 teaspoon salt
1/2 teaspoon dried oregano
1/4 cup shredded Parmesan cheese

Cook macaroni according to package directions. Meanwhile, in a large saucepan, cook beef over medium heat until no longer pink; drain. Stir in the soup, tomato sauce, onion, parsley, salt and oregano; heat through. Drain macaroni; top with the beef mixture and sprinkle with cheese. **yield:** 4 servings.

linda sawin
sterling, massachusetts

This hearty meal is my mom's creation and ranks among my kids' favorites. I cook the sauce on the weekend and keep it in the freezer to save time during the week.

biscuit tostadas

prep/total time 30 minutes

 This beef recipe is lighter in calories, fat and sodium.

terrie stampor
sterling heights, michigan

Refrigerated biscuits and just four other ingredients make it easy for children to help assemble these kid-size tostadas. They're best eaten on a plate with a fork.

1 pound ground beef
1 jar (16 ounces) salsa, *divided*
1 tube (17.3 ounces) large refrigerated biscuits
2 cups (8 ounces) shredded Colby-Monterey Jack cheese
2 cups shredded lettuce

In a large skillet, cook beef over medium heat until no longer pink; drain. Add 1-1/2 cups salsa; heat through.

Split each biscuit in half; flatten into 4-in. rounds on ungreased baking sheets. Bake at 350° for 10-12 minutes or until golden brown. Top with meat mixture, cheese, lettuce and remaining salsa. **yield:** 16 servings.

nutrition facts: 1 biscuit tostada equals 205 calories, 11 g fat (5 g saturated fat), 26 mg cholesterol, 528 mg sodium, 14 g carbohydrate, 1 g fiber, 10 g protein.

speedy taco feast

prep 15 minutes | **bake** 40 minutes

janice steimer
rochester, new york

I've found that teenagers love the Southwestern taste of this hearty main dish. It's not as messy as tacos can be because the ingredients are all combined into an easy-to-eat casserole.

2 pounds ground beef
2 envelopes taco seasoning
1-1/2 cups water
1 jar (16 ounces) salsa
1 can (8-3/4 ounces) whole kernel corn, drained
2 cups (8 ounces) shredded taco *or* Mexican cheese blend
2 packages (8-1/2 ounces *each*) corn bread/muffin mix
Sour cream, optional

In a large skillet, cook beef over medium heat until no longer pink; drain. Add the taco seasoning, water, salsa and corn; cook and stir until heated through, about 15 minutes. Transfer to a greased 13-in. x 9-in. x 2-in. baking dish. Sprinkle with cheese.

Prepare corn bread mix according to package directions. Spoon batter evenly over cheese. Bake, uncovered, at 350° for 40-45 minutes or until a toothpick inserted near the center of the corn bread comes out clean. Serve with sour cream, if desired. **yield:** 8 servings.

chili mac casserole

prep 15 minutes | **bake** 30 minutes

1 cup uncooked elbow macaroni
2 pounds lean ground beef
1 medium onion, chopped
2 garlic cloves, minced
1 can (28 ounces) diced tomatoes, undrained
1 can (16 ounces) kidney beans, rinsed and drained
1 can (6 ounces) tomato paste
1 can (4 ounces) chopped green chilies
1-1/2 teaspoons salt
1 teaspoon chili powder
1/2 teaspoon ground cumin
1/2 teaspoon pepper
2 cups (8 ounces) shredded reduced-fat Mexican cheese blend

marlene wilson
rolla, north dakota

I use many of my family's favorite foods, including macaroni, kidney beans, tomatoes and cheese, to make this nicely spiced dish. Just add a green salad to the menu, and supper's done.

Cook macaroni according to package directions. Meanwhile, in a large nonstick skillet, cook the beef, onion and garlic over medium heat until meat is no longer pink; drain. Stir in the tomatoes, beans, tomato paste, chilies and seasonings. Drain macaroni; add to beef mixture.

Transfer to a 13-in. x 9-in. x 2-in. baking dish coated with nonstick cooking spray. Cover and bake at 375° for 25-30 minutes or until bubbly. Uncover; sprinkle with cheese. Bake 5-8 minutes longer or until cheese is melted. **yield:** 10 servings.

campfire stew

prep/total time 20 minutes

1 pound ground beef
1 can (15 ounces) mixed vegetables, drained
1 can (10-3/4 ounces) condensed tomato soup, undiluted
1 can (10-1/2 ounces) condensed vegetable beef soup, undiluted
1/4 cup water
1/4 teaspoon garlic powder
1/4 teaspoon onion powder
1/4 teaspoon salt
1/8 teaspoon pepper

In a large saucepan, cook the beef over medium heat until no longer pink; drain. Stir in the remaining ingredients. Bring to a boil. Reduce heat; cover and simmer for 8-10 minutes or until heated through. **yield:** 4 servings.

eva knight
nashua, new hampshire

This speedy, single-pan meal brings back childhood memories of my days at Girl Scout camp. The stew is so hearty and flavorful, it was an instant hit with my family.

scrabble soup

prep 20 minutes | **cook** 35 minutes

This beef recipe is lighter in calories, fat and sodium.

mina dyck
boissevain, manitoba

Make a game of eating a good meal by serving this nutritious alphabet soup. Children have fun finding different pasta letters and spelling simple words.

1 pound ground beef
1 cup chopped onion
6 cups water
2 cans (14-1/2 ounces *each*) diced tomatoes, undrained
1 cup *each* chopped celery, carrot, turnip and potato
1 tablespoon dried parsley flakes
2 teaspoons beef bouillon granules
2 garlic cloves, minced
1 teaspoon dried oregano
1 teaspoon salt
1/2 teaspoon pepper
1/2 teaspoon dried basil
1/2 teaspoon Worcestershire sauce
1 cup uncooked alphabet pasta

In a Dutch oven or soup kettle, cook beef and onion over medium heat until meat is no longer pink; drain. Add water, vegetables and seasonings; bring to a boil. Reduce heat; simmer for 20 minutes or until the vegetables are crisp-tender. Add pasta; simmer for 15 minutes or until the pasta and vegetables are tender. **yield:** 12 servings (3 quarts).

nutrition facts: 1 cup equals 153 calories, 5 g fat (2 g saturated fat), 25 mg cholesterol, 426 mg sodium, 17 g carbohydrate, 2 g fiber, 10 g protein.

snowman party stew

prep 30 minutes | **cook** 15 minutes

**taste of home
test kitchen**

greendale, wisconsin

*Make a winter party extra
special with this playful pie.
We packed it with beef stew
ingredients, then shaped the
whimsical snowmen with
mashed potatoes, veggies,
peppercorns and ketchup.*

1   pound ground beef
1   package (16 ounces) frozen
    vegetables for stew, *divided*
1   can (10-1/4 ounces) beef gravy
2   cups mashed potatoes (prepared
    with a small amount of milk)
16 whole black peppercorns
1/4 cup ketchup

In a skillet, brown beef; drain. Remove 24
peas and one carrot chunk from the stew
vegetables; set aside. Add the remaining
vegetables to beef. Cook until vegetables
are thawed. Add gravy; mix well.

Pour into an ungreased 9-in. pie plate.
Top with eight mashed potato snowmen,
using 1 tablespoon of potatoes for each
head and 3 tablespoons for each body.
Bake, uncovered, at 350° for 20 minutes.

Meanwhile, with a sharp knife, cut the
reserved carrot into eight strips. Insert one
strip into each snowman for a nose. Place
three reserved peas on each for buttons.
Add peppercorns for eyes. Drizzle ketchup
between head and body to form the scarf.
yield: 6-8 servings.

editor's note: If serving the stew to small children,
remove the peppercorns.

tater taco casserole

prep 20 minutes | **bake** 30 minutes

ronna lewis
plains, kansas

Our family lives and works on a ranch, and we build up big appetites by the time dinner rolls around. This nicely seasoned casserole is great with a tossed salad or nacho chips and dip.

2 pounds ground beef
1/4 cup chopped onion
1 envelope taco seasoning
2/3 cup water
1 can (11 ounces) whole kernel corn, drained
1 can (11 ounces) condensed fiesta nacho cheese soup, undiluted
1 package (32 ounces) frozen Tater Tots

In a skillet, cook beef and onion over medium heat until meat is no longer pink; drain. Stir in taco seasoning and water. Simmer, uncovered, for 5 minutes. Add corn and soup; mix well.

Transfer to a greased 13-in. x 9-in. x 2-in. baking dish. Arrange Tater Tots in a single layer over the top. Bake, uncovered, at 350° for 30-35 minutes or until potatoes are crispy and golden brown. **yield:** 8 servings.

bacon cheeseburger rice

prep/total time 30 minutes

1 pound ground beef
1-3/4 cups water
2/3 cup barbecue sauce
1 tablespoon prepared mustard
2 teaspoons dried minced onion
1/2 teaspoon pepper
2 cups uncooked instant rice
1 cup (4 ounces) shredded cheddar cheese
1/3 cup chopped dill pickles
5 bacon strips, cooked and crumbled

joyce whipps
west des moines, iowa

My husband and I changed a skillet dish to suit our tastes, and this was the hearty result. I've had teenage nieces and nephews request the recipe after their first bite!

In a large saucepan, cook beef over medium heat until no longer pink; drain. Add water, barbecue sauce, mustard, onion and pepper. Bring to a boil; stir in the rice. Sprinkle with cheese. Reduce heat; cover and simmer for 5 minutes. Sprinkle with pickles and bacon. **yield:** 4-6 servings.

hot dog pie

prep/total time 30 minutes

1/2 pound ground beef
4 hot dogs, cut in half lengthwise and sliced
1 can (16 ounces) baked beans
1/2 cup ketchup
2 tablespoons brown sugar
2 tablespoons prepared mustard
2 ounces process cheese (Velveeta), cubed
1 unbaked deep-dish pastry shell (9-inches)
4 slices American cheese

amy bullis

henryville, pennsylvania

A co-worker who loves hot dogs shared this recipe with me. Baked in a purchased pastry shell, the pie is easy to assemble and is on the table in just 30 minutes.

In a large saucepan, cook beef over medium heat until no longer pink; drain. Add the hot dogs, beans, ketchup, brown sugar, mustard and cheese cubes. Cook and stir until cheese is melted.

Meanwhile, prick pastry shell with a fork. Bake at 400° for 10 minutes. Fill with hot beef mixture. Cut each cheese slice into four strips; make a lattice topping over pie. Bake 5-10 minutes longer or until cheese is melted. **yield:** 4-6 servings.

jack-o'-lantern burgers

prep/total time 20 minutes

vicki schlechter

davis, california

It's fun to "carve" silly jack-o'-lantern faces in the cheese slices I put on these burgers. The spooky sandwiches went over big at my Halloween party.

1 envelope onion soup mix
1/4 cup ketchup
2 tablespoons brown sugar
2 teaspoons prepared horseradish
2 teaspoons chili powder
2-1/2 pounds ground beef
10 slices American cheese
10 hamburger buns, split

In a large bowl, combine soup mix, ketchup, brown sugar, horseradish and chili powder. Crumble beef over mixture; mix well. Shape into 10 patties. Grill, broil or pan-fry until the meat is no longer pink.

Cut eyes, nose and mouth out of each cheese slice to create a jack-o'-lantern. Place cheese on burgers; cook until cheese is slightly melted, about 1 minute. Serve on buns. **yield:** 10 servings.

choosing CHEDDAR

Extra-sharp and sharp cheddar cheeses are used in recipes when a bolder flavor is desired. If you'd prefer a more subtle flavor for Haystack Supper, just substitute shredded mild or medium cheddar cheese for the sharp cheddar.

haystack supper

prep/total time 25 minutes

1-3/4 cups crushed saltines (about 40 crackers)
   2 cups cooked rice
   3 pounds ground beef
   1 large onion, chopped
1-1/2 cups tomato juice
 3/4 cup water
   3 tablespoons taco seasoning
Seasoned salt, salt and pepper to taste
   4 cups shredded lettuce
   3 medium tomatoes, diced
 1/2 cup butter, cubed
 1/2 cup all-purpose flour
   4 cups milk
   1 pound process cheese (Velveeta), cubed
   3 cups (12 ounces) shredded sharp cheddar cheese
   1 jar (10 ounces) pimiento-stuffed olives
   1 package (14-1/2 ounces) tortilla chips

Divide crackers between two ungreased 13-in. x 9-in. x 2-in. baking dishes. Top each with rice.

In a large skillet, cook beef and onion until meat is no longer pink; drain. Add the tomato juice, water and seasonings; simmer for 15-20 minutes. Spoon over rice. Sprinkle with lettuce and tomatoes.

In a large saucepan, melt butter. Stir in flour until smooth. Gradually add milk. Bring to a boil; cook and stir for 2 minutes or until thickened. Reduce heat; stir in American cheese until melted.

Pour over the tomatoes. Top with cheddar cheese and olives. Serve with chips. Refrigerate any leftovers. **yield:** 2 casseroles (6 servings each).

jill steiner
hancock, minnesota

Served as the main course at our family reunion, this layered, taco-style supper appealed to young and old alike. People are pleasantly surprised when they discover the rice, and everyone enjoys the creamy cheese sauce.

pizza tot casserole

prep 10 minutes | **bake** 30 minutes

chris stukel
des plaines, illinois

This upside-down pizza casserole requires ground beef and only six other ingredients. The Tater Tots make this simple supper a guaranteed kid-pleaser.

1 pound ground beef
1 medium green pepper, chopped
1 medium onion, chopped
1 can (10-3/4 ounces) condensed tomato soup, undiluted
1 jar (4-1/2 ounces) sliced mushrooms, drained
1 teaspoon Italian seasoning
2 cups (8 ounces) shredded part-skim mozzarella cheese
1 package (32 ounces) frozen Tater Tots

In a skillet, cook the beef, pepper and onion over medium heat until meat is no longer pink; drain. Add soup, mushrooms and Italian seasoning.

Transfer to a greased 13-in. x 9-in. x 2-in. baking dish. Top with the mozzarella cheese and potatoes. Bake, uncovered, at 400° for 30-35 minutes or until golden brown. **yield:** 6-8 servings.

cheeseburger chowder

prep/total time 30 minutes

- 1 pound ground beef
- 1/4 cup chopped onion
- 1-1/2 cups water
- 3 teaspoons beef bouillon granules
- 1/2 teaspoon salt
- 2 cups cubed red potatoes
- 1 celery rib, thinly sliced
- 3 tablespoons all-purpose flour
- 2-1/2 cups milk, *divided*
- 1 cup (4 ounces) shredded cheddar cheese

In a large saucepan, cook beef and onion over medium heat until meat is no longer pink; drain. Stir in the water, bouillon and salt. Add potatoes and celery. Bring to a boil. Reduce heat; cover and simmer for 15-20 minutes or until potatoes are tender.

Combine flour and 1/2 cup milk until smooth; gradually stir into beef mixture. Bring to a boil; cook and stir for 2 minutes or until thickened and bubbly. Stir in the remaining milk; heat through. Stir in cheese until melted. **yield:** 7 servings.

rebecca mccabe
ekalaka, montana

On cold, blustery days, my family requests this creamy soup. Serve it with oven-fresh corn bread or biscuits for a complete and filling meal.

cheesy potato beef bake

prep 10 minutes | **bake** 35 minutes + standing

nicole rute
fall river, wisconsin

As a teenager, I created this layered casserole one day when my mom asked me what I wanted for supper. Using packaged potatoes speeds up the preparation.

- 1 pound ground beef
- 2 cans (4 ounces *each*) mushroom stems and pieces, drained, optional
- 2 packages (5-1/4 ounces *each*) au gratin potatoes
- 4 cups boiling water
- 1-1/3 cups milk
- 2 teaspoons butter
- 1 teaspoon salt
- 1/2 teaspoon seasoned salt
- 1/2 teaspoon pepper
- 1 cup (4 ounces) shredded cheddar cheese

In a skillet, cook beef over medium heat until no longer pink; drain. Place in a greased 13-in. x 9-in. x 2-in. baking pan. Top with mushrooms.

Combine potatoes and contents of sauce mix packets, water, milk, butter, salt, seasoned salt and pepper. Pour over beef and mushrooms. Cover and bake at 400° for 30 minutes or until heated through.

Sprinkle with cheese. Bake, uncovered, for 5 minutes or until the cheese is melted. Let stand 10 minutes before serving. **yield:** 8 servings.

general recipe index

• recipe includes nutrition facts

• recipe includes nutrition facts

• recipe includes nutrition facts

• recipe includes nutrition facts

• recipe includes nutrition facts

alphabetical recipe index

• recipe includes nutrition facts

• recipe includes nutrition facts

• recipe includes nutrition facts

• recipe includes nutrition facts